THE ETHICS OF SPORTS COACHING

- Is the role of the sports coach simply to improve sporting performance?
- What are the key ethical issues in sports coaching practice?

Despite the increasing sophistication of our understanding of the player–sport–coach relationship, the dominant perspective of the sports coach is still an instrumental one, focused almost exclusively on performance, achievement and competitive success. In this ground-breaking new book, leading sport scholars challenge that view, arguing that the coaching process is an inherently moral one with an inescapably ethical dimension, involving intense relationships between players and coaches. *The Ethics of Sports Coaching* critically examines this moral aspect, develops a powerful idea of what sports coaching ought to be, and argues strongly that coaches must be aware of the ethical implications of their acts.

The book is structured around four central themes: the nature of coaching, the character of the coach, coaching specific populations and specific coaching contexts. It explores in detail many of the key ethical issues in contemporary sports coaching, including:

- coaching special populations
- the ethics of talent identification
- understanding the limits of performance enhancement
- coaching dangerous sports
- expatriate coaching
- setting professional standards in sports coaching.

Combining powerful theoretical positions with clear insights into the everyday realities of sports coaching practice, this is an agenda-setting book. It is essential reading for all students, researchers and practitioners with an interest in sports coaching or the ethics and philosophy of sport.

Alun R. Hardman is Senior Lecturer and Discipline Director in the socio-cultural aspects of sport at the University of Wales Institute Cardiff. His academic focus is on the philosophy of sport and physical education, with particular interests in the area of applied sports ethics and how change and its moral implications impact upon sporting practices and their communities.

Carwyn Jones is Reader in Sports Ethics at the Cardiff School of Sport, UWIC. He has published widely in the area of sports ethics in both peer-reviewed journals and books. His particular expertise is fostering and developing moral virtue through sport and the role of the pedagogue therein.

Ethics and Sport

Series editors

Mike McNamee
University of Wales Swansea

Jim Parry
Charles University in Prague

Heather Reid
Morningside College

The Ethics and Sport series aims to encourage critical reflection on the practice of sport, and to stimulate professional evaluation and development. Each volume explores new work relating to philosophical ethics and the social and cultural study of ethical issues. Each is different in scope, appeal, focus and treatment but a balance is sought between local and international focus, perennial and contemporary issues, level of audience, teaching and research application, and variety of practical concerns.

Also available in this series:

THE ETHICS OF SPORTS COACHING

*Edited by Alun R. Hardman
and Carwyn Jones*

Routledge
Taylor & Francis Group

LONDON AND NEW YORK

First published 2011 by Routledge
2 Park Square, Milton Park, Abingdon, Oxon, OX14 4RN

Simultaneously published in the USA and Canada
by Routledge
711 Third Avenue, New York, NY 10017

Routledge is an imprint of the Taylor & Francis Group, an informa business

Typeset in ITC Stone Sans and Bembo by
Keystroke, Station Road, Codsall, Wolverhampton

British Library Cataloguing in Publication Data
A catalogue record for this book is available from the British Library

Library of Congress Cataloging in Publication Data
The ethics of sports coaching / edited by Alun R. Hardman and
Carwyn Jones.
    p. cm.
1. Coaching (Athletics). 2. Sports—Moral and ethical aspects.
I. Hardman, Alun. II. Jones, Carwyn, 1967–
GV711.E84 2011
796.07′7—dc22   2010025698

ISBN13: 978–0–415–55774–0 (hbk)
ISBN13: 978–0–415–55775–7 (pbk)
ISBN13: 978–0–203–86844–7 (ebk)

CONTENTS

CONTRIBUTORS

Richard Bailey is a writer and researcher working primarily in the fields of sport and education. He has been a teacher, coach, and academic, and now acts as a consultant for agencies like Youth Sport Trust, sportscoach UK and the PGA.

Anne-Mette Bredahl is a clinical psychologist and doctoral researcher. Her fields of interest are existential perspectives on disability and sport. She works at the Norwegian School of Sport Sciences and is a seven-times Paralympic participant and champion in cross-country skiing and biathlon.

Michael Burke is Senior Lecturer in Sport Ethics at Victoria University, Australia. He is also an Associate of the Institute of Sport, Exercise and Active Living (ISEAL) there, with research interests in performance-enhancing drugs in sport and women's position and participation in sport.

Paul Davis's background is in philosophy. He was Senior Lecturer in the Philosophy of Sport at the University of Wales Institute Cardiff, between 1996 and 2004, and is now Lecturer in the Sociology of Sport and Exercise at the University of Sunderland.

Alun R. Hardman is Senior Lecturer in Applied Ethics of Sport in the School Sport at University of Wales Institute Cardiff. He has published in the *Journal of the Philosophy of Sport* and *Sport, Ethics, Philosophy*.

Liv B. Hemmestad is a doctoral candidate at the Norwegian School of Sport Sciences and Lecturer in Elite Sports Coaching at Telemark University College. She has extensive experience of elite-level coaching and works as Head of the Top Sports Coaching Department at the Norwegian Olympic and Paralympic Committee and Confederation of Sport.

Dennis Hemphill is Associate Professor in Sport Ethics and also Head of the School of Sport and Exercise Science at Victoria University, Australia. Dennis, also an Associate of the Institute for Sport, Exercise and Active Living (ISEAL) there, undertakes research in areas such as technology, doping, and human values in sport.

Carwyn Jones is Reader in Sports Ethics at the Cardiff School of Sport, University of Wales Institute Cardiff. He has published widely in the area of sports ethics in both peer-reviewed journals and books. His particular interest is in the relationship between sport and virtue.

Sigmund Loland is Professor and Rector at the Norwegian School of Sport Sciences. He has extensive experience from coaching alpine skiing from the novice to the international elite level.

Irena Martínková is Lecturer in Philosophy of Sport in the Faculty of Physical Education and Sport, Charles University in Prague, Czech Republic. Her principal interests are phenomenology, different conceptions of human being and the human body, and Eastern thinking.

Mike McNamee is Professor of Applied Ethics at Swansea University. He is the Founding Editor of *Sport, Ethics and Philosophy*, was the Founding Chair of the British Philosophy of Sport Association and is a former President of the International Association for the Philosophy of Sport.

Steve Olivier is the Pro Vice-Chancellor for Academic Development at the University of Abertay. He was previously the Head of the School of Social and Health Science. He is an active researcher in research ethics and the philosophy of sport. He played first class rugby in his native South Africa and is now an active participant in adventure sports.

Jim Parry is former Head of the Department of Philosophy at the University of Leeds. He is now Visiting Professor in the Faculty of Physical Education and Sport, Charles University in Prague, Czech Republic, and Vice-Chair of the British Philosophy of Sport Association.

John S. Russell chairs the Langara College Philosophy Department in Vancouver, British Columbia. He is editor of the *Journal of the Philosophy of Sport* and publishes in this area and on topics related to philosophy of law and ethics.

Emily Ryall is Senior Lecturer in the philosophy of sport at the University of Gloucestershire. She is the author of *Critical Thinking for Sport Students* and plays rugby for Bristol.

Øyvind F. Standal is Associate Professor at the Department of Physical Education at the Norwegian School of Sport Sciences in Oslo. His research interests lie in the intersection between practical knowledge, embodied learning and pedagogy.

Martin Toms is a former professional cricket coach and Lecturer in Coaching and Sport Education at the University of Birmingham. His area of research and teaching is the sociological aspects of participant development and grassroots youth sports participation. He works closely with organizations such as the Professional Golfers' Association looking at talent and participant development.

Cesar R. Torres is Associate Professor in the Department of Kinesiology, Sport Studies, and Physical Education at The College at Brockport, State University of New York. He is currently the President of the International Association for the Philosophy of Sport (IAPS).

ACKNOWLEDGEMENTS

We are very grateful to the contributors for providing us with excellent essays in a timely fashion, to the Ethics and Sport series editors, Mike McNamee, Jim Parry and Heather Reid, for their encouragement and guidance, and to both Simon Whitmore, Routledge's commissioning editor for sport and leisure, and Joshua Wells, editorial assistant, for their enthusiastic support throughout the project.

In addition, we would like to thank members of both the British Philosophy of Sport Association and the International Association for the Philosophy of Sport for their scholarly fellowship, which helped plant the seed from which this book grew.

Thanks also to Dave Cobner and the Cardiff School of Sport UWIC for giving us the time and resources to put this book together. Finally, thanks to Heather Sheridan for her diligence in proofreading the manuscript. Diolch yn fawr i chi gyd.

ACKNOWLEDGMENTS

INTRODUCTION

Alun R. Hardman and Carwyn Jones

This book breaks new ground. It provides the first systematic study of sports coaching which has ethics at its core. The book does not simply discuss ethical issues that might surface in the practice of sports coaching, but uniquely, it examines the very nature of sports coaching using the academic discipline of ethics. It brings together the original thoughts of leading international scholars in the field of sports ethics and its parent discipline of the philosophy of sport. In addition to their recognized academic expertise, these contributors bring a depth of sport-specific experience and understanding to bear on their chosen topics. The result is a collection of theoretically informed essays on sports coaching ethics illustrated by a range of practitioner-based examples. For the first time, this book offers a concentrated analysis of coaching as an inherently ethical enterprise and interrogates a range of key moral issues implicated therein.

Although sports coaching is an increasingly common and significant academic field, the range of approaches and perspectives adopted within its study is relatively narrow. This narrowness is characterized by a somewhat uncritical view of coaching as largely a technical practice. Courses in coaching focus almost exclusively on 'how to coach' methods with little reflection on the nature of coaching goals or ends. Technical professional development needs take priority and scholarly activity aimed at providing the subject with authoritative academic foundations is replaced with more prosaic discussions of the practical needs of coaches. The product is an evidence-based body of knowledge and skills that merely inform coaches how best to perform their role (Cross and Lyle 1999; Lyle 2002; Martens 2004).

Given that the view of sports coaching is one principally dominated by talk about improvement, it is not surprising that the academic discourse on sports coaching reflects such an outlook. As a result, the academic study of sports coaching is one inhabited by fields of knowledge and methodological approaches that prioritize the advancement of an empirical account of how coaches can best improve performance (McMorris and Hale 2006). Academic qualifications and degree programmes produce different forms of 'know-how' that aim at perfecting such things as an athlete's motor skills, mental disposition, tactical knowledge and physiological conditioning (Cross and Lyle 1999). The outcome is an academic orthodoxy in sports coaching , often branded as 'coaching science', that endorses a practice-based profession aimed at improving athletic performance. Despite arguments to the contrary (Loland 2001; Breivik 2010), this conventional outlook takes for granted that sport is mainly about competitive success and that sports coaching is unequivocally geared towards winning. The upshot is that good coaching is reduced to meeting fairly narrow, measurable and quantifiable performance criteria such as won–lost records, league positions, player rankings, personal bests and medals won. In this environment, the coach's role and outlook are confined to implementing the most effective means to best achieve largely unquestioned ends.

This book takes a radically different approach. It starts by examining the very nature of sports coaching, asking 'What are the aims of coaching?' before addressing 'How should a coach proceed?' The view advanced in this book is that coaching is fundamentally a moral practice. Coaches work with persons, not machines. Coaching involves human relationships and interpersonal interaction, therefore the moral dimension of sports coaching is unavoidable.

A number of important implications follow from accepting the premise that coaching is a moral enterprise. At its heart, sports coaching aims to affect the attitudes, values and behaviours of athletes towards each other and how they play sport. Most, if not all, coaching exchanges have a moral dimension to them. This premise is predicated on the fundamental Kantian principle that all persons are first and foremost ends in themselves (Tuxhill and Wigmore 1998; Fry 2000). As a consequence of our personhood – of what it means to be human – the pursuit of autonomy and the desire to exercise free will, therefore, is a powerful ideal that drives how we want to live our lives. In the context of sports coaching, then, notions of autonomy and freedom of choice are the cornerstones of ethical discourse. This is evident first in the way that coaches express value judgements in deciding what, why, whom and how they coach. Such normative choices are then further manifest in the manner a coach interacts with those they coach in the sports setting. This applies not merely in terms of enhancing tactical and technical proficiency, but more crucially in terms of engendering a shared sense of motivation and meaning towards how one ought to participate in sport. In such a morally saturated environment, the ethical dimension is pervasive, and morally praiseworthy coach–athlete relationships that aim to be honest and sincere and to promote autonomy, should be the gold standard. Coach–athlete relationships ought to reflect mutual respect in ways that ensure the integrity of participants and their sporting practices. As prominent coach–athlete relationships are often intense, complex, highly contextual and involve struggles for power and control (Bergmann Drewe 2000), judicious and proper conduct is vital to safeguard the interests of those who have entered into a mutually dependent relationship.

The existing academic orthodoxy is not without its critics. Recent interpretive social scientific analyses provide a far more complex and nuanced description of the coach and their role (Sparkes 1997; Jones, R.L. 2006; Denison 2007; Cassidy *et al.* 2009). This literature is linked to earlier work conducted in sports education and sports pedagogy (Evans 1993; Hastie and Sidentop 1997; Kirk and Tinning 2000), which regards sports coaching as rooted in 'nurturing' practices that emerge in formal and informal education. Alongside these other approaches, this book directly challenges the functional role undertaken by the vast majority of academics who embrace a technical approach to the study of sports coaching. We believe that the academic study of sports coaching must encompass more than just the technical elements of coaching practice.

Although these emerging and established dissenting discourses on sports coaching are to be welcomed, they are deficient in an important sense. While such literature provides a more insightful and sympathetic reading of the nature of sports coaching, and in particular may articulate the quandaries experienced by a particular politics, culture or population involved in sports coaching, it does so principally at the descriptive rather than the normative level. A clear example of this is the way in which the well-established distinction between participation and performance coaching is presented to the coaching profession (Cross and Lyle 1999; Markula and Martin 2007). Participation coaching is articulated as humanistic and athlete-centred. In contrast, performance coaching is dominated by the ethos of winning and competitive success. Coaches are made aware of the differences between the two and the implications of following either path for coaching behaviour. This information, however, is often presented uncritically as the natural order of things. This descriptive framework for coaching is driven by a particular set of sporting convictions and beliefs derived from more fundamental socio-cultural ideals. Coaches are rarely encouraged to question either the legitimacy of such a framework and its values or the ensuing normalized behaviours that arise in coaching contexts. This book goes beyond describing the technical complexities of coaching. It argues for particular moral stances in relation to hitherto ignored complexities. The book encourages critical reflection and promotes careful moral judgement as the appropriate response to the inescapable value-laden nature of coaching.

The notion that sport and other social practices are inherently moral activities has been argued by a number of philosophers (MacIntyre 1985, 1988; Taylor 1989; Sandel 1998). In an attempt to further understand sport as a moral enterprise, many sport ethicists have drawn on ideas from ancient Greek philosophy (Jones, C. 2008; McNamee 2008; Reid 2010). Of particular value, we believe, are insights which can loosely be described as neo-Aristotelian. Such Aristotelian-inspired accounts of both modern social practices and the nature and development of moral virtue help us understand and explain the character and scope of ethical conduct in complex interpersonal activities such as sports coaching. Such theoretical insights help us make good moral judgements in relation to coaching, too. Of particular relevance is Aristotle's discussion of *technê*, understood as the rational method(s) involved in producing an object or accomplishing a goal or objective. He warns of an overt focus on pursuing such methods as an *art* (i.e. as an end in itself), for *technê* only has value when undertaken as a *craft* which necessarily involves both careful consideration of goals or objectives and the appropriate practical application of the best means towards the achievement of such goals. For Aristotle, therefore, *technê* or rational method requires both *episteme* (theoretical knowledge) and the virtue of *phronesis* (the ability to do the right thing in the right way at the right time). This book by no means offers a unified account of sports coaching from a neo-Aristotelian perspective; however, we believe that such a perspective provides a valuable framework for understanding the inherently moral nature of the practice and provides an insight into the kind of people coaches should strive to be (Clifford and Feezell 1997; Carr 1998; Carr and Steutel 1999; Jones and McNamee 2000). It is a view that acknowledges the value of rules and principles, but argues that they can only do so much for the development of (morally) good coaching. The remainder is a matter of cultivating practical coaching wisdom (*phronesis*) and other virtues such as trust and integrity through a complex process involving emulation, initiation, training, education and critical reflection.

Throughout the book, as in any text of normative ethics, argument and critical reflection are paramount. There is a strong emphasis on evaluation and judgement in a range of conceptual and moral issues. The 'normative' point of view takes prominence and each author provides the reader with philosophical arguments that support a particular position which may run counter to custom and practice. Moreover, one objective of the book is to reject the view that ethical judgements can be derived uncritically from custom and practice, or worse, from self-interest. Examples of coaching behaviour performed conventionally are numerous. Conventions may be mistaken and the custom simply wrong or undesirable. What counts as an intellectually satisfactory account of sports coaching is one that enables coaches to differentiate what is justifiably part of our moral beliefs from what may be the sediment of particularity and arbitrary convention. This is not to say that convention can never provide ethical guidance, but only that such answers may be correct because of convictions that flow from something other than convention.

Self-interest provides another common source of reason for coach behaviour. When players are asked to fake an injury, to manipulate the officials, or antagonize an opponent through acts of gamesmanship or physical aggression in the interests of the team in order to secure the win, they do so because, from the coach's standpoint, the action is justified. Like reasons based on convention and custom, reasons of self-interest face serious difficulty because they carry the inherent and inevitable reality of conflict. When the behaviour of opposing coaches is motivated by the same mutually exclusive goal (winning), in the absence of any other normative authority coaches will resort to deception or force to get their own way. The need for moral authority as the basis for a legitimate ethics of sports coaching is therefore clear and this book explores the normative grounds beyond custom and self-interest upon which coaches can construct good reasons for acting in certain ways and rejecting others. To summarize, the book completes two crucial tasks. First, it articulates an alternative conception of coaching as a moral enterprise.

Second, it exemplifies how ethical reflection might proceed in a variety of morally-laden contexts.

The structure and content of the book

The book is organized in a sequential framework that proceeds from more universal and broader conceptual considerations to more particular contextual issues in sports coaching. There are a number of core premises established in the early chapters which are subsequently evidenced through the more specific discussions in the latter sections of the book. Together they provide logical lines of reasoning that serve to consolidate the overall philosophical arguments throughout. It is important therefore that the book be understood as an integrated project, where each chapter builds upon themes and issues discussed earlier. In order to get a comprehensive sense of the significance of ethics to the theory and practice of sports coaching, therefore, the book should (unlike many edited collections where one may choose according to one's preferences) really be read from beginning to end.

There are a number of ways of demarcating the subject matter and focus when studying the ethics of sports coaching, but the book provides a four-step model of the conceptual terrain. These four parts of the book are: (1) the nature of coaching; (2) the character of the coach; (3) coaching specific populations; and (4) specific coaching contexts. These four themes form a broad framework which both allows for a detailed examination of central philosophical concepts of sports coaching, and permits the reader to explore a number of enduring practical coaching issues with important philosophical ideas in mind.

The nature of coaching

In the first chapter, Sigmund Loland discusses the conceptual terrain of coaching, and in particular articulates the normative ends towards which the coach should operate. He suggests that the methods of natural and social sciences are often taken for two contrasting accounts of the proper ends of sport. His main argument is that the proclaimed objectivity of the natural sciences and the descriptive sociology of the social sciences are disingenuous as to their neutrality. Neither approach tackles the evaluative dimensions of sports coaching head-on; instead, they provide self-justifications as to their own significance and normative primacy.

He argues, from Aristotelian principles, that a good coach is an 'enlightened generalist' – an individual who pursues the ideals of ethical of perfectionism in terms of the Greek idea of *eudaimonia*, or living the good life. Such an approach, he argues, provides the coach with both the necessary perspective and *phronesis* (a concept examined in detail in Chapter 3) to respond to the potentially excessive demands and pressures of contemporary competitive sport. Loland points to the significance of *phronesis* as an important notion, but what is not so clear is the extent to which such a concept can be effectively recast to have the same authority and respect for us moderns as it had for the Ancient Greeks.

In Chapter 2, the socio-cultural setting in which sports coaching ought to take place is examined in more detail. Here, we represent a seminal piece of work in the ethics of sports coaching by Mike McNamee, which stood for a long time as one of the few essays of quality to seriously examine the nature and purpose of the practice of sports coaching. McNamee argues that central to an understanding of coaching as a profession is that it must be underwritten by exacting moral standards. He directs initial criticism towards the preponderance of coaching organizations that rely on an unexamined and superficial use of codes of conduct to do the bulk of their ethical work. Again, drawing on broadly Aristotelian insights, he suggests that if such codes are to be of any merit, they must be built on the central virtue of trust, which requires not merely that coaches are professional in name, but that such central virtues carry over into the authoritative and regulatory functions of coaching institutions.

The character of the coach

In Chapter 3, we shift attention to the second theme and examine the character and conduct of the coach. Part II raises philosophical questions related to the embodied identity of the coach and their role-specific function. It examines the relationships between personhood, character, and how coaches manifest these qualities in behaviour. Øyvind Standal and Liv Hemmestad focus on the Aristotelian notion of *phronesis* (practical wisdom) as an appropriate coaching disposition and contrast it with the more familiar notion of *technê*, that aspect of coaching that holds means–ends relationships to be uncomplicated strategic instrumental problems to be couched in, and addressed by, scientific knowledge. The authors argue for a re-evaluation of our understanding of the coaching domain where *phronesis* yields the necessary route for responding to the unexpected, the human, and the 'messiness' of coaching. Allowing room for less determinacy in coaching can foster better coaching.

In Chapter 4, Paul Davis develops some of these ideas further by investigating the realms of objectivity and subjectivity of judgements in coaching. Here, he presents and examines the nature of the 'truth' to be ascribed to different types of decisions that coaches make in performing their role. Using Nagel's (1986) graded conceptions of objectivity and subjectivity, he argues that, on the one hand, the coach inhabits the universal objectivity of science, when, for example, they draw on results from max VO_2 tests and, on the other, how they properly inhabit the objectivity of universal morality when, for example, they condemn the physical abuse of young athletes. This normative understanding demands that the coach ought to question and reject the kinds of norms of sport coaching practice that are often accepted because 'that's the way it is'. He then goes on to illustrate how, with the comparative domains of objective science and objective morality operating, much of what goes on in terms of a coach's life involves making choices that are either ontologically subjective or subjectively neutral. This means that the coach must reconcile more carefully moral issues such as fair play, the use of performance-enhancing substances, and the (in)appropriate use of gamespersonship alongside those of lesser importance such as their preferred football formation, style of play or warm-up activity.

In Chapter 5, drawing on neo-Aristotelian virtue ethics (MacIntyre 1985), Hardman and Jones attempt to illuminate what has often been implicit with regard to the coach's position as a positive moral role model. Their argument, founded on two related premises, is that a coach necessarily exhibits a range of physical, technical and moral excellences. The first premise is that the moral imperative or essence of sport, derived from its intrinsic nature (McFee 2004), requires participants and those who coach it to be preoccupied with central principles such as fairness and justice. The second argues that in order for coaches to execute their task fully, regardless of the coaching environment they inhabit and the competitive demands that are placed on them, they must take care to initiate players into the intrinsic values or goods of sport. The authors identify and illustrate here the important instructional role that a range of virtues can play in the coaching process. Finally, it is argued that a number of practical implications follow – that coaching involves being the right sort of person and that coaches must set a good example and have ethically admirable ideals.

Coaching specific populations

The core idea of Part III is that those who play sport ought to be treated as persons who are ends in themselves (Tuxhill and Wigmore 1998). A corresponding duty befalls those who have a responsibility to ensure that this right to think and act autonomously is upheld for all sports participants. The coach, in particular, is positioned at the heart of how those who participate in sport can do so without undue coercion. While autonomy is a crucial moral concern for all who participate in sport, this section of the book examines the issues presented with coaching identifiable populations where, historically at least, ensuring respect for autonomy has been most challenging.

In Chapter 6, John Russell develops a strong critique of the role of the coach in competitive children's sport. He orientates his critique around the claim that the intrinsic nature of competitive sport involves the morally problematic aim of attempting to *win over others*. He argues that regardless of what kind of interpretation is given about the value of sport, competition cannot be separated from the aim to be better and dominate others. From this, he claims, the viciousness of 'jealousy of emulation' emerges as a flawed moral character of sport itself, which can, unless carefully mediated by coaches, be transformed into a dark personal ambition that dominates all others. While remaining fairly pessimistic about the coach's chances, he advocates a conception of sport that encourages children and coaches to pursue what he presents as *absolute* rather than relative standards of perfection in sport.

Many of the underpinning philosophical themes identified by Russell are continued in Chapter 7, where Dennis Hemphill assesses the moral dimensions of coaching youth sport – a context where the boundaries between childhood and adulthood are uneven, cross over, and become blurred in a variety of ways. Here too, the concept of autonomy features strongly in Hemphill's argument, and in particular is linked to how the coach can better facilitate sporting autonomy to enable athletes to become creative and intelligent game players. He argues that coaches have a duty to free players from the narrow instrumental constraints of competitive sport, and the pressures from pushy parents, even if this may place victory at risk. His view is that the overall goal of the development of personhood through sport is far more important.

In Chapter 8, Michael Burke tackles the difficult issues that abound in coaching contexts where the adult coach is a male and the coached athlete is a young female. After acknowledging that many have highlighted that the sports environment is a fertile place for (mostly male) predatory coaches to engage in harassing or abusive behaviour (of male/female child athletes), he goes on to address the more complicated terrain of coaches forming consensual sexual or other relationships with their adult players. He grounds the moral concerns on the presence of a power imbalance which encompasses more than just an age differential. Drawing on literature and evidence from therapeutic and educational settings, he argues for modifications to coach education and accreditation processes that are more sensitive to, and thus aim to prevent, predatory paedophiles from infiltrating the coaching environment.

The ethics of coaching Paralympic sport is the focus of Chapter 9. Here, Anne-Mette Bredahl argues that the predominant, and thus normalized, philosophy of importing and adapting coaching principles from 'able-bodied' sport fails to take into account the range of unique problems encountered in coaching Paralympic sports. She points out how categorization, commercialism, and the varying nature and seriousness of disability mean that doing what is 'normal' does not apply when coaching Paralympic sports. After discussing the Paralympic Games and their history, she examines a range of problems faced by Paralympic coaches. The chapter further highlights the specificity or contextually anchored nature of coaching knowledge and experience, or, to use the concepts developed in earlier chapters, *phronesis* and *techné*.

Specific coaching contexts

In the fourth and final part, attempts are made to locate the coach in the broader ethical landscape. Although the coach's immediate ethical attention is properly focused on their athletes, they cannot simply ignore wider ethical issues or the 'bigger picture'. The value of sport and the value of coaching must not be excluded from the ethical reflections of even their most enthusiastic advocates. The topics included here are by no means the only, or necessarily the most significant, ones, but we consider they provide a taste of how different coaching contexts impact upon coaches' moral decision making.

In Chapter 10, Richard Bailey and Martin Toms examine the ethical issues related to the processes of 'talent identification' that occur in most bureaucratically structured and performance-orientated sports systems. In particular, they examine the gap between the political rhetoric and sociological reality of 'investing in sport' endemic to the kinds of large corporate/state-funded sport programmes that pursue a range of political and economic goals. They argue that coaches should become more aware of, and examine more carefully, those factors that are based on luck, and over which they have no control in their coaching practice. They argue that contingent factors such as sex, race and ethnicity, education, class, and geography are the more likely determinants of sporting success rather than those more directly associated with the coached physiological and psychological demands of the sport. In short, sporting success is dependent on those factors over which the coach may have little control, and are largely a matter of luck or chance (country, family, class, wealth). Bailey and Toms ask why we intensely admire coaches when in reality they have negligible control over and limited impact upon sporting success. Their position calls into question the entire premise of coaching sciences – that coaches are about developing effective micro-managed interventions – and suggests that there is a much stronger role for ethics in maximizing greater access to sporting opportunities.

In Chapter 11, the well-trodden arena of performance enhancement ethics in sport is addressed by Irena Martínková and Jim Parry. They offer a critical summary of the existing philosophical literature that focuses on the use of banned doping products and processes in sport; theirs is a broader account of the concept of performance enhancement. They highlight the tension of performance enhancement in sport where the coach finds him or herself, on the one hand, striving to improve the performances of their athletes through the most efficient means possible, and, on the other hand, accepting that these means must reside within certain acceptable limits. They discuss the coach's role in relation to the use of illicit performance-enhancing drugs, the use of permissible supplements, and physical and psychological abuse in training.

In Chapter 12, Emily Ryall and Steve Olivier explicitly tackle the means–end distinction, highlighted earlier in this Introduction, in the context of dangerous sports. Two views are explored. The first suggests the coach's role is simply to provide the athlete with the means necessary for them to achieve their goals, regardless of how risky or dangerous they might be (focusing on the means only). The second demands that the coach reflect on the potentially harmful goals (ends) an athlete has chosen and consider their duties to protect those in their care from harm. After presenting a typology of sport that attempts to separate out the ontological differences in kind and degree between various forms of risky and dangerous sporting activity, they suggest an approach to coaching that demarcates the individual (autonomous) athlete from the team (and co-dependent) sportsperson. They suggest that a more libertarian position applies to individual participation in dangerous sports, but when coaching participants are involved in team sports, a more paternalistic stance ought to prevail. They argue that the presence and participation of others, along with a tacit agreement that individuals relinquish aspects of their autonomy in order to be coached as a team, justify the differentiated approach.

In the final chapter of the book, Cesar Torres confronts the issues arising from the growing trend of hiring foreign coaches to lead national teams. In particular, he examines the view that hiring foreign coaches violates a putative unwritten principle of international sport which mandates that national teams be led by compatriots. He presents the concept of 'moderate patriotism' supported by the writings of Dixon (2000), Nathanson (1989) and Nussbaum (2002), and argues that the expatriate coach is particularly well situated to promote a set of desirable values that enhance international sport competition and foster intercultural interaction and national solidarity. With moderate patriotism in place, expatriate coaching is not anti-patriotic and has many potential beneficial effects for the coach's home country as well as the adopted one.

Although the book covers a broad spectrum of concerns, we believe a consistent message about the ethical nature of sports coaching emerges. The contributors share a commitment to establishing ethics as fundamental to, and at the forefront of, the study of sport coaching. The book's content provides practitioners and academics alike with a vital resource that will provoke discussion and debate on the very nature of the activity. This debate, we believe, ought to have a significant impact on the design and development of sport coaching curricula and the working practices of committed and reflective coaches, whether amateur or professional.

References

Bergmann Drewe, S. (2000) 'Coaches, ethics and autonomy', *Sport, Education and Society*, 5(2): 147–162.

Breivik, G. (2010) 'Philosophical perfectionism – consequences and implications for sport', *Sport, Ethics and Philosophy*, 4(1): 87–105.

Carr, D. (1998) 'What moral educational significance has physical education? A question in need of disambiguation', in M. McNamee and S.J. Parry (eds) *Ethics and Sport*, London: Routledge.

Carr, D. and Steutel, J. (1999) *Virtue Ethics and Moral Education*, London: Routledge.

Cassidy, T., Jones, R. and Potrac, P. (2009) *Understanding Sports Coaching: The Social, Cultural and Pedagogical Foundations of Coaching Practice*, London: Routledge.

Clifford, E.C. and Feezell, R.M. (1997) *Coaching for Character*, Champaign, IL: Human Kinetics.

Cross, N. and Lyle, N. (1999) *The Coaching Process: Principles and Practice for Sport*, Edinburgh: Butterworth-Heinemann.

Denison, J. (2007) *Coaching Knowledges: Understanding the Dynamics of Sport Performance*, London: A. and C. Black.

Dixon, N. (2002) 'A justification for moderate patriotism in sport', in T. Tansjo and C. Tamburrini (eds) *Values in Sport: Elitism, Nationalism, Gender Equity and the Scientific Manufacture of Winners*, London: Routledge.

Evans, J. (ed.) (1993) *Equality, Education and Physical Education*, London: Falmer Press.

Fry, J. (2000) 'Coaching a kingdom of ends', *Journal of the Philosophy of Sport*, 27(1): 51–62.

Hastie, P and Sidentop, D. (1997) 'An ecological perspective on physical education', *European Physical Education Review*, 5(1): 9–29.

Jones, C. (2008) 'Teaching virtue through physical education', *Sport, Education and Society*, 13(3): 337–349.

Jones, C. and McNamee, M.J. (2000) 'Moral reasoning, moral action, and the moral atmosphere of sport', *Sport, Education and Society*, 5(2): 131–144.

Jones, R.L. (2006) *The Sports Coach as Educator: Reconceptualising Sports Coaching*, London: Routledge.

Kirk, D. and Tinning, R. (2000) *Physical Education, Curriculum and Culture: Critical Issues in the Contemporary Crisis*, London: Routledge.

Loland, S. (2001) 'Record sports: an ecological critique and reconstruction', *Journal of the Philosophy of Sport*, 28(2): 127–139.

Lyle, J. (2002) *Sports Coaching Concepts: A Framework for Coaches' Behaviour*, London: Routledge.

Markula, P. and Martin, M. (2007) 'Ethical coaching: gaining respect in the field', in J. Denison (ed.) *Coaching Knowledges: Understanding the Dynamics of Sport Performance*, London: A. and C. Black.

MacIntyre, A. (1985) *After Virtue*, 2nd edn, Notre Dame, IN: University of Notre Dame Press.

MacIntyre, A. (1988) *Whose Justice? Which Rationality?* Notre Dame, IN: University of Notre Dame Press.

Martens, R. (2004) *Successful Coaching*, 3rd edn, Champaign, IL: Human Kinetics.

McFee, G. (2004) *Sport Rules and Values: Philosophical Investigations into the Nature of Sport*, London: Routledge.

McMorris, T. and Hale, T. (2006) *Coaching Science: Theory into Practice*, Chichester: John Wiley.

McNamee, M.J. (2008) *Sports, Virtues and Vices: Morality Plays*, London: Routledge.

McNamee, M.J. and Parry, S.J. (eds) (1998) *Ethics and Sport*, London: Routledge.

Nagel, T. (1986) *The View from Nowhere*, Oxford: Oxford University Press.

Nathanson, S. (1989) 'In defense of "moderate patriotism" ', *Ethics*, 99(3): 535–552.

Nussbaum, M. (2002) *For Love of Country*, Boston, MA: Beacon Press.

Reid, H. (2010) 'Athletic virtue: between East and West', in M.J. McNamee (ed.) *Reader in Sports Ethics*, Abingdon: Routledge.

Sandel, M. (1998) *Liberalism and the Limits of Justice*, 2nd edn, Cambridge: Cambridge University Press.

Sparkes, A.C. (1997) 'Ethnographic fiction and representing the absent other', *Sport, Education and Society*, 2(1): 25–40.

Taylor, C. (1989) *Sources of the Self: The Making of the Modern Identity*, Cambridge: Cambridge University Press.

Tuxhill, C. and Wigmore, S. (1998) ' "Merely meat"? Respect for persons in sport and games', in M.J. McNamee and S.J. Parry (eds) *Ethics and Sport*, London: Routledge.

PART I

The nature of coaching

1

THE NORMATIVE AIMS OF COACHING

The good coach as an enlightened generalist

Sigmund Loland

Introduction

The vast majority of children and youth take part in school and club-based sport. A significant portion of adults report exercising regularly. In terms of elite sport, events such as the FIFA World Cup and the Olympic Games attract global interest and reach the top of international TV viewer ratings. The impact of sport on society is immense.

To a certain extent, sport reflects and reinforces the predominant norms and values of the societies of which it is a part. Mass sport is justified as a potentially positive arena of socialization of the young, and as a means towards health and social integration. Elite sport is considered great entertainment and as an arena for building positive collective identities. Sport may also reflect, however, more destructive and marginal social values. Children's sport can be cynical and socially exclusive. Elite sport is challenged by doping, chauvinism, aggression and violence.

The point is that sport is not good or evil in itself or 'by nature'. As such, sport is a morally contested terrain and a sphere of both vice and virtue (McNamee 2008). A key question, then, is how the positive potential of sport can be realized, and how negative outcomes can be avoided.

The simple response is that it all depends upon the way sport is practised. Practice is influenced by many factors. First, the significance of the social and cultural context is obvious. In a Chicago ghetto, the boxing club can be an oasis of order and morality in a world of chaos and crime (Wacquant 2004). In well-off suburban Scandinavian culture, combat sports may challenge the existing order (Endresen and Olweus 2005). Second, the characteristics of different sports seem to play a role. The individual sport of full-contact karate probably cultivates norms and values other than those available through the non-contact collective sport of volleyball. Third, and perhaps most importantly, the basis for sport values among participants is shaped in action, at the concrete and embodied level of sport practice.

The key figure in this respect, or what sociologists would call a 'primary agent', is the coach. In addition to setting the performance standards, he or she also sets the motivational climate and the moral standards to be respected and acted upon (Ommundsen *et al.* 2003). In what way can coaches take the responsibility that follows from their significant role? What are the competencies and necessary knowledge to develop into a good coach? What does an ethics of coaching look like?

In this chapter, I will try to answer such questions. My discussion will be limited to coaching in competitive sport with an emphasis on developing athletic performance. More specifically, I will examine three kinds of coaching competence and examine how they relate to the challenge of ethically sound coaching. Summing up, I will sketch how various competencies are interrelated and constitute a basis from which a good coach acts. Above all, a good coach needs what Aristotle called *phronesis*: practical wisdom (see Standal and Hemmestad, Chapter 3 in this volume). I will argue for the ideal of the good coach as an enlightened generalist.

Coaching: the possibilities and limitations of natural science

Sport, it is often said, deals with physical abilities and skills. In sporting games we test more or less quantifiable physical performances. In typical record sports, such as track and field and weightlifting, emphasis is on basic motor abilities such as endurance, speed and power. In team games such as soccer, bio-motor abilities constitute a basis for technical and tactical movement, but again the image is bodies in advanced physical movement.

The fact that sport is a bodily practice has exerted significant impact on the way it is analysed and understood. The predominant scientific approach is that of the natural sciences: biology, physiology, biomechanics. The body is seen as a mechanistic object and as part of deterministic nature in which movements can be quantitatively described and explained by causal relationships. The basic premise is a dualistic worldview in which body and mind are considered to belong to two different spheres of reality. The mind is seen as pure thinking substance with no extension and as completely independent of nature. This is where freedom, creativity, rationality and reflection are to be found.

Dualism has long been rooted in the intellectual and religious history of the West, from ancient Greek Platonic philosophy to the seventeenth-century thinker Descartes, who gave a secular and rationalistic version of dualism that became a basis for the development of natural science (Stricker 1970). The dualistic scheme has had an impact not only on our understanding of human physicality but also on the Western view of reality. Conceptual distinctions are made between fact and value, practice and theory, and physical labour and intellectual work. The term 'physical activity' (as distinct from 'intellectual activity') is a standard example of dualism.

As a working hypothesis in the understanding of the body and its functions, the dualistic understanding has proved extremely powerful. One early example is

William Harvey's (1578–1657) 1628 description of the cardiovascular system. Harvey's work made a profound impression on Descartes, who saw it as an empirical confirmation of the dualistic scheme. Since Harvey, both medical and natural science have developed immensely and still today form the epitome of what 'real science' is all about.

No wonder that knowledge of sport from a natural science perspective is considered a significant element of coaching expertise (Gilbert and Trudel 2004). Exact descriptions and causal explanations serve to predict later chains of events and have a direct, applied side. 'Everything else being equal, if a long jumper increases his speed in the run-up, the jump will be longer.' 'Everything else being equal, if an alpine skier increases the angle of the ski towards the snow, friction and grip will increase.' The natural science approach also has an influence on the didactics of learning sport techniques. Attention is given to particular parts of the body and their movements: the lift of the knee in running, the high elbow in swimming, kicking with the inside of the foot in soccer. The premise seems to be that the mind determines movement. Athletic performances are matters of cognitive control.

In spite of its many merits, however, natural science only tells part of the story. In coaching practice, the view of the body as an object and a property of the mind is highly incomplete. When giving a strong performance, athletes report on the experience of being 'in the zone'. The experience is one of transcendence in which objective distinctions between the body, the mind and the environment seem to merge into one unified whole (Loland 1992). The cyclist becomes one with his bike, the surface and the task to be performed; the skier experiences the body, the equipment, the course and the surface as a single, powerful gestalt. These are 'peak experiences', to use a classic Maslow term, of which the good coach needs insights and understanding.

The perspective of natural science is limited. The aim is to describe and explain reality without interpreting human experience and subjectivity of any kind. Natural science is objective and 'neutral'. However, the history of elite sport tells a story not only of the blessings of natural science but also of how it can be used to manipulate and degrade human biology. What is needed here is moral reflection on the nature and values of sport. Where can coaches turn to for such insights?

Coaching: the possibilities and limitations of a socio-cultural understanding

A next step, then, could be to go from natural to social science. In the past few decades, a significant body of knowledge has developed in which sport has been examined from a social and cultural perspective. Sport is not necessary for human survival but serves a series of significant social and cultural interests and goals. What characterizes sport as a social and cultural practice?

The *credo* in competitive sport is that of performance and progress (Coakley 1994). As demonstrated in the Introduction, the interests and goals of coaches and athletes are not naturally given but the result of socio-cultural context and influence. Athletic performances are given high socio-cultural value, and some sports offer professional careers together with the possibility of fame and fortune. Athletes and coaches are constantly searching for new dimensions of technical movements, new tactical insights, and how to develop training methods that lead to improvement. In elite sport settings at least, this striving easily becomes all-encompassing; it becomes a lifestyle.

To better understand this, socio-cultural perspectives can be of help. Inspired by the work of pioneers such as Norbert Elias (1897–1990) and Michel Foucault (1926–1984), the body and movement are understood as social constructions. The intention is different from that of natural science. Now the body and its movements are to be interpreted as expressions of human intention and search for meaning, and not as objective phenomena to be described in quantitative terms and explained causally. Culture and society not only influence the way we think and act, but also shape our bodies and movement in significant ways. A few examples can illustrate the point.

Different sports are embodied in different ways. The rugged and forward-leaning position of the boxer is considered a key quality in a fight and indicates an attitude of aggression and will-power. The straight gymnast is an expression of ideals of aesthetics, discipline and health. With lean upper body and powerful legs, the expert cyclist masters rapid and tactical movement over long distances and provides an image of deep human interaction with technology. Team games such as football and basketball are explorations of the possibilities and limitations of embodied collective action and cooperation.

Coaches socialize athletes into the movement schemes of their sport. This is done by instruction and by using good athletes as role models for imitation. Although largely ignored in traditional sport science, the good coach's reflective understanding of embodied norms and values is impressive. In talent selection and development, interpretation of body posture and movements seems at least to a certain extent more important than quantifiable physical tests. In some technical sports, experienced coaches can even see by whom and where athletes have been trained. Alpine coaches can recognize a coach by a skier's technique; the style of Spanish soccer players is different from that of Italian and Northern European ones.

This socialization is embedded in normative judgements. Technical and tactical evaluations are based on more general ideas of the values and meaning of a sport; its schemes of fairness and its qualities as a sphere of human excellence. In their dealing with normative issues, most coaches strengthen existing schemes. In the English Premier League, so-called 'diving' – 'play-acting' to fake an offence and get a free kick and perhaps provoke the booking of an opposing player – is considered an unacceptable form of conduct. Norwegian cross-country skiing has a culture of traditionalism and often considers new techniques to be 'unhealthy' and 'non-aesthetic'.

The best coaches go further than reproduce existing normative schemes. On the one hand, athletes are taught a sport with respect for its histories and ideals.

On the other, athletes are taught independence and are stimulated towards creativity and a constant quest for improvement. Good coaches are sensitive to situational aspects and unpredictability. The key question is not whether a training method is in accordance with established norms and values, but whether it enhances performance. The innovative coach is what the philosopher Richard Rorty calls a 'strong poet' who is able to change the 'language' of his or her practice (Roberts 1995). A good coach is constantly searching for change.

But again, moral issues arise. Embodied norms and values are not always ethically sound. Strong efforts to succeed may lead to ethical problems. Competitive sport, especially at elite levels, is a borderline activity. Some athletes use extreme performance-enhancing means and methods that threaten both their own and others' health and well-being. Some athletes cheat and search for the rewards of victory in illegitimate ways.

Can social and cultural insights help the coach in dealing with these challenges? To a certain extent the answer is yes. Socio-cultural perspectives add to the understanding of human intention and action and of the formation of human values and attitudes. At the same time, they are ambiguous and can be used in many ways. Coaches with insights in attitude development can use their competence in cynical and manipulative ways. Young athletes can be socialized into a liberal drug culture in which doping is considered unproblematic since 'everyone else is doing it'. An ice hockey team can be taught the efficiency of brutality and violence.

As with natural science, socio-cultural approaches have no normative focus. The question for the social scientist is not whether doping is right or wrong but how values and attitudes can develop and be understood. The question is not whether cynical and violent behaviour should be sanctioned but what its causes and driving forces are. We are still left with the question of an approach that enables the coach to make morally sound decisions in practice.

Coaching and perfectionist ethics

The good coach not only searches for scientific knowledge but is engaged in a practical search for reflective and good choices in the many dilemmas of his or her profession. In split decision situations, the good coach has morally sound intuitions and reaction patterns. In a moral dilemma, the good coach attempts to consider all sides of the issue and weighs them against each other before finding a solution. What is at stake here is practical wisdom, or *phronesis*, to use a classic Aristotelian term (see Standal and Hemmestad, Chapter 3 in this volume). Practical wisdom refers to the ability to act in accordance with virtues such as justice and fairness, temperance and enthusiasm, empathy and understanding. Where does coaching wisdom come from?

Ethical frameworks for sport are as old as sport itself. Since ancient times, there has been the vision that sport builds character. According to Plato, the gods gave two gifts to humankind: music and gymnastics. For more than a thousand years, the ancient Olympic Games were the primary meeting spot for all free Greek men and for the consolidation of Greek ideals and identity (Finley and Pleket 1976).

The idea of sport as a sphere of morality is deeply rooted in modern sport culture, too. The development of modern sport in nineteenth-century Britain was influenced by the ideological framework of 'muscular Christianity' as developed by historical figures such as Thomas Arnold, headmaster of Rugby School (Mangan 1981). In our time, politicians and public authorities seem to consider sporting activities as *a priori* good. Perhaps the clearest articulation is found in the Olympic ideal of sport as a physically, socially and morally cultivating force both for the individual and for society.

In coaching practice, however, these overriding ideals are not always helpful. There is a need for concrete judgements in practical situations. The 800 m runner is pushed by an opponent and responds with an even harder push back. Is this an acceptable tactical move in an athletic race? The soccer goalkeeper tries his best to 'psych out' the penalty shooter by staring, talking a load of rubbish and flapping his arms. Is this acceptable and part of the game? The racing cyclist has the choice of adopting a performance-enhancing doping regime like many of his team-mates, or rejecting the regime. Which will he choose?

The hard-core response is that it is all about winning. 'Nice guys finish last', as the saying goes. Media constructions of elite sport emphasize conflict and aggression (Raney and Bryant 2006). Pushing, talking rubbish and even drug use are acceptable if this gains winning chances. In relativistic schemes, the idea is to follow the minimum requirements on morality, but nothing more. This is a tit-for-tat strategy: 'If the others are doing it, we have to respond with the same.'

These responses are problematic from an ethical point of view. Hard-core and relativistic moral schemes will ruin sport if they become the common norm. The mass media has a deceptive role in this respect. The fact is that these attitudes are not particularly common in sport. Empirical studies of elite sport cultures point to value systems in which there is a strong drive to improve and excel in admirable ways (Ronglan 2007). In fact, passionate performance cultures are sometimes described according to a classic definition of play as activities with pure intrinsic value. At its best, sport offers a sphere for intense engagement in which athletes, teams, coaches, support systems and spectators are fully absorbed in a search for excellence in competitions with 'a sweet tension of uncertainty of outcome' (Fraleigh 1984). Good and tight competitions appear as a phenomenological field of complex communication and interdependencies (Kretchmar 1975). Experiences of sporting play are said to be among the most valuable experiences we can have (Hyland 1990).

A reflective coach with a sense for such values rejects cynical and relativistic schemes of morality. What counts is not only the result but the manner in which it has been achieved. This is perhaps best expressed with the ideals of ethical perfectionism (Hurka 1993). The core idea is that each individual has a moral obligation to develop in virtuous ways his or her natural talents and predispositions, and that each individual has the obligation to stimulate and encourage similar developments in others. In the Aristotelian tradition, perfectionism is a key element of *eudaimonia*, or living a good life. In a perfectionist coaching scheme, the overall ideal is the empowering of athletes to explore their own talents through hard training, and effort. Good coaching stimulates the development of athletes as moral agents with freedom of choice and responsibility for their choices. In light of this, Murray (2007) talks of sport as 'the virtuous development of natural talent towards human excellence'.

Perfectionist normative premises have direct implications for practice. A good coach creates a moral climate in which aggression, cheating and excessive psychological warfare are considered unacceptable forms of conduct as they undermines athletes' status as free and responsible moral agents. In a similar vein, ethical perfectionism implies a critical attitude towards the use of performance-enhancing drugs and the transfer of responsibility towards external expertise. Again, athletes' status as moral agents is threatened.

Ethical perfectionism in coaching has an additional distinct feature. The athlete is not the centre of the performance developmental scheme. In proper interaction with athletes, a good coach is also developing his or her own natural talent. Sport history is full of tales of how this process may take place. The history of the relationship between the sprinter Harold Abrahams and the professional coach Sam Mussabini before the 1924 Paris Summer Olympics, or the relationship between tennis star Bjørn Borg and late coach Lennart Bergelin, or the international success of the Norwegian handball team with the original and inclusive coaching style of Marit Breivik, are some examples. In a perfectionist scheme, the coach and the athlete or team are engaged in a mutual virtuous striving for excellence by realizing different but complementary natural talents. In this way, sport can provide images of the possibilities of human interaction, images that carry moral significance far above and beyond the realm of sport.

The coach as an enlightened generalist

I started this chapter by asking what an ethics of coaching might look like. What are the competencies involved in good coaching, and how do they interrelate? In the first two sections, I discussed the good coach as knowledgeable in the context both of natural science perspectives and of socio-cultural approaches. In the third section, I pointed at an additional competence in terms of an anchoring of coaching practice in ethical perfectionism and in the concrete and embodied ideals of sport itself.

To handle the many moral dilemmas and challenges of competitive sport, a good coach needs practical wisdom: *phronesis*. He or she has the ability to weigh different kinds of facts and insights against each other in sound and reasonable ways. The good coach is an enlightened generalist and engages with his or her athletes in a virtuous mutual quest for not just sporting excellence but human excellence.

References

Coakley, J.J. (1994) *Sport in Society: Issues and Controversies*, St Louis, MO: Mosby.

Endresen, J.M. and Olweus, D. (2005) 'Participation in power sports and antisocial involvement in preadolescent and adolescent boys', *Journal of Child Psychology and Psychiatry*, 46(15): 449–450.

Finley, M.I. and Pleket, H.W. (1976) *The Olympic Games: The First Thousand Years*, London: Chatto and Windus.

Fraleigh, W.P. (1984) *Right Actions in Sport: Ethics for Contestants*, Champaign, IL: Human Kinetics.

Gilbert, W. and Trudel, P. (2004) 'Analysis of coaching science research published from 1970–2001', *Research Quarterly for Exercise and Sport*, 75(4): 388–399.

Hurka, T. (1993) *Perfectionism*, Oxford: Oxford University Press.

Hyland, D. (1990) *Philosophy of Sport*, New York: Paragon.

Kretchmar, R.S. (1975) 'From test to contest: an analysis of two kinds of counterpoints in sport', *Journal of the Philosophy of Sport*, 2: 23–30.

Loland, S. (1992) 'The mechanics and meaning of alpine skiing', *Journal of the Philosophy of Sport*, 14: 55–77.

Mangan, J.A. (1981) *Athleticism in the Victorian and Edwardian Public School: The Emergence and Consolidation of an Educational Ideology*, Cambridge: Cambridge University Press.

McNamee, M.J. (2008) *Sport, Virtues and Vices: Morality Plays*, London: Routledge.

Murray, T.H. (2007) 'Enhancement', in B. Steinbock (ed.) *The Oxford Handbook of Bioethics*, Oxford: Oxford University Press.

Ommundsen, Y., Roberts, G., Lemyre, N. and Treasure, D.C. (2003) 'Perceived motivational climate in male youth soccer: relations to social-moral functioning, sportspersonship and team norm perceptions', *Psychology of Sport and Exercise*, 4: 397–413.

Raney, A.A. and Bryant, J. (2006) *Handbook of Sports and Media*, Hillsdale, NJ: Lawrence Erlbaum Associates.

Roberts, T.J. (1995) 'Sport and strong poetry', *Journal of the Philosophy of Sport*, 22: 94–107.

Ronglan, L.T. (2007) 'Building and communicating collective efficacy: a season-long in-depth study of an elite sport team', *The Sport Psychologist*, 21(1): 78–93.

Stricker, S.F. (ed.) (1970) *The Philosophy of the Body: Rejections of Cartesian Dualism*, New York: Quadrangle.

Wacquant, L. (2004) *Body and Soul: Notebooks of an Apprentice Boxer*, Oxford: Oxford University Press.

2

CELEBRATING TRUST

Virtues and rules in the ethical conduct of sports coaches

Mike McNamee

Introduction

When people talk of professions and professionalism, they most commonly refer to a limited number of occupations whose objects refer to the highest of civilized goods, such as education, health, justice, salvation and security. Currently, there appears to be a new move towards the establishment of a variety of codes and rules to govern conduct within these professions. Into these codes of conduct can be read a moral conservatism; a flight back to the language of moral certainty, of duties, obligations, principles and rules. The task of how we should understand these codes of conduct and what we may properly expect of them in the context of sport is the object of this chapter. In order to carry out this task, I will set out a caricature of professionalism that is partly at odds with the rule-based conceptions of ethics and, utilizing the concept of 'trust', I will offer a virtue-based account of moral life that underwrites the notion of sports coach as professional.

Professions and professionals

In a recent work on professional ethics (Koehn 1994), Koehn analyses certain practices that are commonly thought to be paradigmatic of professions: the clergy, medicine and law. Many would argue that the list, though traditional, is somewhat incomplete. There is already, however, a significant literature in sports regarding professions and professionalism whose arguments I do not intend to review here (Morgan 1993: 470–493; Schneider and Butcher 1993: 460–469). Instead, I will take the spirit of Koehn's analysis and situate it in the context of sports coaching.

Koehn argues that the concept of 'professional' is inherently normative since any attempt to describe the boundaries of the concept is at the same time to recommend a particular version of the powers of a person under that description. Mindful of

George Bernard Shaw's quip that all professions are conspiracies against the laity, Koehn sets out to ground the moral authority of professionals in contradistinction to two alternative models that are not uncommonly characteristic of relationships in sporting contexts: (1) the professional as expert; and (2) the professional as service-provider for fees. Neither of these conceptions can underwrite the trust we place in professionals that is, following Baier,[1] at their very heart. The notion of professional as possessor of expertise deals only with techniques or means and is not tied to proper ends, among which is the client's good; in this conception, the expert pursues a private agenda. The professional as service provider for a fee is similarly untrustworthy. This contractual model places the client's agenda in the foreground, obscuring the proper end of the profession; the professional, placed in the service of the client, becomes little more than a hired hand.

Koehn sets out seven conditions that are intended to ground the moral authority of a given profession, and professionals therein, in a trustworthy relationship:[2]

1. The professional must aim at the client's good (whose desires do not simply entail that good).
2. The professional must exhibit a willingness to act towards this aim.
3. Such willingness to act thus must continue for as long as is necessary to reach a determination.
4. The professional must be competent (in the appropriate knowledge and skills).
5. The professional must be able to demand from the client (specific appropriate knowledge and performances).
6. The professional must be free to serve the client with discretion (which, as with (1) above, need not be consistent with their desires).
7. The professional must have a highly internalized sense of responsibility.

From these conditions, the grounds for trusting the professional are given moral authority, the like of which enables a fairly catholic definition that *prima facie* does not disqualify sports coaches. As professionals, sports coaches aim towards the production of relative and absolute excellence of their performers; this is the proper end of sports and what is to be aimed for within the framework of the relevant practices. Moreover, the coaches have been initiated into a body of knowledge and skills in areas ranging from physiology, skill acquisition, motivation to goal setting. Further, and reciprocally, the coaches demand from their athletes appropriate performances; the 'client' is not the master of the entire agenda. Finally, some authority, often paternalistic authority (with old and especially with young athletes), is invested in coaches whose powers are effected with discretion in a framework of responsibilities to self, performer and sport. Not in reference to sports, but applicable to them, Koehn summarizes:

> A professional is an agent who freely makes a public promise to serve persons . . . who are distinguished by a specific desire for a particular good . . . and who have come into the presence of the professional with or on the

expectation that the professional will promote that particular good. In other words, agents become professionals by virtue of what they profess or publicly proclaim before persons lacking particular goods.[3]

(1994: 59)

And later: 'Professionals must have some way of establishing that they are worthy of the client's continuing trust. Adherence to the professional pledge in each and every interaction with the client constitutes a solution to this problem' (ibid.: 68).

The notion of a public pledge is one that finds no home in sporting practices. What is presumed is that the coach always acts in the interest of the performer and, indeed, of the sport. Where the paradigmatic professions have been thought to be related to essential social goods (justice, health and salvation), their import might be such that the public pledge was a strong normative lever. Sport seems by comparison to be trivial. Why would such a pledge be necessary? Yet sport is thought to be a good in and of itself (that is, independently of other ends to which it may serve as a valuable means), athletes stand before coaches in need of particular sporting goods, and coaches are the repository of conventional wisdom in that sphere. It may be the case that to trust them requires not merely that they are, *qua* professional, virtuous but perhaps that they have been legitimized by the appropriate authority and are regulated in proper ways by that authority. It is in this lacuna, then, that codes of conduct in sport may find their *raison d'être*.

Codes of ethical and professional conduct

Why should professionals adopt a code of practice to govern their conduct? It is a commonplace, in moral philosophical circles at least, to search for authoritative support for ethical commitments in order to avoid caprice or arbitrariness. Likewise, it is often thought that moral rules allow us to point up most clearly the clashes between permissible and impermissible conduct. We can still ask, though, why we need a *code* of rules to guide ethical conduct in professional life.

In answer to this question, a number of reasons recommend themselves: first, they offer *apparent* clarity and simplicity in a confusing world; second, they set out standards and criteria to evaluate provision and expectation in relationships which are consistent over time; third, they offer a neutral framework for resolving conflict or ambiguity to those under the authority of the organization; and fourth, in constraining certain actions, they allow exclusion from that organization anyone who will not conform to the code.[4] In short, we might say that codes of conduct franchise 'blameability' and consequently 'punishability' to their respective organizations. The closeness of these quasi–ethical objectives to a legal mindset is apparent. 'Blame', as Williams reminds us, 'is the characteristic reaction of the morality system' (Williams 1985: 177); it invites us to think of the whole of ethical life in terms of a series of obligations of increasing power that must be met for fear of incurring blame and possible retribution.

Characteristic of these guides to professional conduct is the codification of a set of rules that describe, prescribe and, more commonly, proscribe the actions of professionals. The codes are a pastiche of eclectic moral positions. But one particular portion of the picture dominates: a 'common-sense' view of morality as a set of rules or principles which stop people from acting *purely* in the pursuit of their interests to the detriment of others. The sum of these rules or principles, both negative and positive, constitutes the moral code enshrined in rights, duties and obligations. To what extent does this common-sense picture recommend itself above others?

The sheer range of ethical theories in this pastiche makes the task of summarizing difficult. In keeping with the brevity of this argument, albeit following many philosophers before, we may separate ethical theories into two categories: those that concern themselves with actions and those that concern themselves with agents, or, put another way, those that focus on what it is right to do and those that focus on what sort of agent it is good to be. In keeping with the above, I will eschew felicity for the sake of brevity and generalize further by calling them rule-based and virtue-based theories of ethics. I will now consider how these caricatured positions underwrite codes of conduct.

Rules, rule-following and rule-based ethical theories

My compass here is necessarily broad and the targets I aim at are less than well focused. The name 'rule-based ethical theories' is not intended to be definitive in any final manner. What it points to is the fact that the ethical considerations belonging to a theory under that description are centred around considerations to do with actions governed by something like a set of rules, rules which are designed to frustrate the worst of people's desires and are grounded in reason such that they have an authoritative voice. In rule-based theories, being largely modern, there is no appeal to a deity; the rules are human constructions. Given that professionals are faced with problems of how to decide between competing courses of action in a way that is not merely capricious or God-given, the rules are supposed to point us towards what any reasonable person would agree is right.

Perhaps the best-known theories of right actions are deontological in character, and the most celebrated of these belong to Kant.[5] To act rightly is to refrain from things that can be known, before the fact, to be wrong. The rules are effectively negative, whether as constraints, proscriptions, prohibitions or norms. They prevent us from doing, with good conscience, things that are known to be wrong, irrespective of all consequences, including good ones. Characteristic of deontological theories is the prioritization of the right over the good. The fact that my harming one person may save the lives of several others does not weigh with the strict deontologist; the rules guide my conduct, which is good or bad *in itself*, and not in respect of other considerations. A deontologist writing a code of conduct would not be directly concerned with maximizing happiness or minimizing pain, or indeed with any of the range of considerations that an emotivist, intuitionist or virtue-based theorist would necessarily appeal to. Instead, what would inform the rules of conduct is the distinction between that which is and is not permissible. This distinction enables agents to perceive what is the right thing to do. Again, this may be stated negatively; I am obliged *not* to do that which is not permissible. This negative characterization of morality is captured well in Mill's *Essay on Liberty*:

> Its ideal is negative rather than positive; passive rather than active; Innocence rather than Nobleness; Abstinence from Evil, rather than the energetic Pursuit of the Good; in its precepts (as has been well said) 'Thou shalt not' predominates unduly over 'thou shalt'.
>
> *(Mill 1859, cited in Warnock 1962: 177)*

Deontological constraints are paradigmatic of such rules. Three considerations show their nature and structure (Davies 1991). First, though it is possible to formulate these rules or constraints positively (for example, one might say that 'never lie' can be translated into 'always tell the truth'), they are negatively formulated and there is neither entailment nor equivalence between them. Additionally, the rules are narrowly framed and directed. One is not permitted to act in ways that are wrong. Not only does this give a form of specificity to the rule but it also puts into context the distinction between actions intended to bring about certain outcomes intentionally and those where, for example, bad outcomes result from foreseen and unforeseen consequences from our *prima facie* permissible action. For the deontologist, writing or indeed enforcing a code of conduct, wrong action (rule-breaking) is necessarily intentional action.

In many ways the moral value of games and sports has resided in rather opaque accounts of rule-responsibility. It is thought that if we can develop children (or coaches for that matter) who follow the rules (moral and non-moral), then we will thereby develop moral maturity (or professional conduct). But all this is a far cry from the idea of a moral *code*, a systematized set of principles, not merely aggregated and ultimately reducible to one. Thus, we often find reductions from many rules to the 'Golden Rule', and this is instanced in more than one type of ethico-religious system and, perhaps, most famously in philosophical terms by Kant's Categorical Imperative: 'act so as to treat rational beings always as ends and never as means only'. Yet the elegance of Kant's formulation of moral actions motivated by impartial duty with universality of application under the assent of practical reason is not mirrored in codes of conduct. Where Kant attempted to achieve a non-conflicting order of moral principles (notwithstanding the distinction between perfect duties that oblige all rational beings to act in specific ways that observe the rights of all rational beings, and imperfect duties that are not categorical but are selective and do not have corresponding rights), codes of conduct tend to be more eclectic. They have maintained, perhaps implicitly, the idea that rule-responsibility is at the heart of ethical conduct.[6]

From here it is but a short step to the assertion that the heart of the rule-based ethics, especially deontological ones, is negative; moral behaviour consists in the avoidance of wrong acts.[7] This is one reason why codes of conduct are framed explicitly or implicitly in rule-like ways, but another is their legalistic nature and the blameability they offer. Where there are rules, we should be able to distinguish right from wrongdoing and wrongdoers.

There are, however, weaknesses in this way of thinking. I shall take, for the purpose of exposition, merely one principle from the code of conduct of the most important coaching organization in the United Kingdom, the National Coaching Foundation (NCF).[8] The code displays a wide variety of rules, principles, duties and general exhortations, the type of which are likely to be familiar to the reader, and therefore the one exemplar is chosen merely as representative of the kind of analyses that might be made of the remainder of the code and, indeed, any other code of its kind. Consider, then, principle 3.3 in the Code of Practice for Sports Coaches: 'Coaches should not condone or engage in sexual harassment . . . with performers or colleagues. It is considered that sexual relationships with performers are *generally* inappropriate to the professional conduct of coaches' (emphasis added).

There is no reasonable person who would not want to say that sexual harassment is wrong. Surely part of what 'harassment' actually means is the negative evaluation; 'wrongful' (in the same way that someone could not condone murder, which is *defined* as 'wrongful killing'; if it were not wrongful, it would have to be an act that fell under some other description). Surely this principle is heading in the right direction at least; it sets out wrongful conduct and allows us to blame would-be wrongdoers and enable sanctions to be taken against them.

What, though, are we to think of this principle? First, let us be clear that it is an odd principle that admits of exceptions.[9] What is the function of the word 'generally' in its midst? Isn't a principle something which is absolute? Consider some classic deontological principles that are commonplace to those in a Judaeo-Christian tradition at least: 'thou shalt not kill' or 'thou shalt not steal'. Imagine now, then, 'thou shalt not lie, generally speaking'. This would appear an odd commandment were Moses to have brought it down from Mount Sinai. This might appear a trivial point but it is not. It kicks out at the very idea of establishing principles which are designed to function as universal rules, not mere guidelines.[10] This is, again, a very general difficulty with the universalization of moral rules. Perhaps it would be better to follow Hart's jurisprudential idea that we have rules which are indeterminate (Hart 1983). In special circumstances, things that we might normally disapprove of or even abhor may become permissible. This is the function of the word 'general'; perhaps it could be more strongly put.

By contrast, the American Psychological Association's updated code is less equivocal. It forbids sexual intimacies with existing clients or patients and minimally for two years after professional contact. Of course, the client or patient relationship is of a different kind than that of coach and athlete, yet the potential for abuse is also there. What is significant about the APA's code regarding sexual harassment is the further, explicit, rule that its members shall accord the complainant dignity and respect. The idea that the victim of sexual harassment should be taken seriously – morally seriously, that is – is an interesting one. What it points to is the institutional recognition of norms of acceptable and unacceptable practice in areas that can be ignored or ridden roughshod over because of the sometimes macho ethoses of sporting practices. Stories are legion in sports of sexual harassment being ignored, not taken seriously or considered as part and parcel of the whole package of elite sport. Again, there are salient differences between coaching and psychology, not least of all in respect of the control exercised over its members by a governing legislature. So much of sports coaching is carried out on a voluntary basis and there is little hope of exercising such a degree of control as could be exercised by the APA or the British Medical Council or the Law Society in Great Britain. Perhaps codes of conduct in sport are best viewed as forms of institutional posturing; important but without real bite.[11] I shall return to this point later.

Second, let us also be clear, as Wittgenstein points out in the *Philosophical Investigations*, that a rule cannot determine its own application. The sophistication of this insight is one that will be underdeveloped here.[12] I will explicate a little of the import of this remark by way of discussion of the scope, application and interpretation of rules and also by noting the different aspects of rule-following as distinct from merely acting in apparent accordance with a rule.

How should I conceive of the scope of any given rule that I am supposed to follow? Is it properly the place of a code of conduct to govern the conduct of its members outside the role of coach, given the many related and unrelated roles that a coach has to play? These roles range from parent, friend and counsellor merely in the coaching relationship; there are a plethora of others. Would it really be unethical, or 'inappropriate professional conduct', for someone to have sexual relations with a colleague? This is one of the points at which there is a salient distinction between coaching and psychology; we refer to those who seek their service as clients, yet the service they offer, though conceivably similar in certain contexts, *is* clearly different. So, then, let us agree that sexual harassment is wrong, but how did the formulation of the 'rule' concerning sexual harassment lead us here?

Perhaps we should ask 'what is the concept of "rule"?' or 'what does "rule" actually mean?' in order to begin. Fortunately, that question has already been asked. Baker and Hacker make the Wittgensteinian point that the concept of a rule does not adequately allow for an essentialist analysis; there are no common features to all the things we call 'rules' in virtue of which we call them 'rules'. The recognition of such need not paralyse us, though, for even if it opens up a certain generality, that generality is of a specific kind, as Baker and Hacker write:

> The generality of a rule lies in its use, not (or not necessarily) in its form. We guide our actions by reference to rules: we teach and explain rule-governed activities by citing the rules that govern it. When in doubt as to how to proceed we consult the rules . . . *But the forms of guidance by a rule are most varied.*
> (Baker and Hacker 1985: 45)

An important cautionary note is embodied in the final sentence regarding the variability of the forms of guidance that rules take. A cursory glance at the types of rules in any particular code of conduct would make this evident. That the rules refer to so many different types of activities and interests, from confidentiality and safety to informed consent, makes this inevitable. For present purposes, let us take the type of rule that is of direct concern to codes of conduct: moral rules. This theme has been taken up by Edmund Pincoffs, in his tirade against reductivism in ethics. He warns us to be wary of asking of moral rules what they cannot deliver by attending to their divergent powers:

> Rules may be like general standing commands or like general standing orders; analogously they may be like general standing specific and non-specific prescriptions. They may allow no leeway in compliance or they may allow a great deal of compliance.
>
> Some moral rules are more like general standing orders than like general standing commands: for example, 'Love thy neighbor' or 'Do not cause suffering.' They say what is wanted but do not say what to do. If, however, we concentrate upon rules that are like commands, such as 'Do not kill' or 'Never break promises,' we are likely to think of moral rules much like criminal laws, in that they will consist for us, largely of specific injunctions and directions. But if we recognize that they can also be like orders, we will be more aware of the discretion they sometimes allow. They do not tell us exactly what to do so much as they indicate what we should struggle toward in our own way.
>
> *(Pincoffs 1986: 25)*

We can see now, perhaps, the unavoidable disparity of the *kinds* of rules that are on offer in codes of conduct. For attention must be paid not only to their differing roles, but also to the comparative directness and ambiguity of their application.

Third, following one of Wittgenstein's major theses against the 'private language' argument, Baker and Hacker offer exegesis on the distinction between rule-following and acting merely in accordance with the rule. (It will repay attention for my present purpose even if I attend only to the consequences of this point, though its original target is significantly different, and significantly more profound in philosophical terms, than that which I aim towards.) The distinction is apposite; it points to the discontinuity between the vogue for codes of professional (and therefore ethical) conduct and much current practice in elite sports that is characteristic of behavioural accordance rather than rule-following proper. Baker and Hacker write:

> It is not at all necessary that for an activity to be guided by a rule the rule should enter into the activity or even cross the minds of those engaged in it (chess players do not think about the rules of chess as they play; they know them too well . . . But neither is it enough that the behaviour of someone following a rule merely conforms with the rule (a chess computer follows no rules). Nor is it sufficient that he once learned the rule – for that is past history . . . and the issue here is his present possession of an ability, not its genesis. Nor would it

suffice that the rule might be encoded in his brain (whatever that might mean); for being caused to act by the encoding of a rule is precisely *not* to follow a rule . . . That a person's action is normative, that he is following a rule, that he is guided by a rule (or better, guides himself by reference to a rule) is manifest in the manner in which he uses rules, invokes rule-formulations, refers to rules explaining what he did, justifying what he did in the face of criticism, evaluating what he did and correcting what he did, criticizing his mistakes, and so forth.

(1985: 45)

As with the actions of our sports coaches, so with codes of conduct. Why do we need a *rule* like that concerning sexual harassment? Well, let us be clear that such actions are wrong and that we scarcely need a code to tell us this. We can no more sexually harass our colleagues or athletes than we can any other person in the street. So the rule, in this sense, tells us nothing new. No, to follow the rule with regard to sexual harassment is to understand the psychology of the situation: its thick, substantial richness. Rule-based theories do not work that way. What is the point, then? Well, as an organization, the NCF recognizes clearly and properly that situations in which coaches and athletes find themselves can introduce temptations into human relationships. Such vicious behaviours as exploitation, domination, extortion or bribery can occur. And with specific reference to sexual harassment, oftentimes athletes are scantily clad and situations where the coach is required to physically manipulate body positions are not rare. The rules are intended to preserve proper human relationships in the coaching situation. We use them for a variety of purposes, as Baker and Hacker note: to explain, justify, evaluate, correct and criticize. An example will better illuminate this point.

Consider the following scenario. I am the coach of some elite female adolescent gymnasts. You are one of these gymnasts, aspiring to a full-time sporting career. Mine is a privileged position. The children are with me two or three hours nearly every day of the week. They respond to me. I am a power figure; I know my sport; its history; its techniques and skills; its hierarchy; I hold a privileged position within that hierarchy; I am the gate through which the successful gymnast must go first; I am esteemed in the community; I am strong physically; I can catch you, literally, when you fall; I can lift you up psychologically or I can destroy you and your career by various means; you need me; above all, perhaps, you trust me; your parents trust me. The sexual harassment of you by me through the powers of my station violates that trust. We do not need the rule book to guide our actions; we do not consult it to see whether we do right or wrong, good or bad, nor to explain, criticize or justify those actions. (Though here again we must ask how, even when rules are clear and unambiguous, such as that for sexual harassment, there are difficulties; 'it wasn't harassment,' says the coach; 'of course that's wrong. But she gave me the come-on, she wanted it; that's not harassment', as the unfortunate script too often goes.) Instead we enquire as to what sort of person the coach is (we often ask for character witnesses); what his or her motivations might have been; whether he or she was disposed to other kinds of abuses; what his or her biography or institutional affiliations point towards, and so on. The rules may allow us to blame, but they do not do the job of determining the context or evaluating the person; other considerations must come into play.

To consider the actual abuses that codes of professional conduct seek to highlight, enables us to see the laudable work that the word 'generally' was trying to perform in our principle above. No rule book can anticipate all actions; nor can it describe, or predict, all possible actions that may be considered professional and unprofessional. Rule books just cannot do that sort of thing. And so what we have is an eclectic mix; some rules we make can perform specific tasks, others have more general application. We cannot expect them to be like a calculus table to be consulted prior to performance, nor is this how they work in real life. And to capture coaches who are unprofessional in their conduct, we may very well wish to distinguish those who are genuinely following the rules (of course, not in the calculus-like parody) from those whose behaviour merely *appears* not to break the rule while they are appearing to act in accordance with it.

What becomes clear from this brief consideration of rules in codes of conduct in addition to the diversity of rules and their action-guiding implications is the need for something beyond mere rule-observance where this means the avoidance of rule-breaking actions. We can imagine, quite wrongly, that rule responsibility is at the centre of ethical life. This is why Koehn's condition that a professional must have a highly developed sense of responsibility, though true, falls short of the mark. It is clear that it is not merely an important professional virtue, but an essential social virtue; how could we get along if there were social anarchy or mere unpredictability and randomness of behaviour? What, of course, does not follow is the idea that ethics and ethical conduct can be simply *reduced* to the idea of rule responsibility. To see why this is the case, we need to return to our earlier distinction of being and doing; of agency and acts. By turning to a non-reductivist vocabulary of the virtues, we can prize open the reasons why such unprofessional conduct is reproachable; for the coach in our scenario is left in the care, or striking distance, of someone who is valuable in and of his or herself, and that trust has been violated by the coach. I shall develop this point in the sections that follow.

One of the central reasons why we need either to replace or to augment the notion of rules as exhaustively descriptive of ethical theory and conduct is, so to speak, their under-determination. Put simply, though they commonly tell us what not to do, often what to aim towards and, occasionally, what to do, they leave so much else in the void. Fried (1978: 13) captures this point well: 'One cannot live one's life by the demands of the domain of the right. After having avoided wrong and doing one's duty, an infinity of choices is left to be made.'

When, therefore, we consult the rules, to examine conduct that is under question, just as when we wish to commend conduct, the rule book will not do the work for us. The rule cannot determine its own application; we must do that from within the forms of life we inhabit. And in so doing we must try to work our way through the unavoidable pitfalls and fallibility of character evaluation in a spirit devoid of capriciousness or any of the forms of bias. But such actions as we will attempt to inspect and label 'professional' and 'unprofessional' will admit various, perhaps conflicting, interpretations. We are left to ask, 'how we can possibly ground our interpretations, to know we have seen a situation aright?' and 'what underwrites our confidence?' to avoid the vertigo of subjectivity. These particular questions must be left for another day, but one thing is certain: if we are to discuss more fully such conduct as is to be characterized 'professional' and 'unprofessional', we must move to the language of virtues.

Virtue-based ethical theories

Let it be clear, however, that in making transparent some of the difficulties of rules-based ethics and in commending virtue-based ethics, at least with respect to my present concern with the theoretical and practical limitations of codes of conduct, I must make similar caveats. First, the term 'virtue-based ethics' is itself a caricature, for there are many modern and pre-modern theories of virtue and the good life. Second, I am not in any way committed to the thesis that rule-based considerations are necessarily either inferior, or reducible, to virtue considerations. It will be one of my conclusions that they may happily coexist for the purposes of guiding professional conduct. I hold, instead, to the rather weaker claim that rules, principles and their like are not exhaustive of the basic facts of moral life, a picture of which is incomplete without reference to the virtues.

The tendency to think of morality in terms of duties and principles has been challenged recently by a powerful array of neo-Aristotelians.[13] Their point of departure is to be found not in specific behaviours governed by rules or principles of right conduct, but in the character of good persons living good lives. The pursuit of *eudaimonia* (human well-being or flourishing) is better served by certain sorts of characters rather than others. We prefer the just to the unjust, the courageous to the cowardly, the honest to the dishonest, and so forth. It is these virtue-based considerations that guide my conduct, not the moral rule book. In a sporting context there is a clear analogy. Are we not to prefer those who merely keep the rules for fear of being punished but those who keep them in order that the contest is a fair and equal test of relevant abilities and powers? And if sports are to flourish too, must we not have trustworthy coaches and wise administrators as well as honest performers, all of whom keep the sporting faith; the spirit of the game?

The picture of the good life is one that is lived in accordance with virtue against a given background, for example of the proper nature of human being (as in the pre-modern work of Aristotle) or the cultural and historical traditions I am heir to (as in the modern works of MacIntyre). *Arete* (excellence) is that which enables persons to achieve their *telos* (proper end) of flourishing, yet *arete* is also an ingredient of the attainment of that goal at the same time. What constitutes the good life is socially and historically located, yet it will be achieved by persons who are possessed of a core of virtues that are acquired, displayed and reproduced in a variety of shared social practices that are themselves constitutive of broader cultural traditions.

When I am faced with a quandary, on a virtue-based account it is not that I can simply consult a moral rule book that tells everyone, irrespective of context, not to do this and not to do that. I cannot write off the particularity of quandary. It is 'me', a grounded self, with particular goals, desires, needs, habits and roles. What will *I* do here in the light of what I conceive myself to be: just, cowardly, arrogant, sensitive, untrustworthy?

One of the key points in such a scheme is the notion of a virtue conceived not as an isolated act but as part of a narrative that is my life. This consideration points us towards the psycho-social aspects of my agency because the virtues or vices I display in this or that situation flow from relatively settled dispositions in qualitatively different ways. Virtues and vices are displayed in the *manner* in which I am disposed to act in regular and interrelated ways. This point is usually developed by remarking, first, that one cannot simply possess a virtue in isolation, and, second, that the moral sphere is thereby extended to include a wider range of acts and appraisals that are found in rule-based accounts. MacDowell develops the point:

> Thus the particular virtues are not a batch of independent sensitivities. Rather, we use the concepts of the particular virtues to mark similarities and dissimilarities among the manifestations of a single sensitivity which is what virtue, in general, is: an ability to recognize requirements which situations impose on one's behaviour. It is a single complex sensitivity of this sort which we are aiming to instil when we aim to inculcate a moral outlook.
>
> *(1981, cited in Holtzman and Leich 1981, 332–333)*

But if there is no rule to guide us, how do we know which virtue, which sensitivity, ought properly to be triggered by this or that situation? One resort, analogous to the reduction to the 'master rule', is to pick out a 'master virtue' such as the disposition to be just. What can assure that my acts tend towards the appropriate amount of each virtue and fail not in excess or deficiency? Time and space do not allow further elaboration but a second example will show the more complete range of ethical considerations that virtue accounts would bring to the surface over and above mere rule-responsibility.

Trust and the virtuous coach

To enact and to evaluate trusting relationships necessarily requires a range of dispositions from courage, to wickedness, spite, generosity, foolhardiness, benevolence and beyond. To dislocate trusting from the fuller gamut of dispositions and the contexts in which they are triggered is to focus on a partial aspect of the picture and thus to distort the grasp we have of it. There are, therefore, two reductive temptations that are to be avoided. We should neither consider isolated acts in our evaluation of the professional conduct of coaches, nor focus too resolutely on single dispositions in evaluations thereof.

What is it, then, for the parent and performer to trust a coach? Social scientists have often talked about trust merely as a reliance on another person or thing to perform some kind of act or function under conditions of limited knowledge (Gambetta 1988). But this understanding of trust is economistic; it lacks an explicit moral dimension. Sisela Bok was one of the first philosophers to recognize this dimension when she wrote, '*Whatever* matters to human beings, trust is the atmosphere in which it thrives' (Bok 1978: 31). It is precisely because activities like sport are inherently social that virtues like trust are ineliminable. Developing this point, Baier (1994) has offered an account of the moral concept of trust and its close conceptual relations. Among other things, she highlights the importance of considering the notions of value and vulnerability in addition to reliance:

> [L]ook at the variety of sorts of goods or things one values or cares about, which can be left or put within the striking powers of others, and the variety of ways we can let or leave others 'close' enough to what we value to be able to harm it. Then we can look at various reasons we might have for wanting or accepting such closeness of those with power to harm us, and for confidence that they will not use this power.
>
> *(1994: 100)*

Now the coach is someone in whom discretion is invested. Parents value their children more than just about anything in the world. When they entrust the coach with their children, they place within his or her sphere of influence a vulnerable person, one who can be damaged in a variety of ways. Yet they necessarily trust the coach as a professional. Expectations issue from the status of coach *as* professional, as we have seen. Parents properly expect the coach not merely to be the bearer of expertise, either with or without a fee. Loaded into the coaching situation are a set of normative expectations whereby the coach, implicitly at least, aims towards the good of the performer with appropriate knowledge and skills utilized in a framework of accumulated wisdom generated within the practice.

Consider, then, another scenario. My young gymnast, Johnny, shows great promise. He has the potential to be an Olympian. His parents are exceptionally keen. Perhaps their zealous guidance is motivated by their lowly socio-economic status (this would be a route to a good college scholarship, a lucrative career, and so forth); perhaps it is a desire for vicarious success that makes them want their child to succeed. Whatever the motivation, I am told in no uncertain terms that I am to do whatever it takes to make Johnny the best gymnast that he can be. He is struggling with his flares on the pommel horse; he cannot perform sufficient repetitions and their quality is lacking owing to his own deficient amplitude in the adductors. And this afternoon he is tired after a heavy conditioning session this morning. Various options compete in my mind: shall I make him try that routine one more time? Is he too tired? Have I succeeded in achieving all I wanted in this session? Have I done enough for next week's championship? All these questions are invoked in everyday contexts that commonly fall well outside the rule-governed jurisdiction of the code of conduct (or perhaps better, beyond even the most comprehensive rule book), yet in each, as coach, I may have to ask myself, 'what sort of person am I/would I be to act in this way or that?' And the range of replies may range from considerate, sympathetic and supportive, to insensitive, myopic, arrogant, intolerant, vindictive and spiteful. How could any rule book cover such a range without tearing down all the rainforests in order to attempt to write rules for every possible occasion or eventuality? And yet the exaltation of the rule-book mentality – 'moral minimalism', to invent a term of art for the occasion – is precisely that mentality whose character is raised by the exclamation 'we have done nothing wrong or immoral; we have broken no rules', as if the latter entailed the former.

I decide that the only way Johnny will succeed is if I 'help' him gain the amplitude by further stretching exercises. I ask Johnny to go down into the splits and to get his chest as close to the floor as possible. He fails to get close. I continue to urge him with greater vociferousness. He complies, he utters no words of complaint. Then, while he is unaware, I come behind him and, with all my strength, force his chest down to the floor and hold him down. I prove to him his body's capabilities; I chastise him for his laziness and lack of willpower; I rebuke him for the ingratitude for his parents' sacrifices for his kit, travel expenses, coaching fees, and so forth. And all the time I *may* have broken no rule. I may have complied with every consenting wish of his parents (perhaps even Johnny himself, after he has recovered from his tearful fit) and I have reinforced the 'no pain, no gain' ethic in him. Yet on the way home I reflect; what sort of person am I that I should do such a thing? Shall I convince myself that I have done nothing wrong since I have broken no rules and in any case it is all in the child's long-term financial and performative interests; his parents sanctioned it? Without my intervention there is no way he would have . . . and so on. Such a view *may* be underwritten by our rule-based ethic. I am comforted. But perhaps I reflect upon considerations that perhaps should have weighed with me as the boy's coach, a figure esteemed in the community, a role model. I think to myself, 'Johnny trusted me, and his parents trusted me with a son whose respect I have complied with only under the auspices of potential star performer.'

What are we to think of this, not uncommon, scenario? Let us accept that there is no clear application of a rule that will help us unequivocally here. The situation, if not a moral dilemma, is deeply ambiguous. Given that we impart to the trusted coach a valued child, within the limits of discretionary power we run the risks of verbal, physical or psychological abuse. Anyone who has been engaged with elite sport knows how cruel it can be. Yet this is not something that can be avoided lest we attempt to live in a bubble, or indeed to wrap our children in cotton wool; it comes as part and parcel both of sports and of trust itself:

> To understand the moral risks of trust, it is important to see the special sort of vulnerability it introduces. Yet the discretionary element which introduces this special danger is essential to that which trust at its best makes possible.

To elaborate Hume: ''Tis impossible to separate the chance of good from the risk of ill.'

(Baier 1994: 104)

Trust, then, on Baier's analysis, is characterized as letting persons take care of something that is cared for or valued, where such caring involves the use of discretionary powers about the reliance and competence of the trusted. Risk, as she reminds us, is of the very essence in trusting. But there are good and bad bets. In accepting this, Baier builds in a normative dimension that inescapably requires good judgement. To leave your baby with the nearest passer-by while you go into a store to buy some provisions while on a shopping trip to London or New York is not trusting but, *ceteris paribusm,* foolishness. We should be wary of jumping to the conclusion that the proper attitude to adopt in such a situation is to distrust. The consequences of distrust are dire; it is, as Baier reminds us, a fragile plant which does not long survive the inspection of its roots. This point is reinforced that we must view trust as any other disposition in the context of the person as a whole and the community in which they reside.

We do not, of course, expect to read in any code of ethics a rule confirming the trustworthiness of the coach. Under the cloak of moral minimalism, coaches may sell themselves the story that where no rules are broken, there is no moral difficulty. Yet, as we have seen, the rules under-determine the ethical sphere in everyday life as well as in professional interactions. There is no rule to trust; it is almost a matter of volitional necessity. We have no choice in the matter most of the time. Like our health, which is foregrounded as a concern only when we are ill, so we attend to trust only when it is broken. And what would be the cost of continual distrust? Is not paranoia the name for such a condition?

The latter considerations are brought before us *only* under the aspect of a proper consideration of the place and role of virtue in ethical situations, whether everyday or climactic. Moreover, these considerations are to be prioritized not simply by asking whether I have broken any rules but by asking what a person in my situation might do in the light of the kind of life that they consider 'good'. And this cannot be done by the methodological trick of making dispositions generalizable under principled propositions, though this is, I think, precisely what codes of conduct illicitly do; code writers attempt to make rules do the work of virtue requirements by replacing the need for particularity. They attempt to relegate context-sensitive judgement to the rule of law.

One needn't throw the baby out with the bathwater. What we might say by way of temporary conclusion is, first, that the scope of rule-based ethics is under-determining; there is still oftentimes a wide range of options and corresponding dispositions to fill the void after the rules have been laid out. Second, the rules do not specify their own scope and interpretation; agents, who are variously virtuous and vicious, do. Likewise, third, even after the rule is specified, it will only be *followed*, in the strong sense, by the virtuous agent. Mere robot-like rule observance is an inappropriate point of departure for our description of ethical lives, professional and otherwise. And worse, it can lead to the further entrenchment of the ethos of rule-bending in its extreme as is characteristic of so much conduct in modern sports.

This is precisely the case of our gym coach, whose actions are those of the technocrat. His reasoning is instrumental. He sets out his ends unreflectively in accordance with the relevant dominant ethoses and cants slogans around his workhouse: 'no guts, no glory', 'just do it', 'nobody remembers who came second'. What justifies the selection of means is technical efficiency and economy. Ethical discourse is suspended under various guises such as 'nice guys come last'. Bend the rules as much as you can but don't break them, or if you do, whatever else, don't get caught. Here the professional as craftsman finds no home; his or her dedication, care and commitment to the defining excellences of the practice, moral *and* technical, are relegated to the sole, justifying, end: winning performance whose services have been bought and paid for; whose contractual labour measured only against that reductivist end.

Conclusion: virtues and rules in professional life

What kind of communities are developed in professional sports practices? This is a question insufficiently asked in the education of coaches, whose agendas are narrowly conceived in instrumental and technicist terms. Two witticisms spring to mind. First, I think it was Samuel Beckett who once said that, at 50, we get the face we deserve. Perhaps, at the close of the twentieth century we are getting the sporting milieu we deserve too. Too readily, journalists, administrators, performers and coaches refer to sports and athletes as professionals merely by virtue of their grossly inflated remuneration or their expert knowledge, without recognizing what by virtue of that normative description is entrusted to them; the demands that the term places upon them. Their mien is too often characteristic of Molière's remark about writing, a profession 'like prostitution: First you do it because you enjoy it; then you do it for a few friends; then you do it for money'.[14] We must remind ourselves continuously that professionalism demands much more.

I am conscious that the burden of my argument has rested on the explication of theoretical weaknesses as applied to a single principle for professional conduct Ironically enough, my argument requires that it be taken on that trust which I have briefly argued is definitive of professionalism; that, indeed, extrapolation can further be made to other principles, rules and codes.[15] This is one of the areas that needs far greater explication, as does the need to explicate more fully the relationships that exist between rules and virtues themselves. There is, of course, no use in philosophers who favour rule-based ethics castigating their otherwise inclined colleagues as 'allergic to principles', nor in virtue theorists characterizing adversaries disparagingly as 'psychologically phobic'. The debate must instead focus on the complexity of their unavoidable relations. I have not eschewed rules altogether from codes of conduct but have instead focused on their variety, the difficulties necessarily entailed in their interpretation and application, as well as their characteristic under-determination.

Codes of conduct are indeed indispensable to the safety-net task of catching those who will be unprofessional in their conduct and enabling their punishment and/or expulsion. What they cannot do, and what they should not be expected to do, is to have any great effect in ensuring ethical behaviour *per se*. In highlighting this shortfall, I have focused positively on the role that virtues play in professional life and ethical explanation and have argued the necessary incompleteness of ethical evaluation and motivation in their absence. I have hinted at difficulties entailed in conceiving professionals as technocrats, whether merely as hired hands or providers of expertise, and how, following Koehn, we might more profitably look to the notion of trust as characteristic of the basis of professionalism rather than to mere rule responsibility and the legally inspired 'moral minimalism' that so often accompanies it. In the particularity and richness of personal relationships that exist most commonly between coach and performer, the rules, I fancy, play very little motivating or explanatory roles.[16]

Notes

1 Koehn cites Annette Baier's original (1986) essay 'Trust and Anti-trust', which appeared in *Ethics*, January, 96: 231–260. All references to that essay heretoforward are from the version of it that appears in Baier's (1994) *Moral Prejudices: Essays on Ethics*.
2 Koehn offers etymological support for this normative account:

> The word 'profess' comes from the Greek verb *prophaino* meaning 'to declare publicly.' The Greek *prophaino* became the Latin *professio*, a term applied to the public statement made by persons who sought a position of public trust.
>
> *(Koehn 1994: 59)*

3 I have made amendments, and incorporated Koehn's own augmentations without distinction, in parentheses.
4 These points are synthesized and amended from Dawson (1994) and Brackenridge (1994). Whether or not any code can, as Dawson asserts, offer a neutral framework seems to be highly dubious. Time and space, however, do not permit further comment.
5 The *locus classicus* of this view is Kant's *Groundwork of the Metaphysic of Morals*.
6 It is precisely this point, that rule-responsibility should not be thought of as the heart of morality, that is one of the main targets in Pincoffs (1986).
7 Any utilitarian would properly object that this negative characterization, though it fits the utilitarian rule to minimize pain, misses entirely the corresponding rule to maximize happiness or pleasure. It should be clear that the general target here is the deontological one.
8 I am particularly grateful to Coachwise for sharing a draft copy of their code of conduct before publication.
9 For an account of the idea of a moral principle, see Schneewind (1970, cited in Hauerwas and MacIntyre 1983). He articulates three features of a classic moral principle: relative context-freedom, unexceptionability and substantiality. To these, he adds a fourth, a foundational or basic feature, which, in combination with the others, gives what he calls a 'classical first principle' (ibid.: 114).
10 An amusing anecdote illuminates the point. I hope it does not offend my feminist friends and colleagues; it ought not to. In the smash hit film *Ghostbusters* the fraudulent psychology professor Venkman has gone to see a would-be client who has been citing paranormal activity in her flat (the sort of activity a code of conduct might properly comment upon), whereupon he finds her body lying on the bed with another identical

figure floating invitingly above her in a provocative fashion. Venkman at first says, 'I make it a rule never to go to bed with more than one person at the same time' (or something very similar), but upon further exhortations gives in with a spurious self-justification: 'it's more of a guideline than a rule'!

11 I am grateful to John Lyle for this observation.

12 This is not the place for Wittgensteinian exegesis. See instead Baker and Hacker (1985); also Holtzman and Leich (1981).

13 The most prominent of whom is MacIntyre (1981). I have elsewhere offered a critical account of what parts of his thesis might look like in the context of sport (McNamee 1995).

14 As reported by Solomon (1993).

15 Though, for the untrusting, I have elsewhere explored a different and greater range of principles and rules in a paper presented to the Leisure Studies Association 1995 Conference, entitled 'Theoretical Limitations in Codes of Ethical Conduct' and published in McFee *et al.* (1996). This chapter is an extended version of that presentation.

16 I am very grateful to Graham McFee, Gordon Reddiford and Tony Skillen for their helpful comments.

References

Baier, A.C. (1994) *Moral Prejudices: Essays on Ethics*, London: Harvard University Press.

Baker, G.P. and Hacker, P.M.S. (1985) *Wittgenstein: Rules, Grammar and Necessity*, Oxford: Blackwell.

Bok, S. (1978) *Lying*, New York: Pantheon Books.

Brackenridge, C. (1994) 'Fair play or fair game? Child sexual abuse in sport organisations', *International Review for Sociology of Sport*, 29(3): 287–299.

Davies, N. (1991) 'Contemporary deontology', in P. Singer (ed.) *A Companion to Ethics*, Oxford: Blackwell.

Dawson, A.J. (1994) 'Professional codes of practice and ethical conduct', *Journal of Applied Philosophy*, 11(2): 145–154.

Fried, C. (1978) *Right and Wrong*, Cambridge, MA: Harvard University Press.

Gambetta, D. (ed.) (1988) *Trust*, Oxford: Blackwell.

Hart, H.L.A. (1983) 'Problems of the philosophy of law', in H.L.A. Hart (ed.) *Essays in Jurisprudence and Philosophy*, Oxford: Clarendon Press.

Holtzman, S.H. and Leich, C.M. (eds) (1981) *Wittgenstein: To Follow a Rule*, London: Routledge and Kegan Paul.

Kant, I. (1953) *Groundwork of the Metaphysic of Morals*, trans. H.J. Paton, *The Moral Law*, London: Hutchinson.

Koehn, D. (1994) *The Ground of Professional Ethics*, London: Routledge.

MacDowell, J. (1981) 'Virtue and reason', in S.H. Holtzman and C.M. Leich (eds) *Wittgenstein: To Follow a Rule*, London: Routledge and Kegan Paul.

MacIntyre, A.C. (1981) *After Virtue*, London: Duckworth.

McFee, G., Murphy, W. and Whannel, G. (1996) *Leisure Cultures: Values, Genders, Lifestyles*, Brighton: CSRC.

McNamee, M.J. (1995) 'Sporting practices, institutions and virtues: a critique and a restatement', *Journal of Philosophy of Sport*, 22–23: 61–82.

Mill, J.S. ([1859] 1962) 'On liberty', in M. Warnock (ed.) *Utilitarianism*, Glasgow: Fontana.

Morgan, W.J. (1993) 'Amateurism and professionalism as moral languages: in search of a moral image of sport', *Quest*, 45: 470–493.

Pincoffs, E. (1986) *Quandaries and Ethics: Against Reductivism in Ethics*, Lawrence, KS: University of Kansas Press.

Schneewind, J.B. (1970) 'Moral principles and moral knowledge', in S. Hauerwas and A.C. MacIntyre (1983) *Revisions: Changing Perspectives in Moral Philosophy*, Notre Dame, IN: University of Notre Dame Press.

Schneider, A.J. and Butcher, R.B. (1993) 'For the love of a game: a philosophical defense of amateurism', *Quest*, 45: 460–469.

Solomon, R.C. (1993) *Ethics and Excellence: Co-operation and Integrity in Business*, Oxford: Oxford University Press.

Williams, B. (1985) *Ethics and the Limits of Philosophy*, London: Fontana.

PART II
The character of the coach

3

BECOMING A GOOD COACH

Coaching and *phronesis*

Øyvind F. Standal and Liv B. Hemmestad

Introduction

The *Oxford English Dictionary* (2006) lists over 20 meanings of the word *good*, two of which are particularly relevant for our chapter: (1) 'good' as in successful or skilful, i.e. a coach who consistently achieves good results; and (2) 'good' as in doing what is morally right, i.e. a coach whose coaching is virtuous. It would not be out of place to suggest that in the abundance of literature on coaching, the first meaning of good has received most attention. Though the two meanings of the word should not be viewed as competing or mutually excluding, it is the second sense of good that will be our topic.

In this chapter, we will first briefly review some of the literature on coaching. This literature suggests that coaching is a complex domain of professional practice, where a science-driven, technical approach dominates. This is an approach that favours the first meaning of the word 'good' over the second. In order to bring the second meaning of 'good' into sharper focus, we suggest that the Aristotelian notion *phronesis* (practical wisdom) is useful. We will try to make the case for the relevance of *phronesis* in sport coaching, and we will also take up the question of how *phronesis* is learned.

Coaching: a complex domain

It is argued that the skilful coach must have extensive sport-specific knowledge about the techniques and tactics of the given sport (Isberg 2001). In addition, s/he must have administrative leadership, psychological insight and the training expertise of a physiologist (Martens 1996). In working with athletes, the coach must simultaneously be able to retain a long-term perspective in planning for a season, and make immediate decisions on the training ground and in the heat of the game. In addition, the coach is held accountable not only for the performance of the team and the individual athletes, but also for the well-being of the team members (Coakley 1994; Portrac *et al.* 2000; Ronglan 2000). As the body of scientific knowledge in all these domains is rapidly growing, the skills needed to cope with the coaching situation consequently become increasingly complex.

One way of overcoming the complexities in the coaching situation is to break down the coaching process into manageable goals, performance targets and work tasks for the athletes. Doing so provides structure, direction and focus for the coaches' work. This approach is advocated in textbooks with a 'how-to-coach' approach, and is characterized by general recipes and checklists for successful coaching, or by models that attempt to analyse the coaching process from a chosen and purportedly superior framework (see Lyle 2002). These 'how-to-coach' approaches have been challenged, for instance by Jones and Wallace (2006), for being idealized and providing a false and seductive sense of security and control, thus ignoring the variability and unpredictability of human interaction. It is also argued that one should be warned not to reduce a complex process into something one-dimensional (Hemmestad *et al.*, accepted for publication).

Another way for the coach to deal with the complexities of coaching is to seek scientific knowledge to support his or her work. Knowledge about sports coaching has been closely related to the methodological preoccupations of natural science (Gilbert and Trudel 2004; Locke 2004). This kind of research has been fed into the theory and methodology of training and labelled 'coaching science' (Nash and Collins 2006; Woodman 1993). However, Jones (2007: 163) maintains that coaching science adopts 'a rather narrow, rationalistic bio-scientific approach to coaching giving precedence to physiological, psychological and nutritional "facts", [thus presenting] coaching as an almost autonomous body of information, which just needs to be given, unquestioned, to the performer.' Thus, in Jones' perspective, coaching science has failed to take into account the complexities and context-dependent features that are at play in every coaching situation.[1]

This is not to say that coaching science is unable to inform the practical, everyday work of the coach. However, in both coaching science and the how-to-coach approaches, the coach is viewed as simply applying his/her means towards the realization of the goals in an objective manner, and as such the difficulties of situational decision making are underestimated. In addition, this way of viewing the work of the coach fails to give sufficient attention to the challenges faced by the coach in the swampy lowlands of practical situations where technical solutions are defied (Schön 1983). By reducing the practical work of coaches to value-neutral and technical questions about finding and implementing the best means to achieve victory, little room is left to discuss the value-laden and ethically charged dimensions of the coaching profession.

In order to frame our understanding of the actions of a good and virtuous coach in everyday encounters with athletes, we will draw on the Aristotelian distinction between *technê* and *phronesis*, and we will relate this distinction to the rationality of coaching practices.

Phronesis: a brief introduction

Although Aristotle's philosophy is over 2000 years old, it is still seen as relevant today because, among other things, of its nuanced conception of knowledge and rationality (Dunne 1993, 2005; Gallagher 1992; Saugstad 2002, 2005). In the *Nicomachean Ethics*, Aristotle (1998) distinguished between two different categories of knowledge, namely theoretical and practical knowledge. Theoretical knowledge (*episteme*) concerns the invariable laws of nature, i.e. those things that exist out of necessity, uninfluenced by human beings (e.g. astronomy, mathematics). Since *episteme* concerns the eternal and invariable, it is possible to give demonstrative proof of this kind of knowledge. Practical knowledge, on the other hand, is distinguished from the theoretical, in the sense that it is a domain of knowledge that human beings influence through their actions. Because it is variable and influenced by human actions, no demonstrative proof can be given of practical knowledge. Indeed, it is an important aspect of the Aristotelian theory of knowledge that the different forms of knowledge admit of different degrees of security, so that one should not expect the same degree of exactness in practical knowledge as in theoretical: 'it is evidently equally foolish to accept probable reasoning from a mathematician and to demand from a rhetorician demonstrative proof' (Aristotle 1998: 3).

The domain of practical knowledge is further divided into two, and encompasses *techné*, which is a form of productive knowledge (i.e. regarding the capacity to make), and *phronesis*, which is most often translated as practical wisdom. Aristotle defines practical wisdom as 'a reasoned and true state of capacity to act with regard to human goods' (ibid.: 143). It is this capacity that we want to link to the professional practice of coaching.[2]

The hallmark of *techné* is that the end product can be evaluated without reference to the maker of the product and the process of making it. When it comes to *phronesis*, on the other hand, there is no clearly definable result that can be separated and identified apart from the act and the acting agent. Therefore, the goal of *phronesis* is to be found in the practice itself. That is, *phronesis* is a form of performative knowing (Dunne 2005).

As an example, one can say that making a piece of furniture is an outcome of *techné*. The quality of a table is evaluated with reference not to the way it was made, but to the quality of the end product; if it is a good and useful (or beautiful) table, the way it was made is not of particular concern. *Phronesis*, on the other hand, has specific reference to the way that the act of doing something is performed. *Phronesis* concerns the capacity to act in accordance with virtues such as justice, courage, wisdom and temperance (Vetlesen 2007). Whereas *techné* is an act of applying means towards the realization of an external end, *phronesis* is an end in itself.[3]

Different forms of rationality in coaching

On the basis of this account, one could say that there are two different forms of rationality at play in *techné* and *phronesis* (Dunne 2005). We are quite familiar with the rationality of *techné*, because we have retained that word in our language (e.g. technology). Technical rationality has achieved hegemonic dominance in society in general, and, as we argued above, it also has a strong position within the field of sports coaching. Its dominance over other forms of rationality is so strong that 'it is no longer seen as *a* form of rationality, with its own limited sphere of validity, but is coincident with *rationality as such*' (ibid.: 374), to the extent that other modes of rationality appear to be a- or irrational.

In its nature, technical rationality adheres to a kind of objectivity that seemingly guards against the interference of the coaches' subjectivity. Its procedures are transparent and explicit, thus establishing unambiguous criteria for accountability and success. In the fields of sports coaching and physical education, the idea of technical rationality finds a clear expression through the so-called linear model of professional practice, where the coach first explicitly specifies the goals and then selects a strategy for his/her intervention. Preferably this choice is made on the basis of scientific evidence for what works. Next, the coach intervenes and performs the planned training session, before s/he assesses the outcomes of the intervention (see Hammersley 2001 for a critique).

Though this way of thinking about coaching practice is intuitively appealing and has some truth to it, it also hides or overlooks important aspects of sport coaching. More specifically, it ignores the interpretations and judgements made on the micro level of interaction (Biesta 2007; Jones 2007). Sport coaches work in dynamic conditions where one cannot know for sure what will happen next, and where coaches' actions do not necessarily have immediate and knowable effects (Saury and Durand 1998).

Practical rationality is concerned with those subject matters that are variable and unruly, in the sense that they do not lend themselves easily to pre-designed plans (Dunne 2005). The complex situation of human interaction is an example of such a subject matter. Though these situations display some amount of regularity, they may also deviate from each other in any number of ways. The characteristic feature of practical rationality, according to Dunne (ibid.: 376), is judgement, i.e. the 'ability to recognize situations, cases, or problems of this kind (which are perhaps of *no* clearly specifiable kind) and to deal with them adequately and appropriately'. Practical rationality aims at mediation between general principles and the particular case at hand, without subsuming the interpretation of the particulars under the laws of the general. This means that whenever the good coach faces a given situation, s/he does not try to understand the situation from within a specific theoretical framework that can prescribe the proper action. It is the specific case at hand which guides the interpretations. These interpretations are of course made with some general principles as a backdrop that may be formed by theoretical knowledge. But, importantly, the interpretations are also made in light of the coach's previous experience.

Thus, it may seem that there is a clear and strict separation between *techné* and *phronesis*, where the former concerns technical efforts aimed at reaching certain results and the latter concerns the ability to act in an ethically good way. On this account, *techné* concerns production and *phronesis* concerns acting. Dunne (1993) refers to this as the official notion of *techné* and *phronesis*, but through his detailed examination of Aristotle's work, he also argues that the distinction between *techné* and *phronesis* is not that clear-cut in Aristotle's texts. Though this kind of philosophical exegesis lies outside the scope of the present article, two relevant points can be made in this regard.

First, in some places, Aristotle speaks of a form of *techné* where a durable result is achieved, but where this result should not to be seen as a material product, but more like a state of affairs. This is important and relevant to coaching, because in the context of coaching, this state of affairs could be thought of as an outcome of the coach 'intervening in a field of forces, or as immersing himself in a medium, in which he seeks to accomplish a propitious end' (ibid.: 254). Clearly, a major part of a coach's work consists of this kind of intervention into 'fields of forces'. It is our argument that coaching – due to its complex nature – is a domain where one must operate with a notion of *techné* that leaves room for practical judgement and *phronesis*. As Gallagher (1992: 186) points out, 'We would propose that *techné* should be actually practiced under the guidance of *phronesis*.' This means that although there clearly is a productive outcome of coaching in the sense that one works to effect a change in (or among) the athletes, this process is value-laden and has ethical implications.

Second, even if the distinction between *techné* and *phronesis* is less clear-cut, one must, as David Carr (2003, 2007) points out, resist the temptation to treat *phronesis* as a skill of situation-specific reasoning. *Phronesis* is not a skill, but should be thought of more as a character trait, something inextricably bound up with the self of the acting agent (Gallagher 1992; Carr 2003). The distinction between *techné* and *phronesis*, between technical and practical rationality, should be upheld because it grounds an important difference between technical and moral ways of dealing with the world. As such, acting in a morally good way cannot be reduced to a set of skills at all (Carr 2003).

Coaching and *phronesis*

Now, what does this mean in terms of the practicalities of coaching? In their study of high-level sailing coaches, Saury and Durand (1998) showed that coaching knowledge performed in real-life situations requires improvisation and opportunistic adaptations because the training sessions were highly unpredictable. In sailing, this is obvious, because weather changes influence how training sessions evolve and which tasks and goals can be worked with. But they also showed how coach–athlete interactions were unstable and unpredictable, and as such put constraints on the training sessions. Saury and Durand (ibid.: 263) therefore concluded that coaching is a domain characterized by 'complexity, uncertainty, dynamism, singularity, and conflicting values'. The constraints put on the coaches produced problems that were complex, ill-defined and sometimes contradictory. The coaches thus had to act and make decisions under conditions of uncertainty and time pressure.

A discourse about coaching that emphasizes a technical application of pre-established means towards the realization of ends (e.g. improved performance or victory) fails to sufficiently recognize: (1) the flux inevitably involved in this kind of work; and (2) the value-laden nature of working with human beings. Given the complexity of coaching situations, technical rationality is insufficient because it fails to address the judgement and interpretations that are continuously at play in every encounter between coach and athlete.

The everyday practice of sports coaching demands the coaches to be master of spontaneous response (Launder 1993). Unlike the case of technical rationality, the relation between input and output in coaching is therefore unclear and not a matter of causality. Rather, much as Biesta (2007) argues in the context of education, the relation between input and output in coaching is to be found in the interpretations and sense-making performed by coaches and athletes in the situations they encounter.

Jones (2007) has argued that coaching science should be redefined as an educational relationship of teaching and learning in order to capture the complex, everyday encounters occurring within coaching. This way of framing the coaching situation is congenial to an understanding of *phronesis*, because educational relationships of teaching and learning are also characterized by ambiguity and incompleteness, and as such they require *phronesis* (Gallagher 1992). The teacher (or coach) is interpreting the goals, the subject matter and the diverse group of people s/he is working with. The learners (or athletes) for their part also interpret the goals, the subject matter, and the teacher's presentation of the subject matter. The acts of understanding performed by teachers and learners are always incomplete, and this incompleteness makes teaching and coaching interpretational processes.

The hermeneutical structure of these processes requires, according to Gallagher (1992), that professional practice involving teaching and learning should be modelled on *phronesis*. Unlike technical rationality, where the particularities of the situations are subsumed under a predetermined (theoretical) framework, the phronetic approach is committed to the idea that good actions cannot be calculated in advance. As Gallagher (1992: 153) puts it, '*phronesis* calls for an application in light of the existing situation within which the actor finds herself. In *phronesis* one approaches an understanding of the universal in light of the particular, rather than the other way around.'

Phronesis provides the coach with a 'habit of attentiveness' that makes the coach's past experiences available to him/her, and 'at the same time allows the present situation to "unconceal" its own particular significance' (Dunne 1993: 305–306). When coaches find themselves in problematic, ethically challenging situations, the coaches with *phronesis* will not appeal to predetermined, universal rules for the right actions. Instead, they will approach the situation with a sound balance between universal principles and the particular characteristics of the situation.

Returning to the sailing coaches introduced in the beginning of this section, Saury and Durand (1998) showed how the interactions between coaches and athletes were unstable, due, for instance, to states of fatigue, motivation and conflicts. Saury and Durand do not address this from an ethical point of view, but they do, as we have already mentioned, point out that the coaching domain is characterized by conflicting values. Thus, in the heat of action, the virtuous coach has to navigate between conflicting values.

The guiding principle in an Aristotelian ethics would be that of the rationally and emotionally well-balanced mean (Carr 2007). Exactly what this would entail depends on the situation where the conflicts arise, but good professional judgement characterized by *phronesis* involves precisely the balancing act of integrating knowledge of the universal with a keen understanding of the particular. Not only will the coach who has *phronesis* be able to determine the action needed to achieve a particular end, but he/she will also see to it that the action is morally right.

How is *phronesis* learned?

As mentioned earlier, Aristotle distinguished between theoretical and practical knowledge. We have been concerned with the latter, because we see coaching as a practical domain where human beings intervene in a field of forces in order to change other human beings and the state of affairs between them. As such, we would argue that sport coaching primarily concerns the variable – that which can be otherwise – rather than the invariable knowledge of *episteme*.[4]

An important point with the Aristotelian distinctions between forms of knowledge is that *phronesis* cannot be learned in the same way as the theoretical knowledge needed by the coach. Whereas theoretical aspects of coaches' knowledge can be learned on the school bench in an academic institution, neither *techné* nor *phronesis* can be learned that way. Aristotle points out that

> it is from playing the lyre that both good and bad lyre-players are produced. And the corresponding statement is true of builders and all the rest; men will be good or bad builders as a result of building well or badly . . . It is well said, then, that it is by doing just acts that the just man is produced, and by doing temperate acts the temperate man; without doing these no one would have even a prospect of becoming good.
>
> *(1998: 29, 35)*

For Aristotle, practical knowledge in general, and *phronesis* in particular, can only be learned by taking part in the practice one is concerned with. Just as builders learn to become builders by building houses, coaches will become good and virtuous by coaching in a good and virtuous way; they will not have the remotest chance of becoming good without actually practising good coaching.

But this sounds paradoxical! If you are already able to do good actions, there is no need to learn them, and if one is not capable of good actions, it is impossible to perform them in the first place. It seems that the learning process already presupposes the finished result. This paradoxical situation is known as 'Meno's paradox' (Marton and Booth 1997), which takes its name from a dialogue by Plato (1994). The dialogue is a conversation between Socrates and a young aristocratic visitor, Meno, who asks Socrates whether virtue comes from teaching, practice or from nature. Socrates appears to be puzzled by the question, because he claims to be unable to tell what virtue is in the first place. Since Meno himself is not able to define virtue, Socrates wants to inquire about what virtue is, and this leads to Meno's paradox:

> [H]ow it's impossible for a person to search either for what he knows or for what he doesn't? He couldn't search for what he knows, for he knows it and no one in that condition needs to search; on the other hand he couldn't search for what he doesn't know, for he won't even know what to search for.
>
> *(Plato 1994: 47)*

White (1994: 161) suggests that one moral we can draw from Meno is that '[w]e must choose between paradoxes on the one hand and indeterminacy on the other.' This points to a fundamental aspect of *phronesis*: it is a form of knowledge that can be acquired and put to work first when one acknowledges the incompleteness and fallibility of knowledge. Since the domain of coaching admits of variation, its knowledge is not certain and general.

If it is at all appropriate to talk about teachers of *phronesis*,[5] then these are teachers *qua* their position, status and actions as good people. *Phronesis* is learned through gaining the right experiences, i.e. one becomes good by doing good deeds (Dunne 1993), and this in turn is dependent on being in the presence of good role models. As Gallagher (2006: 38) puts it, *phronesis* is learned by 'hanging out with the right people – good people who provide good examples of good actions'. In addition to the opportunity of being in the presence of good coaches, one also needs to imitate them, 'to act as they do and to do the kinds of things that they do' (Gallagher 2006: 38).

We would therefore suggest that *phronesis* could be learned through some form of apprenticeship in coaching. Part of coaching education should perhaps be moved out of the classroom and into a real-world practice, where budding coaches work as assistants to coaches who have a reputation for being good – in the ethical sense. This suggestion is supported by Jones (2008) in the sense that he underscores that virtues are learned by a critical initiation into a practice. The initiation into an ethically sound coaching practice takes place through a cultivation of a moral atmosphere and imitation of good and just acts.

Conclusion

In line with recent literature on coaching, we have argued for the importance of transcending the narrow and limiting focus on coaching as a technical process of applied (natural) science. Our aim has been to give attention to the problematic, context-dependent judgements that coaches are faced with on an everyday basis. These judgements are ethically charged, and we have argued that the knowledge needed in this regard can be understood with the Aristotelian concept *phronesis*, a form of practical wisdom that enables the coach to take account of the particularities of the situation, and act upon them without subsuming them under a predetermined theoretical and universal framework. Some parts of the knowledge needed by coaches are theoretical and technical, and can be learned in schools and academic institutions. This is not the case with *phronesis*. *Phronesis* is learned by immersing oneself in the field of coaching together with experienced, good coaches that one tries to imitate.

We have been trying to make a case for *phronesis* and practical rationality within sports coaching because we think that *phronesis* provides an illuminating way of understanding the ethical dimensions of professional judgement in coaching. But one might well ask if *phronesis* is possible at all in the competitive world of sports. Isn't top-level sport a game where winning is everything, and the coach should apply only the means strictly necessary to achieve victory? Talking about actions that are not productive in themselves – as phronetic actions seem to be – sounds like misguided ideology that will not be lived up to in real life, precisely because it is unproductive.

In our view, this objection is incorrect. Top-level sport is not a domain where 'anything goes'. There are already ethical guidelines for sports, such as fair play principles, and most of us do condemn coaching practices that treat people in an inhumane way. Thus, ethical judgements are always being made, even within top-level sport, and there will continue to be borderline cases that call for ethical reasoning. Just to mention one, we can ask ourselves how much pain one can inflict on athletes with the aim of improving their performance. It is our argument that the coach with *phronesis* is better suited to deal with such dilemmas in a good way.

On the other hand, we have sought to make the case that top-level sport could be viewed as a *techné* that is under the guidance of *phronesis*. This might be seen as problematic, because we then accept the current logic that top-level sport operates within. A more critical perspective would perhaps hold that the whole logic of top-level sport needs to be questioned from an ethical point of view, and that our insistence on *phronesis* is but a vain rescue operation for a practice that is lacking in ethical standards.

However, precisely because *phronesis* operates in the domain of the variable, the possibility is always open that states of affairs can become otherwise. Therefore, we think that a phronetic approach to sport coaching would be able to question hegemonic assumptions of what is right and wrong, possible and impossible, within sports. Indeed, this is the strength of the phronetic approach: *phronesis*, and, as we have argued elsewhere (Hemmestad *et al.*, accepted for publication), phronetic social science have the potential to critically question the fundamental assumption of elite sport coaching.

Another worry might be that it is unclear precisely how *phronesis* guides the coach. The reader might find that we talk about ethical problems in general and unspecific terms: it might appear that *phronesis* does not given any directions for action apart from somewhat unclear statements like 'not subsuming the particulars of the situation under a predetermined, universal set of rules' or 'follow a well-balanced mean'. This is a common critique of Aristotle's ethics: it is so general that it tells us nothing specific about how to act (Vetlesen 2007). From an Aristotelian perspective, the answer to this critique would be that those who expect clarity and precise guidelines expect more than *phronesis* can provide. The domain of *phronesis* (i.e. praxis, actions in inter-personal fields) does not lend itself to clear and general formulations of what is ethically right or wrong. If *phronesis* says too little, then, as Vetlesen (ibid.) points out, this is far better than promising too much. The problem with the technical rationality that dominates coaching is that – precisely because it overlooks the flux and unpredictability of human interaction – it promises too much in terms of clarity and control. *Phronesis*, on the other hand, provides the openness and the proper flexibility needed to deal with these situations.

Notes

1 This is related to the 'how-to-coach' approach in the sense that it follows the rationalistic logic of applying objectively defined means to an end, albeit now with the aid of scientific evidence of what works to support the decision-making process. The similarity is that in both cases the coach becomes a managerial expert (Carr 2003).
2 Yet another important aspect of Aristotle's account of knowledge is that to each of the different forms of knowledge, there correspond specific modes of activity. The activity form of *episteme* was called *theoria*; in *techné*, the activity was called *poiesis*; and the activity of *phronesis* was known as *praxis* (Aristotle 1998).
3 It should be mentioned, however, that if we think of *phronesis* as a practice that is merely *an end in itself*, we fall short of the full significance of *phronesis*. *Phronesis* transcends the rational logic of means and ends, and as such it involves a modification of the entire means–end framework (Dunne 1993).
4 Of course, coaching also involves aspects that in the Aristotelian account would be considered *episteme*, for example the scientific knowledge about biomechanics and physiology. It must therefore be pointed out that we do not want to reduce the work of coaches to a matter of *phronesis* solely.
5 It follows from Meno's paradox that there can be no teachers of virtue. It would be impossible to consult a teacher of virtue, because if one does not know what virtue is, one cannot know which teacher has the right view on virtue (Day 1994). *Phronesis* is therefore not learned from teachers who are transmitting their knowledge about virtues in a school. When one is concerned with *phronesis*, it will not do to take refuge in theory (Dunne 1993).

References

Aristotle (1998) *The Nicomachean Ethics*, Oxford: Oxford University Press.
Biesta, G. (2007) 'Why "what works" won't work: evidence-based practice and the demo-cratic deficit in educational research', *Educational Theory*, 57(1): 1–22.
Carr, D. (2003) 'Rival conceptions of practice in education and teaching', *Journal of Philosophy of Education*, 37(2): 253–266.
Carr, D. (2007) 'Character in teaching', *British Journal of Educational Studies*, 55(4): 369–389.
Coakley, J. (1994) *Sport in Society: Issues and Controversies*, Boston: Irwin/McGraw-Hill.
Day, J.M. (1994) 'Introduction', in J.M. Day (ed.) *Plato's Meno in Focus*, New York: Routledge.
Dunne, J. (1993) *Back to the Rough Ground: Practical Judgment and the Lure of Technique*, Notre Dame, IN: University of Notre Dame Press.
Dunne, J. (2005) 'An intricate fabric: understanding the rationality of practice', *Pedagogy, Culture and Society*, 13(3): 367–388.

Gallagher, S. (1992) *Hermeneutics and Education*, New York: SUNY Press.

Gallagher, S. (2006) 'Moral personhood and *phronesis*', *Moving Bodies*, 4(2): 31–57.

Gilbert, W. and Trudel, P. (2004) 'Analysis of coaching science research published from 1970–2001', *Research Quarterly for Exercise and Sport*, 75(4): 388–399.

Hammersley, M. (2001) *Some Questions about Evidence-Based Practice in Education*, online. Available at: http://www.leeds.ac.uk/educol/documents/00001819.doc (accessed 10 October 2007).

Hemmestad, L.B., Jones, R. and Standal, Ø.F. (accepted for publication) 'Phronetic social science: a means of better researching and analysing coaching?' *Sport, Education and Society*.

Isberg, L. (2001) *Supercoach på internationell toppnivå i fotball: en kunskapsanalys* [Supercoach at the International Top Level in Football: An Analysis of Knowledge], Research report, Örebro, Sweden: Institutionen för Idrott och hälsa.

Jones, C. (2008) 'Teaching virtue through physical education: some comments and reflections', *Sport, Education and Society*, 13(3): 337–349.

Jones, R. (2007) 'Coaching redefined: an everyday pedagogical endeavour', *Sport, Education and Society*, 12(2): 159–173.

Jones, R. and Wallace, M. (2006) 'The coach as "orchestrator": more realistically managing the complex coaching context', in R. Jones (ed.) *The Sports Coach as Educator: Re-conceptualising Sports Coaching*, London: Routledge.

Launder, A. (1993) 'Coach education for the twenty first century', *Sports Coach*, 16(1): 1–2.

Locke, A. (2004) 'Accounting for success and failure: a discursive psychological approach to sport talk', *Quest*, 56(3): 302–320.

Lyle, J. (2002) *Sports Coaching Concepts: A Framework for Coaches' Behaviour*, London: Routledge.

Martens, R. (1996) *Successful Coaching*, Champaign, IL: Human Kinetics.

Marton, F. and Booth, S. (1997) *Learning and Awareness*, Mahwah, NJ: Lawrence Erlbaum Associates.

Nash, C. and Collins, D. (2006) 'Tacit knowledge in expert coaching: science or art?' *Quest*, 58(4): 465–477.

Oxford English Dictionary (2006) Oxford: Oxford University Press.

Plato (1994) 'Meno', in J.M. Day (ed.) *Plato's Meno in Focus*, New York: Routledge.

Portrac, P., Brewer, C. and Jones, R. (2000) 'Toward an holistic understanding of the coaching process', *Quest*, 52(2): 186–199.

Ronglan, L.T. (2000) 'Gjennom sesongen. En sosiologisk studie av det norske kvinnelanslaget i handball på og utenfor banen' [Through the season: a sociological study of the Norwegian women's handball team, on and off court], doctoral thesis, Norges Idrettshøgskole, Oslo.

Saugstad, T. (2002) 'Educational theory and practice in an Aristotelian perspective', *Scandinavian Journal of Educational Research*, 46(4): 373–390.

Saugstad, T. (2005) 'Aristotle's contribution to scholastic and non-scholastic learning theories', *Pedagogy, Culture and Society*, 13(3): 347–366.

Saury, J. and Durand, M. (1998) 'Practical knowledge in expert coaches: on-site study of coaching in sailing', *Research Quarterly for Exercise and Sport*, 69(3): 254–266.

Schön, D. (1983) *The Reflective Practitioner: How Professionals Think in Action*, New York: Basic Books.

Vetlesen, A.J. (2007) *Hva er Etikk?* [What is ethics?] Oslo: Universitetsforlaget.

White, N.P. (1994) 'Inquiry', in J.M. Day (ed.) *Plato's Meno in Focus*, New York: Routledge.

Woodman, L. (1993) 'Coaching: a science, an art, an emerging profession', *Sports Science Review*, 2(2): 1–13.

4

OBJECTIVITY AND SUBJECTIVITY IN COACHING

Paul Davis

Introduction

This chapter tries to explain and illustrate how sport coaching mirrors human life as a whole by properly combining objective and subjective ingredients. That is not to say that sport coaching unfailingly does combine objective and subjective ingredients in the right way. It is to say that it, like human life as a whole, tends to flourish when it does and tends to falter when the objective or subjective makes imperialist claims upon the territory of the other.

The treatment begins with Nagel's graded conceptions of objectivity and subjectivity, which cast each as a matter of degree. It then tries to illustrate how the coach inhabits the objectivity of science, and how he properly inhabits the objectivity of universal morality. (We can maintain some neutrality on exactly where each of these is positioned on the subjectivity–objectivity continuum.) It is argued, with the help of examples from the literature, that universal morality entails an important rejection of recognizable, intersubjective norms of sport coaching practice. The chapter then tries to show that the comparatively objective domains of science and objective morality leave important spaces which are key to the coach's identity as the coach that he is. These spaces need to be filled by more subjective materials and by materials that critically need to be appropriated as though they were more subjective, whether they are in fact. The latter distinction – between the more subjective and that which needs to be *treated as though* it were more subjective – is marked by the terms 'ontological subjectivity' and 'neutral subjectivity'. These (putatively) comparatively subjective materials are illustrated in notions of sport's value and resultant attitudes on topics such as drugs, sportspersonship, and running up the score; the 'serve-volley' tennis coach; preferred or emblematic styles of play; and the distinctive life that animates a coach.

Nagel

Thomas Nagel characterizes objectivity as one of two directions in which thought can move. When we want to acquire a more objective understanding of something,

> [w]e step back from our initial view of it and form a new conception which has that view and its relation to the world as its object . . . The process can be repeated, yielding a still more objective conception . . . The distinction between more subjective and more objective views is really a matter of degree . . . The standpoint of morality is more objective than that of private life, but less objective than the standpoint of physics.
>
> *(1986: 4–5)*

One might doubt the preceding positionings on the continuum, as Nagel is doubtless aware. Those inclined, for instance, to harden morality and soften physics might wish to collapse or even reverse the respective positionings asserted by Nagel.[1] However, dispute or doubt over such positionings can exist alongside acceptance of the form of the distinction between subjectivity and objectivity proposed by Nagel.

The sport coach

Where, on the subjectivity–objectivity continuum, does the sport coach figure? It is doubtful that the question admits of a unified answer. Different facets of coaching might position the coach at different points, including the extremes. For instance, the imparting of technical and procedural elements of skill is, arguably, as objective as anything about the physical world. It seems to be as objective as anything in physics, indeed a consequence of physics, that if a soccer player leans back while shooting, then the ball will rise. Reality does not in any measure consist in how things appear or are constituted from the standpoint of the coach. The equivalent objectivity seems to apply to performance-relevant features of, say, physiology and biomechanics. I will finish this chapter with a putative illustration of the opposite case, in which reality is constituted by something arguably more subjective than even private life. Before then, I will consider a range of cases that might illustrate coach habitation of intermediate points.

Sport coaching and universal morality

Do the moral requirements of the rest of life apply in the sport world? If so, then the coach is unconditionally normatively required to occupy the standpoint of normal morality. Or is sport an entirely separate normative space? If so, then he is never required to occupy the standpoint of normal morality. Or does sport have an area of normative overlap with the rest of life, and an area of normative discontinuity? In that case, the coach is sometimes required to be the moral agent of the rest of life, and sometimes allowed or perhaps even required to suspend this agency. This is an old discussion.[2] Moreover, the notion that the usual moral pressures are at least substantially suspended is a commonplace defence by performer, coach and spectator of what would otherwise be thought ethically precarious conduct within the sport world. However, there is good reason to believe that this form of defence is itself precarious. In sport, one engages with fellow members of humanity. The second version of Kant's Categorical Imperative, sometimes known as the Formula of Humanity, states that one ought to treat persons as ends and never as a mere means. What exactly does this mean? The precise scope and grounding of Kant's principle admit some contestation, but a key consequence of it is universally agreed. It is that one may not *reduce* another person to an instrument of one's desires or objectives. This does not mean that other persons may not in fact be instruments of one's desires or objectives. Such a consequence would make most human collective activity impossible. It is quite in order that I expect the bus driver to further my ends by driving me to my destination. However, it is impermissible that I consider him to be an instrument of those ends *and nothing else*. He is critically discontinuous with the chair I sit on, the computer I write on and the umbrella I put up. The latter *are* mere instruments of my objectives. It is up to me to treat them any way I like in pursuit of those objectives. For instance, I can bin the umbrella if I go off it. Chairs, computers and umbrellas do not matter *in themselves*. Persons do. I may not, for instance, discharge my frustrations on my bus driver as I do when I needlessly thump my keyboard as I write. He is himself a source of mattering. When one complains of having been used by another, one is effectively complaining that one's status as a person, and therefore a source of mattering, has been overlooked.

Since sport involves engagement with *persons*, strict limits are similarly placed upon how we treat one another in it, regardless of the legitimacy of our expectations that others will help further our individual and collective ends. These limits apply to coach treatment of performers.

Jeffrey Fry (2000: 56–60) has invoked the Kantian framework to argue that certain commonplace coach behaviours and temptations are in fact morally problematic. He offers four examples. In the first, a football coach has privately decided which of two squad members will be his starting quarterback on opening day. But he pretends not to have done, in order to maximize the development of his preferred choice. He therefore prevents the 'loser' from exercising his rationality and self-determination, and uses him as a means to an end. The deception of the 'winner' could well be morally problematic too. In the second example, a high school basketball team is approaching the end of a mediocre season in which it has probably played to the best of its ability. The coach marginalizes the seniors in favour of promising juniors, who (as figured) gain valuable playing time and in fact go on next season to take the championship. The seniors provide useful practice competition for the juniors, and are therefore used to service relatively remote ends. The ends of the seniors, who are in their last season, are not, Fry argues, taken seriously enough. In the third example, a state university football team has had an unusually successful season, resulting in an invitation to a college football bowl appearance. The coach ('Jones') is ready to move on, and knows that victory in the bowl appearance will make him a candidate for a very lucrative coaching vacancy. Two days before the appearance, the starting quarterback sustains a neck injury. Omission from the line-up guarantees full recovery for next season, while special neck padding will give probably adequate but faintly risky protection. The coach opts to play the quarterback. If the ground of the decision is the furtherance of his own coaching career, then the coach, concludes Fry, 'surely uses a person improperly as a means to his end' (ibid.: 59). Again, the ends of another (or others) too heavily influence the treatment of someone. In the final example, it is half-time in a city soccer 'derby', with the score at 2–1. The coach of the losing team instructs one of his midfielders to commit a hard foul at the start of the second half on the opposition's best player. The player, himself an erstwhile victim of such a foul, resists. He offers the reason that he could not endorse the action as universalizable. He is in turn pressured with the counsel that 'it's all a part of the game', but finally refuses. The coach therefore pulls him from the line-up on grounds of insubordination and disloyalty, placing winning above his player's moral ideal and the well-being of the opponent. And by dismissing the player's appeal to universalizability, Fry argues, the coach has failed to respect his rational nature.

Universal morality and hegemonic masculinity

Fry is surely right that the preceding scenarios are familiar. And he makes a compelling case that the respective coach responses are *properly* grounded in a standpoint no less objective than that of global morality (he cites Aristotelian practical wisdom, alongside Kant's framework, as relevant to the second example in particular). The burden of argument is surely with those who believe that sport is a practice that enjoys protection from ordinary moral demands. However, the standpoint that inscribes the *actual*, problematic coach responses seems to be a familiar intersubjective one, constitutive of much of the practice of sport and characterized by unscrupulous instrumentality and a resultant insensitivity to pain of all kinds. Under that description, it rings like the ideology of hegemonic masculinity, which feminists, among others, have found morally unsustainable.[3] The fourth of Fry's examples, in which the coach tells his player that the prescribed action is 'part of the game', is the only one in which this outlook is stated. It might well be that its efficacy requires that it be articulated infrequently, but inhabitants of sport encounter it tacitly and pervasively from within. Frequent articulation courts contestation (and, if Fry is right, most probably defeat in the cases of his examples) from the more objective standpoint of universal morality. The said masculinist ethos, furthermore, is *intrinsically* inhospitable to discussion of issues of psychological, emotional and social salience. Its very *content* therefore arms it against the local articulation which might damage it. Challenging it 'at the coalface' is therefore a fierce task, as Fry no doubt knows. However, objective morality tends not to find a warm welcome or a swift result in the stony habitats of tacitly self-legitimating, intersubjective cultural forms, as a hackneyed catalogue of moral reforms could illustrate. The same catalogue, on the other hand, grounds hopes of some eventual success.

Recall that Nagel characterizes objectivity as a process of detachment from, and examination of, one's view and its relation to the world. This process can be explanatory or evaluative. Fry's objective treatment of his examples is robustly evaluative. In each case, things appear a certain way to the coach. These appearances are supported by an intersubjective normative template. However, the view from the more objective vantage point of global morality – grounded in our very humanity – suggests that these appearances are illusory. The intersubjective template cannot withstand this view from without. At the same time, the more objective view can (at least partially) explain the illusory appearances, in terms of intersubjective norms which are, in turn, explained in terms of a familiar social psychological story connecting sport, hegemonic masculinity and the ontological primacy of the masculine. If Kant is right, then ethics expresses the hope that we can close the gap between explanation and justification, even if we know that this hope cannot be fully realized. Our actions should be explained by reasons that also *justify* them, collapsing the foregoing distinction between the explanatory and the evaluative. In Fry's examples, the explanations of the coaches' actions are not justifications, even if the coaches think that they are.[4]

Objective under-determination

However, the objectifying impulse does not always meet with such a pliant world. It might sometimes be that we can explain normative appearances without clarity on whether they are justified from without. That is, it might be that we can sometimes explain why the world *happens to appear* normatively to agents just as it does, without confidence on whether these appearances converge with normative reality. Conversely, normative appearances, whether rejected or affirmed, need not yield up explanations of themselves. That is, it *need not* be that we can explain a given normative appearance in terms of, say, psychological, social or cultural features. Furthermore, objectivity might have limitations which sometimes mean that the appropriate direction of travel is not from the more perspectival subjective to the less perspectival objective, but is from the latter to the former. For instance, the comparatively objective vantage point of sport coach might leave critical areas of under-determination which can be filled only by more perspectival materials. The examples to follow offer some illustration of these possibilities.

Ontological subjectivity and neutral subjectivity

However, I wish, as a preliminary step, to propose a distinction between what is to be called 'ontological subjectivity' and what is to be called 'neutral subjectivity'. Ontological subjectivity occurs just in case reality is in fact dependent upon perspective. If Nagel is right, it is therefore a comparative notion. For instance, if his positionings are correct, then morality is more ontologically subjective than physics, and private life is more so again. Again, if an aggressive version of ethical subjectivism (moral statements can be translated without loss of meaning into reports of personal dis/approval) is correct, then morality is as ontologically subjective as private life.

Neutral subjectivity is non-committal on the ontological nature of the relevant reality. Whether the relevant reality radically depends upon perspectival appearances is left open. Neutral subjectivity is present just in case *an identity-constitutive stance needs to be adopted within a contested area.* That is, cognitively contestable reactions and responses that partly define someone as the kind of thing that she is (the precise athletics coach that is Jane and not Ann, say) are unavoidable. (The final section explains why these cognitively contestable reactions and responses do not exhaustively define someone as the kind of thing that she is.) Note that the agent need not *feel* any cognitive insecurity or caution with respect to these reactions and responses. She may be unappreciative of their contestable nature, and therefore display them with a bullish certainty. That would not detract from their actual cognitively insecure character.

I add a few brief points of emphasis and illumination. It is by now a familiar point that full-blooded objectivity is not refuted by the existence of contestation, complexity, or even universally and modestly acknowledged ignorance.[5] Neutral subjectivity, first, allows that there is a robustly objective and as yet undiscovered resolution to the question that demands a response. Second, by confining itself to identity-constitutive responses within contested domains, neutral subjectivity is saved from collapse into a popular but worthless conception of subjectivity that does no more than emphasize the fact that judgements and responses tend to be properties of individual judgers and respondents ('that's *your* opinion', viz. *subjective!*). Neutral subjectivity is more substantive, since the responses are both unavoidable and constitutive of someone as the kind of thing, or a kind of thing, that he is. Most token judgements do not have this quality. Indeed, most token judgements within heavily contested areas do not have it. Consider the judgements of most people on, say, the heavily contested area of the morality of capital punishment. For most, there is no existential necessity for consideration of it. And if a conclusion is reached or tactically presumed, it is usually in no sense constitutive of an identity that one has.

Some brief reinforcement of the immediately preceding point is helpful. This is because the legitimacy of neutral subjectivity might be questioned on the ground that it is explicitly consistent with full-blooded objectivity. What licence do we have for taking 'neutral subjectivity' to be subjectivity at all, when any given reality in which it figures might be in fact objective? Neutral subjectivity is properly considered a form of subjectivity because of two, related, features: first, the situatedness of the agent means that he cannot opt out of finally trusting in the relevant areas to how things appear; and, second, these unavoidable calls are quite radically constitutive of a perspective itself – they heavily define the very vantage point of the individual agent. This vantage point is more perspectival than the general situatedness that demands navigation of contested territory. Being a sport coach illustrates the latter; being coach Tom with his precise reactions and responses to this contested territory illustrates the former.

The coach has, as already intimated, no choice but to negotiate much normative space that manifests neutral subjectivity. Since neutral subjectivity is non-committal with respect to ontological subjectivity, this space might contain regions of ontological subjectivity. Each region can be investigated. If Fry is correct, then coaches who respond to his examples through ontologically subjective spectacles are mistaken (and many, as we saw, probably view them through ontologically intersubjective spectacles). One should, instead, respond to Fry's dilemmas from the vantage point of objective morality, which can both refute and explain the (inter)subjective outlook operating. However, it should be clear that the distinction between ontological and neutral subjectivity is of secondary existential relevance here. Both forms of subjectivity entail the need for critical, identity-constitutive calls. If it is on occasion revealed to a coach that her calls admit of scrutiny from a standpoint more objective than she previously realized, then she is at liberty to revisit them. We can now elaborate a few examples of these identity-constitutive calls.

Objectivity and the value of coaching sport

Can we offer an objective specification of the role of coach? Is there something it is to be a coach, independently of how it appears to any coach? The coach, *qua* coach, attempts to impart or consolidate or develop or better use physical skills needed for competition in games or performances of physical skill.[6] (It can be left open that the objective specification involves other elements.) Any coach to whom it appears otherwise is surely mistaken about her role, in the same way that a bus driver who thinks he can drive the bus anywhere he pleases is mistaken about his. However, this objective specification leaves open the following questions, at least:

- What is valuable about games and performances of physical skill?
- What skills, individual or collective, are to be imparted or encouraged, and how, if at all, are they to be ranked?

Numerous suggestions have figured regarding the first of these questions. These include the celebration of bodily subjectivity,[7] and aesthetic possibilities for performer and spectator,[8] as well as more generally characterized qualities, such as the existential joy of play;[9] health; fitness; moral education;[10] humanization;[11] and social, cultural and even national objectives.[12] Clearly, there are possibilities of co-habitation within the preceding set. Furthermore, recent discussions about value, both in sport and elsewhere, have highlighted the conceptual complexity entailed in questions of value. Culbertson (2008: 305–314), for instance, in a discussion of sport's value, distinguishes eight notions: final ends, inherent value, instrumental value, non-instrumental value, an intrinsic value (or property), a value (or property) had intrinsically, the ground for value, and enabling features. Few have the conceptual sophistication for a discussion in these terms, and I do no more here than dip my toe briefly in the water. Yet the coach cannot avoid making key, indeed identity-constitutive, calls in this area. For instance, what does she take to be the ground of sport's value, i.e. the features of sport in virtue of which it has value? What does she take in turn to be the enabling conditions of this grounding, i.e. conditions that *allow* the ground to function as a ground for value? In the same way that the spiritual enrichment thought to be the ground of a particular sonata's value might require the absence of chronic toothache, no putative value-grounding feature of sport is likely to enjoy insensitivity to all circumstantial conditions.[13] According to Schmitz (1988: 35–36), for instance, the existential quality of play is a ground of sport's value, a ground in turn disabled by current, contingent conditions of sport, such as an exaggerated emphasis on winning. Does the coach embrace this ground of value? If so, does she agree with Schmitz's allegations of current disabling conditions? Or does the coach regard the celebration of bodily subjectivity as the ground of sport's value? If so, what are its enabling and disabling conditions? To what extent, for instance, is it compatible with pain, injury, and suffering? Might it indeed *require* these ('*Citius, altius, fortius*')? To what extent is it compatible with the gendered structure of current sport arrangements?[14] Queries such as these, about enabling and disabling conditions, could be raised about any of the grounds of value noted at the start of this paragraph, alongside queries about the grounds themselves. And there are important consequences. Coach positioning on value and enabling conditions affects responses on a myriad of questions relevant to the conduct of sport.

Consider, for instance, performance-enhancing drugs and comparable techniques such as blood doping. A coach who regards the ground of sport's value as the open-ended breach of bodily limits is liable to view these techniques as *enabling* conditions of the ground of sport's value. He is also likely to take a high level of pain, injury and suffering as at least compatible with the same ground. Conversely, the coach who, like Schmitz, takes play as the ground of sport's value is liable to view techniques such as drugs and blood doping as *disabling* conditions. He is also likely to regard a high level of pain, suffering and injury as incompatible with the same ground. Consider, also, how coach beliefs about the ground of sport's value and its enabling and disabling conditions influence conclusions on the normative questions surrounding, for instance, rule-breaking, running up the score, sportspersonship, coach–athlete interactions and treatment of minors. For instance, a coach who grounds sport's value in its facility to enhance national prestige will have a very different attitude to the treatment of minors from a coach who grounds sport's value in play, personal expression, or aesthetic possibilities for the performer. For the former, the enabling conditions of sport's value will be (comparative) national success, with (comparative) national failure therefore a disabling condition. He is therefore liable to be willing to coach only those minors whom he thinks likely to be contributors to national prestige, and to be relatively unconcerned with the quality of their experiences under him. He will not be disturbed to think that his performers experience their performance of sport as something essentially repressive, except for the fact that they ought to be so dedicated to national glory that they *should not* feel repressed. His conception of sportspersonship is liable to be one that is confined to the maintenance of honour, ultimately for the glory of the nation.[15] Running up the score on the nation's behalf is liable to be required. The latter coach, on the other hand, is willing to coach a much wider ability range, and is highly concerned with the quality of experience of his performers, which he regards as an enabling condition of sport's value. He loathes the thought that some performers might be desperate to stop sport as soon as they have 'done their bit' for the nation. This, he thinks, disables sport's value. He is liable to regard an honour-confined model of sportspersonship as too stern.[16] He might have a nuanced view of both sportspersonship and running up the score. Similarly, the coach who takes the ground of sport's value to be its moral possibilities might view intentional rule violation as a disabling condition of sport's value, and the constant attempt to keep the rules an enabling condition. His conception of sportspersonship might be similarly inscribed with, for instance, concern for the welfare and experience of opponents. (The view that sport aids or can aid moral development has, of course, more than one version.[17])

Ontological or neutral?

It can be asked whether the question about the value of sport manifests ontological or merely neutral subjectivity. We probably do not have a particularly decisive answer, especially if Nagel is correct in proposing that (ontological) subjectivity is a comparative notion. It seems quite unlikely that the question finally admits of the same objectivity as, say, the preceding question of how to address the ball when shooting in soccer. Perhaps it has the same objectivity as Fry's foregoing examples, i.e. the objectivity of objective morality (no less consummate, for some, than that of physics, pace Nagel)? That should not be ruled out. It might be that we have so far failed to uncover answers that are in fact as objective as those available in Fry's examples. Maybe the admirable efforts of contributors such as Culbertson (2008) are steps on the road to the discovery of those answers, which we have so far failed to land because of, perhaps, the comparative infancy of the enquiry. It would, however, be rash to invest too much in this hope. It might be more dialectically appropriate to cautiously posit sport's value somewhere between morality and private life on Nagel's continuum. But we tend to see the question through a glass darkly.

This comparative ontological opacity is, again, of secondary existential relevance. The coach is not at liberty to sit agog, pending objectivity's jackpot of answers on sport's value. If she is to be a sport coach, then she has no choice but to position herself within this family of questions. It could be that we are *all* normative and even epistemological gamblers to a degree, all of the time. This is the case if truth is always something that outruns the evidence or reasons on its behalf (that is, if realism is true).[18] However, as the preceding illustrations should show, normative gambles of a notably unsparing kind seem impossible for the sport coach to avoid. She places identity-constitutive bets on normative appearances whose confirmation from without is less than decisive.

It might be rejoined that many sport coaches give no conscious thought to the preceding family of questions. That is probably true. However, to fail or refuse to think about them is *ipso facto* to adopt a position, even if merely that of the dominant practice community. (It was noted earlier that the dominant, masculinist sport ethos is in cahoots with an anti-reflective stance towards issues of psychological, social and emotional salience. These clearly include questions about sport's value.) A coach who is not positioned in this normative space is like someone who speaks language in general or who is religious in general. One cannot speak language in general or be religious in general. The language(s) one speaks is constitutive of one's identity as a language speaker, and the religion one affirms is constitutive of one's religious identity. Similarly, if views about the ground and enabling conditions of sport's value, along with their diffuse consequences, are not constitutive of one's identity as the sport coach that one is, then what is?

The insistent demands of objective morality

It is fair to see a 'coaching philosophy' as, in large part, an attempt to coherently respond to questions about sport's value and their consequences (and failure or even aggressive refusal to think about these questions or consequences is itself a philosophy in this sense). And while objective morality might be inadequate to the subjectivity of the questions, it nevertheless bulks large in coach–athlete communication of responses. The respect for the other's humanity that inscribes Fry's treatment of his examples dictates that there should be, as far as possible, no great surprises for athlete or coach. A lack of respect for the athlete's humanity is shown by the soccer coach who tells a recruit insincerely that he is against intentional fouling before instructing him to do it in a crucial match. A lack of respect for the coach's humanity is shown by the athlete who tells her coach that she shares his rejection of performance-enhancing drugs, before proceeding to surreptitiously use them. A mutually honest end to a relationship far better manifests Kantian respect for rational nature than a relationship that continues on pain of deception, and perhaps coercion or undermining.

Skills and the subjective and intersubjective standpoints

What skills, individual or collective, are to be imparted, developed, etc., and how are they to be ranked? Some sports might leave no decisions to be made, and contextual features might dictate their content in other cases. However, where these conditions under-determine, the coach might need to tap into less objective resources than those yielded up at the vantage point of coach. These resources might include a personal philosophy of the sport that he coaches, probably inscribed with some responses on the preceding questions about sport's value, as well as his own abilities and limitations. A tennis coach, for instance, might have discovered that he gets better results from coaching serve-volley players than from coaching baseliners. That might reflect his abilities or experience (perhaps he was a particularly successful doubles player), or an underlying philosophy of how tennis should be played (perhaps inscribed with values about life). He gradually becomes established as an excellent serve-volley coach, but one for baseliners to avoid. Furthermore, he eventually and robustly conceives himself in this way. His coaching identity therefore assumes an irreducibly perspectival element, not in conflict with his perspectiveless identity as a tennis coach but not determined by it either. This precise coach identity seems positioned on Nagel's continuum, again at a point between morality and private life, and at a point less objective than the practice of tennis (and the practice of tennis coaching, if distinct). Reality is irreducibly anchored to a standpoint less objective than the practice of tennis (and the practice of tennis coaching). We can perhaps explain this reality using more objective tools, such as psychological, biographical and temperamental qualities of the coach. However, such objective explanation is, again, of secondary relevance to all concerned (though it might be interesting). First and foremost is the comparatively subjective identity itself. This is a ground on which some players will wish to be coached or avoid being coached by him, and on which the coach will seek to recruit performers. And there is, again, the same, objective imperative to respect the rational nature of the other, manifested in the absence of big and avoidable surprises, deception, coercion and undermining.

A question of style

Other elements can similarly inscribe the perspectival identity of a coach, and in turn dictate the skills he respectively elevates and downgrades. Consider, for instance, the outlooks of soccer managers. (Soccer tends to run the distinction between manager and coach, especially at higher levels. However, managers serve equivalently as illustrations of coaching objectivity and subjectivity.) These outlooks regularly reflect preferred narratives of soccer, sport, and perhaps even life. One narrative is that of simple instrumentality, in which performance outcomes predominate. There are others, however. The legendary, flairful Hungarian national side of the 1950s did not win anything, yet were the biggest influence on Jock Stein, manager of the swaggering Glasgow Celtic of the late 1960s and early 1970s (and, alas, the plodding Scotland of the early 1980s). Former Stoke City manager Alan Durban, on the other hand, is unlikely to have been too influenced in his coaching perspective by the Magnificent Magyars, having famously snarled to a hostile press conference, 'If you want entertainment, go and watch clowns' (Hornby 1992: 133). Stein and Durban present a sharp contrast in their preferred soccer narratives. Stein's relative indifference to goalkeepers is continuous with his, and is unlikely to have figured in the instrumentality of Durban. These respective outlooks are key to the coaching identities of Stein and Durban, and are apparently undetermined from the more objective vantage point of soccer coach. We might, again, be able to explain them from the more objective standpoint of psychology, biography and temperament. That one of them is correct and the other incorrect, or that both are incorrect, should not be ruled out. In such a case, it is merely neutral subjectivity that we see illustrated in Stein and Durban. If there are no resources to ground such a call, then ontological subjectivity is present.

Before leaving the topic of the last paragraph, it is instructive to note that the immediately preceding elements of a coach identity might cohere or clash with existing intersubjective narratives that connect sport to social, cultural or national identities. Stein's Hungarian predilections, for instance, were relatively well suited to management of Celtic, a club whose self-narrative already featured motifs of expression and, indeed, flamboyance. They would have been similarly congruent with the self-narratives of West Ham United and Tottenham Hotspur. Durban's coaching identity – as expressed in the preceding quotation – would have clashed with the intersubjective narratives of Celtic, West Ham or Tottenham. It should be noted that while intersubjective narratives such as the preceding might be taken by adherents to express enabling conditions of value of sport or of a particular sport, they need not do so. They might, instead, express nothing more putatively objective than 'the way we do things *here*'.[19] They might even be thought to require a counterpoint of things done differently elsewhere.[20]

Objective morality again gets a significant foothold with regard to the topics of the last two paragraphs. Respect for the rational nature of others again demands that there are no great (avoidable) surprises, deception or coercion. A soccer manager who has been honest with directors on appointment should not be suddenly told by them that he must send out a team to play in a way that is foreign to his outlook. The manager, similarly, is under moral pressure to communicate any relevant personal playing outlook to employers, players, fellow coaching staff and prospective players. Supporters, too, are sometimes legitimately covetous about the intersubjective narratives of their club, and must therefore be considered – and perhaps consulted – when radical departures from it (Alan Durban's appointment as manager of Celtic, West Ham or Tottenham, say) are considered.

This section's brief reflections on the coach and playing styles perhaps illustrate particularly sharply the fusion of subjective, intersubjective and objective components.

The distinctive life of persons

This chapter has travelled a road of putatively decreasing objectivity, beginning at shooting technique in soccer and stopping off at objective morality, the value of sport, and elements of personal and intersubjective orientation. The stopping points do not purport to be an exhaustive set. The journey ends as indicated at the outset, with the something that is, as soon explained, arguably yet more ontologically subjective than even private life. It is fair to think of it, paraphrasing Cordner (1988: 36–42), as the distinctive life that animates the coach. Under that description, it might seem like an epiphenomenon. However, such dismissal would be a huge error. Cordner is correct that persons are like artworks, insofar as the thing we find most valuable in them is not their views on this or that, but the distinctive life that animates them, and infuses, in turn, their views on this and that. This is the reason we can like people with a lot of views we reject, and rather dislike some whose views we tend to share. A performer might find the coaching philosophies of two coaches indistinguishable. However, she might have a decisive preference never-theless, because of the different ways these philosophies are lit up (or not) in each case. And again, she might even prefer, on the same grounds, one coach over another whose coaching philosophy she embraces to a greater degree. The most definitive thing about persons, whatever their jobs, preferences or philosophies, is the distinctive life animating them. This is realized in, among other things, tone, accent, language, body language, clothing, *ways of* liking and disliking, greetings and valedictions. Indeed, this might be more than usually definitive of those in pedagogic roles (think back to the teachers you remember best, for instance). One's own distinctive life is also a large part of the ground from which one responds to the distinctive life of another.

Why might it be that the distinctive life animating a person is even more subjective than private life? It is quite safe to think that by 'private life' Nagel means a domain of personal orientation, where this includes tastes, preferences and habits. It is also safe to think that he positions this at the subjective pole of the objective– subjective continuum because he takes the appearances of private life to be ineligible for correction by a more objective reality, unlike the appearances that fund moral judgements or judgements about the physical world. And this is certainly a serviceable conception of private life.[21] One either likes the Rolling Stones or one does not, for instance. Greater objectivity cannot show that one's taste is mistaken or that one does not have the taste one thinks one has. The distinctive life that animates a person is arguably more signatory of individual standpoint than even this, since it is an orientation towards (1) the personal orientation of 'private life'; (2) one's views on this and that; and (3) personal philosophies such as a coaching philosophy. It is a *way of having* (1)–(3). For instance, Jack and Jill both love the Rolling Stones. This (strong) taste is part of the 'private life' of both Jack and Jill. However, there are radical differences in *how* this shared, roughly equal love realizes itself. Jack plays and sings the Stones while driving, and Jill does not. Jill sings Stones songs walking along the street, Jack does not. Jack knows multitudinous details of band history, tours, rows, etc., and Jill is turned off by minutiae like this. Jack will involve the band in conversation only with those he already knows to be fellow fans – and then he is hard to stop – but Jill can start a conversation with anyone by asking them if they know certain Stones lyrics. Jack would not wear the T-shirt, but Jill does. After one Stones song, Jill wants to hear a different one, whilst Jack might well play the same one repeatedly. They can each be terrific Stones bores, but Jack's soporific is administered and takes effect quite differently from Jill's. And so on. Jack's love of the band is inflected in a Jack-ish way and Jill's in a Jill-ish way. The distinctive life animating Jack is realized in his love of the Stones, and the distinctive life animating Jill in hers. Therefore, some Stones fans who know each of them and share their passion like the prospect of seeing a Stones tribute band with Jill but not with Jack, while others feel the opposite. This mirrors, again, our varied responses to those who share our views on this and that, and – of course – the preceding performer asymmetry of response to different coaches who share a congenial coaching philosophy.

While explanations of and changes to the distinctive life animating persons are not impossible, and sometimes desirable, the objectifying impulse should in this case be handled with the utmost care. While the uniqueness of persons might be an exaggerated motif of Western modernity, the distinctive life that animates us might embody the most interesting and precious sense in which each of us is unique. It can be very hard to admit that we like or do not like someone on this sort of ground. We fear that it is 'superficial' to respond very significantly to, for instance, someone's vocal inflections, body language or precise way of liking the Stones. We tend to think we are not then responding to the *person*. Conversely, we typically feel indignant if others respond to us on those sorts of grounds (some feel this even when the response is positive). But these attitudes are mistaken. As Janet Radcliffe Richards (1980: 229) has wisely said, 'Persons *are* their qualities.' And these qualities critically include the distinctive life animating them. Responding positively or negatively to it in others is no reason for self-reproach, and being the object of the equivalent responses of others is no reason for indignation. Therefore, there is no transgression in a coach or performer wishing to end a relationship because the other is just not one's 'sort of person'. Nor indeed is there anything transgressive in coach and performer enrichment being substantially heightened by the distinctive life that outruns ability and, say, a shared philosophy of sport and performance.

Objective morality again has its say, however, in how the coach and performer deal with the innocuous and unavoidable responses just illustrated. Respect for the humanity of others, again, means that they cannot legitimately ground coercion, deception, undermining or favouritism.

Notes

1 Russell (2004) might be fairly considered an example. See especially p. 155.
2 For powerful contributions, see Reddiford (1981) and Carr (1998: 119–133), especially pp. 122–127.
3 Giddens (1999: Lecture 4) suggests that our moral awareness is increasingly and properly characterized by a (Kantian-sounding) principle of 'democracy of the emotions'. The perspectives of previously marginalized groups – such as women, children, non-whites and animals – are therefore attributed a moral status closer to what is proper. The coaches in Fry's examples do not seem properly motivated by this principle. This would be unsurprising, in light of the inhospitality of hegemonic masculinity towards a democracy of the emotions.
4 See Nagel (1986: 135).
5 For a compelling discussion of disagreement and ignorance in morality, see Brink (1989: 197–210).
6 Suits, as is well known, first declared that all sports are games, then that all sports are either games or performances. I do not engage in the discussion here. See Suits (1988b: 39–48) and Suits (1988a).
7 See, for instance, Young (1988: 335–341).
8 See, for instance, Arnold (1985).
9 See especially Schmitz (1988: 29–38).
10 The progenitor of this notion is, of course, Plato. For useful discussion of Plato's views on sport and moral education, see Reid (2007).
11 See Young (1988: 335–341) and Boxill (1995: 30).

12 For powerful discussion of the value that sport might have for cultures and nations, see Morgan (1998: 184–204) and Morgan (1999).
13 For Plato, the spiritual fortitude resulting from sport declines into a coarsening of the spirit if not accompanied by music.
14 See, again, Young (1988: 335–341).
15 For illumination of different models of sportsmanship, see Arnold (1983).
16 For a powerful defence of sportsmanship as honour, see Sessions (2004), who argues that the laudable features of alternative models are subsumable within the honour paradigm.
17 See Carr (1998: 122).
18 For compelling discussion, see Hetherington (2005), esp. 'Attempted solutions: eliminating luck'.
19 See Morgan's reflections on Japanese baseball, Basque soccer and Mexican soccer (1999: 58–60).
20 The followers of Celtic and Tottenham Hotspur have tended, historically, to posit their antitheses in the allegedly stuffy approaches of local rivals Rangers and Arsenal, respectively.
21 There are well-known controversies in social and political philosophy about where the private domain so conceived ends and social and political life begins. Discussion of them is not required here.

References

Arnold, P. (1983) 'Three approaches toward an understanding of sportsmanship', *Journal of the Philosophy of Sport*, 10: 61–70.
Arnold, P. (1985) 'Aesthetic aspects of being in sport: the performer's perspective in contrast to that of the spectator', *Journal of the Philosophy of Sport*, 12: 1–7.
Boxill, J. (1995) 'Title IX and gender equity', *Journal of the Philosophy of Sport*, 20–21: 23–31.
Brink, D.O. (1989) *Moral Realism and the Foundations of Ethics*, Cambridge: Cambridge University Press.
Carr, D. (1998) 'What moral educational significance has physical education? A question in need of disambiguation', in M. McNamee and S.J. Parry (eds) *Ethics and Sport*, London: Routledge.
Cordner, C. (1988) 'Differences between sport and art', *Journal of the Philosophy of Sport*, 5: 31–47.
Culbertson, L. (2008) 'Does sport have intrinsic value?' *Sport, Ethics and Philosophy*, 2(3): 302–320.
Fry, J. (2000) 'Coaching a kingdom of ends', *Journal of the Philosophy of Sport*, 27: 51–62.
Giddens. A. (1999) *The Reith Lectures* (BBC 1999), Lecture 4, 'Family', online. Available at: http://www.bbc.co.uk/radio4/reith1999/lecture4.shtml (accessed 12 December 2009).
Hetherington, S. (2005) 'Gettier problems'. Online. Available HTTP: http://www.iep.utm.edu/gettier/ (last accessed 5 September 2010).
Hornby, N. (1992) *Fever Pitch*, London: Victor Gollancz.
McNamee, M.J. and Parry, S.J. (eds) (1998) *Ethics and Sport*, London: E & FN Spon.
Morgan, W.J. (1998) 'Multinational sport and literary practices and their communities: the moral salience of cultural narratives', in M.J. McNamee and S.J. Parry (eds) *Ethics and Sport*, London: E & FN Spon.
Morgan, W.J. (1999) 'Patriotic sports and the moral making of nations', *Journal of the Philosophy of Sport*, 26: 50–67.
Morgan, W.J. and Meier, K.V. (1988) *Philosophic Inquiry in Sport*, Champaign, IL: Human Kinetics.
Nagel, T. (1986) *The View from Nowhere*, New York: Oxford University Press.

Reddiford, G. (1981) 'Morality and the games player', *Physical Education Review*, 4(1): 8–16.

Reid, H. (2007) 'Sport and moral education in Plato's *Republic*', *Journal of the Philosophy of Sport*, 34(2): 160–175.

Richards, J.R. (1980) *The Sceptical Feminist*, Harmondsworth: Penguin.

Russell, J.S. (2004) 'Moral realism in sport', *Journal of the Philosophy of Sport*, 31(2): 142–160.

Schmitz, K.L. (1988) 'Sport and play: suspension of the ordinary', in W.J. Morgan and K.V. Meier (eds) *Philosophic Inquiry in Sport*, Champaign, IL: Human Kinetics.

Sessions, W.L. (2004) 'Sportsmanship as honor', *Journal of the Philosophy of Sport*, 31(1): 47–59.

Suits, B. (1988a) 'Tricky triad: games, play, and sport', *Journal of the Philosophy of Sport*, 15: 1–9.

Suits, B. (1988b) 'The elements of sport', in W.J. Morgan and K.V. Meier (eds) *Philosophic Inquiry in Sport*, Champaign, IL: Human Kinetics.

Young, I.M. (1988) 'The exclusion of women from sport: conceptual and existential dimensions', in W.J. Morgan and K.V. Meier (eds) *Philosophic Inquiry in Sport*, Champaign, IL: Human Kinetics.

5

SPORTS COACHING AND VIRTUE ETHICS

Alun R. Hardman and Carwyn Jones

Introduction

Our opening claim is that sport provides coaches the opportunity to realize a range of technical, physical and moral excellences. In order for coaches to do so, it is necessary for them to pay equal attention to both the inherent morality of sports structures and their own moral agency. It means that the coach, as a central cog in the sports environment, has moral responsibilities reaching far beyond the purely technical and tactical (Jones *et al.* 2004; Jones 2007). In fact, the coach is crucially involved in facilitating the *good* sporting contest because they are responsible for establishing and controlling apposite conduct. The coach's moral responsibilities are to be understood as not merely the immediate or long-term policing of foul play to ensure compliance with sporting etiquette, or the infusion of respect for 'fair-play conventions'. Rather, their role extends to the nurturing and promotion of specific virtues that directly concern the attainment of the values of sport.

Despite evident discrepancies between professional, elite levels of sport and recreational, amateur sport, real and significant normative limits encountered at the core of sport cut across how every coach ought to behave. At its heart, these sporting values provide a 'contingent universal condition of its practice' (Morgan 1994: 215). In all situations, therefore, the coach, regardless of his or her experience, qualifications, personality, pedagogic style and salary, is obligated by moral concerns that are derived from the inherent nature of sporting practices.

The meta-ethical and ethical arguments underlying this claim are perhaps less familiar to coaches, who are more likely to encounter coaching ethics by way of formal guidance and policy interventions dealing with specific issues such as child welfare, sexual abuse and performance-enhancing drug issues (Brackenridge 2001). We argue, more contentiously, that such second-order matters are less important, and that solutions to them ultimately depend upon the more fundamental view that the coach, in all matters, through word and through deed, should behave well, set good examples *and* be committed to the goods and values that make sport uniquely dear to those who play it. This chapter therefore attempts to provide a coherent theory to support such a comprehensive normative view of the coach – a theory that is capable of articulating how the substantial and interconnected metaphysical, existential and ontological claims as to what a coach is, what they do and why they do it all fit together.

We first provide a virtue theoretical account of sport. We draw on the work of the neo-Aristotelian philosopher Alasdair MacIntyre (1985) to highlight both the intrinsic and the extrinsic value of practices such as sport and the significance of moral character. We outline the nature of, and process by which, specific virtues that are constitutive of character aim towards the full realization of sporting experiences. Second, we outline the way in which a virtue-theoretical account of sport informs our understanding of how the coach's character is crucial in order to initiate participants appropriately into the (moral) demands of sporting practices. Finally, we examine how coaches might go about applying the insights from virtue ethics theory into their everyday practices so that they can contribute positively to the sporting experiences of those they coach.

Sport, coaching and 'initiation' into a social practice

Aristotelian virtue ethics can enlighten coaching practice, with regard to both the ethical conduct of coaches and the character development of athletes. Virtue ethics has enjoyed significant popularity as a theoretical framework for moral philosophy in recent times. In the province of coaching, it can provide a lush and fruitful reserve for investigating both the nature of the practice and the moral behaviour of the persons involved. MacIntyre (1985) has been at the forefront of examining this philosophical perspective, and his work has enjoyed significant influence on those interested in the moral status of sport as a social practice (Morgan 1994; McNamee 1995; Jones 2001, 2003, 2005). More recently the trend has been questioned by McFee (2004), but nonetheless many of the core principles of MacIntyre's work (in particular his conception of a social practice) provide an effective and compelling approach to understanding the moral landscape of sport. MacIntyre's conception of a social practice is important because it contains both normative and descriptive elements. Together they provide a robust and ethically powerful critical resource for describing both the 'is' and the 'ought' of sport.

A MacIntyrean understanding of sport in terms of a practice discloses a number of crucial and necessary normative obligations for coaches. When defining practices, MacIntyre has in mind a particular kind of activity:

> By a 'practice' I mean any coherent and complex form of socially established cooperative human activity through which goods internal to that activity are realised in the course of trying to achieve those standards of excellence which are appropriate to, and partly definitive of, that form of human activity, with

> the result that human powers to achieve excellence, and human conceptions
> of the ends and goods involved, are systematically extended.
>
> *(1985: 187)*

Science, education, music, art and sport are broad sets of activities which contain a range of more specific practices such as organic chemistry, guided discovery, flute-playing, ice sculpting and football. By contrast, component activities such as spectrometry, providing feedback, playing scales, using a sculpting knife and shooting are in themselves not practices, but may constitute some of the necessary skills partially definitive of a practice. Practices, by their inherent nature, are constituted by notable ranges and scales of difficulty and intricacy, but more significant, and central to their character, is that those who participate in them are able to apprehend and value those goods which are *internal* and, thereby, definitive of them. The notion of goods *internal* to practices such as sport provides the virtue ethics cornerstone of a normative, rather than a descriptive, theory of a practice. Such goods signify the *raison d'être* of practices in terms of both their ends and their means. A concern for internal goods of a practice spells out that regardless of any other goals pursued by practitioners, the means available are constrained by specific behavioural norms. It entails that ways of achieving and the intended result become indivisible to what it means to participate legitimately in the practice. In reality, this often means that narrower and technically efficient ways for achieving a particular goal are rejected because the means employed are unacceptable on moral grounds. These internal goods are the precious gems of sport participation – sports uniqueness and charm stem from them. Such goods are encapsulated, for example, in the strength, poise, tactical acumen, agility, dexterity, speed of thought and movement required of an elite level football player. Such qualities articulate, and are illustrative of, both what is strived for and what is valuable in sport.

The main priority of the coach, based on a MacIntyrean conception of sport as a practice, should be the initiation of persons into their sport in ways that emphasize those appropriate customs through which internal goods are to be pursued. The coach should help and encourage his or her players in appropriate ways to strive towards the acquisition of these goods to the best of their ability. In football (and all sports), the pursuit of such goods entails that the game must be played in specific ways. For example, a goal scorer's speed and strength are a waste if their ball control is clumsy and lumbering. The player must have patience to develop sensitivity and grace in their 'first touch' play if they are to take into account the likely effect of their football limitations (e.g. being dispossessed easily, not able to find time and space, tempted to foul an opponent). Developing their first touch will allow them to have better and more frequent opportunities to score through skilful and honest play. Doing so preserves a good and fair contest between opponents. To score a goal by a poor or illegal technique (such as an unintended ricochet or handball) is not to fully encounter the fulfilment of the internal goods.

It may be, and often is, the case in modern professional sport that players view contentment in winning whatever the means employed, but such persons cannot also claim to have disclosed 'good' qualities of character in the form of those virtues such as honesty, justice and courage. In such instances, the source of their satisfaction cannot, we argue, be the internal goods. Exercising qualities such as speed, endurance and technical dexterity, to the exclusion of particular virtues and admirable qualities of character such as resoluteness, diligence, and grace in victory and defeat, suggests a one-dimensional and impoverished understanding of sporting excellence, which if pressed upon athletes by their coaches fails them in a significant and discreditable way. Therefore, the coach whose actions are overtly instrumental, born of the hot pursuit of victory, such as those associated with deliberate rule-breaking and gamespersonship, may, in a technical and tactical sense, disclose skilful acumen, sharpness of wit and insight. However, by pursuing such goals without concern for the prescriptive moral boundaries manifest in terms of the exhibition of virtues (particularly those of honesty and fairness), the coach falls considerably short of achieving fully the kinds of sporting excellences understood in terms of internal goods (Fraleigh 1984; Morgan 1994).

MacIntyre (1985) acutely acknowledges this enduring tension, for the descriptive strand to his theory argues that coexistent within practices are not only internal goods of a moral and non-moral kind, but also other external goods. External goods associated with the practice of sport, particularly high-level elite sport, are scarce and therefore only available to a few. The paradigm examples are economic ones such as salaries and prize-money that are available to professional sportsmen and women. Attendant rewards also come in other various commodified forms such as fame, celebrity, reverence and esteem, which in turn may provide athletes with a further resource for financial gain without significant personal investment of time or effort such as endorsement contracts, complementary services and goods, and appearance fees. The common derivatives here are attendant political power, cultural and economic capital, and social privilege.

Coaches, particularly those who work with elite sportsmen and women, play a significant part in ensuring athletes achieve the kind of sporting success that is then rewarded with money, fame, trophies, and so forth. They also recognize that the presence and appeal of such rewards potentially undermine their coaching proposals by distracting and potentially corrupting both their athletes and themselves. A strong empirical case can be made that money, fame and fortune often lead to compromises on principle involving cheating, deception, and a win at all costs attitude in the context of sport. Sport, in this instance, is no different from normal life, where external rewards are often the motive for fraud, malpractice and conspiracy (MacIntyre 1985).

Virtues play an important role in keeping out these corrupting influences. The list of relevant virtues needed for individuals to keep in balance the pursuit of practice goods is contested avidly by moral philosophers. Some, as is the case with MacIntyre (1985), focus on justice, courage and honesty. Others, such as Pincoffs (1986), cast their net much wider. Some (Slote 1997) are more prescriptive in the sense that they attempt to articulate 'the good' of a relevant virtue in terms of a practice-specific context. Such authors even push the idea that there may be practice-specific virtues which may be partly definitive of the activity in question. In the case of sport, Simon (1999) has argued that the particular form of ludic rationality demanded of those who engage in activities that are gratuitous in nature might be considered a virtue. It means that even for the most mercenary of athletes, the attendant rewards that motivate their participation in sport are frustrated (constantly) by having to observe rules and conventions that they would prefer to ignore. In the case of most who coach sport, their projects embrace the kinds of virtues that make for well-rounded athletes. They aim towards the development of integrity, fairness, magnanimity, humility, cooperation and loyalty. In supporting athletes towards their full potential within sport, the coach will both understand and accept that they have a responsibility to nurture strong characters who are fair, honest and brave enough not to have their heads turned by the temptations that arise with material over-indulgence.

A few examples from elite professional sport help demonstrate this point. It is now the norm for coaches and players at post-match televised interviews to be increasingly critical and blaming of officials, primarily when they have lost. Such engagements consist of little more than post-mortem examinations of officials' errors. Blame for losses is often apportioned because officials have been unable to discern genuine from disingenuous intentions to play fairly or unfairly. Such outbursts proceed often without any acknowledgement that players and coaches who adopt a radically instrumental perspective towards the rules have only themselves to blame for muddying the scene. So when Premier League football manager Joe Kinnear describes a top-level official as a 'Mickey Mouse referee' (Ley 2008) for giving what Kinnear thought was an undeserved penalty, he takes for granted the radical instrumental view that the rules are nothing more than obstacles to be manipulated for one's own self-interests. It is a view which takes for granted that, with respect to many normative aspects of the game, the responsibility for ensuring fair play is for the officials alone to determine rather than collectively borne through the interaction between players and coaches. Contrition, humility and magnanimity, and a sense of how one's own responsibilities towards the role of the rules might limit the tarnishing of much of professional sport, are non-existent. Coaches here could set good examples rather than bad ones, but rarely do so.

Although the dominant coaching ideology may often play free and easy with regard to moral concerns, such an ideology can only be seen as contingent upon, rather than logically necessary to, the practice of coaching. This standpoint can be contrasted with the opposite view held by some who argue that the practice of coaching may be inherently corrupt (Burke 2001). While the moral sagacity of coaching at the elite level may draw disapproval and condemnation from those who consider the sphere as one marked by selfish instrumentalism, individual coaches and individual coaching actions of great integrity survive, a fact that provides reformers with some hope. For example, to note are the worthy efforts of individuals such as Dario Gradi, the former coach to the English League Championship side Crewe Alexandra, who is a six-time winner of the Bobby Moore Fair Play Trophy during an eight-year period. Gradi received much praise (though perhaps a mere

£5,000 is not enough reward) for his ongoing efforts to emphasize the moral dimension of football. He considers that strong discipline is not just a matter of manners but also a mark of professionalism:

> We just feel it's in the best interests of the football club to try and get the least number of players suspended as possible. We teach the players, at every level from youth team upwards, the benefits of not giving away unnecessary free kicks and cautions. I read Sir Clive Woodward's book, and in it he talks about how he doesn't understand why so many players make enemies of referees – and I can see his point. He thinks players should be trying to make referees their friend and I agree.
>
> *(Clarkson 2007)*

The important implication of MacIntyre's account is that the moral character of individuals and the cultivation of virtues should stay at the heart of why sporting practices are valued and pursued. This point is well understood by coaches like Gradi. Without such coaches and the values they espouse, sports are reduced to impoverished, radically instrumental activities.

Coaching and character

The pursuit of moral virtues is, we have argued, at the heart of a normative account of sports coaching (Jones 2005). However, for both coaches in particular and sportspersons in general, cultivating such virtues, unfortunately, is difficult for a number of reasons, and mirrors the kinds of moral uncertainty, crises of conviction and tentativeness of action that prevail in civic society in general. In order to ensure that such an ethos of moral indecision and neutrality does not take hold of coaching environments, an effective way to move the moral dimension to the forefront of the aims and objectives of coaching is to focus on the development of character (as opposed to the menu of techniques and tactics that often dominate the coaching outlook). Emphasizing how sport impacts character requires ethical reflection and evaluation from both (morally) good coaches and (morally) good athletes, and for both athletes and coaches, such a goal involves embracing a complex process that includes education, training, instruction, reflection, practice experience and emulation. It is a complex process because character is complex. Character involves habits of perception, cognition, emotion and action such that doing the right thing involves much that is beyond understanding, knowing and wanting to do the right thing. Moral perception, for example, requires coaches to develop awareness, a certain sensitivity or level of attention to particular morally salient features of their practice. This sensitivity is not an *a priori* or assumed human faculty that lies innate within each of us, nor is it a quality of persons that, by the very nature of coaching, goes through organic growth the more we coach. Sensitivity is a realized, and to an extent a practice-dependent and therefore relative, disposition. Similarly, the coach as decision-maker who simply knows the differences between right and wrong, good and bad, what is fair and what is unfair, is an infant in moral terms. Fully formed decision-making will depend on the extent to which the coach is capable of developing human relationships, embracing social conventions and establishing moral obligations and commitments, all of which often fall way outside their more narrow professional and role-specific obligations.

So coaching knowledge (conceived of in narrow terms) is, in itself, insufficient, and, some may argue, largely irrelevant to the formation of a coach's character. Coaches who learn to *feel* a certain way, for example, about certain features or qualities of their coaching environment possess a crucial precursor for moral action. In practice, then, where unfortunate cases of, say, bullying in sport take place, appropriately morally educated persons should be offended by such behaviour. Coaches ought to feel outraged, and their capacity and willingness to address moral indiscretions such as bullying are more likely to develop if coaches are the kinds of characters for whom moral impropriety registers on the emotional radar.

The process of recognition, understanding and purpose, however, does not fully capture the character of coaching either. Coaching dilemmas, particularly those that have moral dimensions (which, by the nature of the activity, means most of them), demand action or intervention. This is neither easy nor an inevitable consequence of qualities of moral perception, knowledge or emotion. If the coach is pusillanimous, the confrontation that such problematic dilemmas inevitably demand may stall or paralyse them, preventing them from effecting an adequate and timely response. Coaches may often experience fear, anxiety and a lack of self-confidence, which may all hinder their best intentions. At a more fundamental level, coaches may exercise flawed judgement and might simply get decisions wrong despite due diligence and attention to all aspects of the matter. Their judgement in some cases, therefore, will be deficient, and they should be considered poor judges of what counts as the 'right' thing to do.

The moral complexities that abound and surround the coaching process at every turn are not just food for academic thought. In the real world of sports coaching, the noteworthy case of Bill Sweetenham, the United Kingdom's former national swimming performance director, who was cleared of bullying allegations in 2005 (BBC 2006), is illustrative of what prevails in many sporting practices. Though Sweetenham was found to have behaved appropriately, the case prompted much reflection in swimming and sport as a whole as to the limits of coaches' actions in the pursuit of improved performance. What transpired from this discussion was that rather than think a transparent, fixed and universally accepted boundary exists between appropriate and inappropriate coaching conduct, in reality sports coaching consists of a continua of highly complex, context-dependent and historically situated behaviours.

In this section, we have argued that a crucial aspect of coaching involves realizing that sport makes demands on moral character, which is not innate and is difficult to develop. The upshot is that coaches should focus greater attention on the ethical implications of their coaching, and consider carefully how the kinds of coaching values and behaviours they hold and exhibit impact upon those they wish to influence. In the final section, we discuss some practical implications this virtue ethics-derived view has for coaching practice.

Sports coaching and virtue ethics: practical implications

The value of virtue ethics as a normative theory resides in whether or not it has the capacity to impact coaching behaviour in three important and interconnected ways. The first emphasizes the significance of character in the coaching context. In particular, it asks those who coach to reflect upon, and develop a self-awareness of, how their own character impacts those they coach. The second involves an examination of the kinds of normative standard of behaviour and action that should inform coaching practice in different sports settings. The third and final issue encourages the coach to examine their own personal goals and values of sport and, in particular, entails clarifying the moral values and aims that shape sport itself. Together these three elements might be constitutive of a virtue ethics-based approach to developing a personal coaching philosophy. How each of these three elements is relevant to the coaching environment is now examined in turn.

Personhood, character and coaching

Our philosophical grounding suggests that without question, coaches are individuals who must conduct their lives reflectively and consciously as moral agents (Carr 1991). In order to develop a morally sensitive self-awareness of one's moral agency, coaches must first view themselves in a particular, embodied way. Central to this holistic outlook is a conception of personhood that resists the deterministic and technocratic compartmentalization of the concept of the coach to that of a service technician engaged in prescribed techno-performative services within narrow spatio-temporal boundaries. It resists an alienating division of coaching labour to narrow specialisms and with it the increasingly professionalized divisions that split apart who they are as a person and what it means to be a coach. Our view is that the role of the coach should deliberatively be self-consciously ambiguous (Carr 1998).

This holistic view of the coach challenges the generally accepted account and professionally sustained model for elite performance in sport that emphasizes the specialist with an eye for minute detail and a capacity to increase tactical and technical know-how aimed at improving competitiveness (Jones 2000; Lyle 2002). It therefore also rails against a fragmentary approach to professional development where progress is measured in terms of the acquisition and application of sports-specific knowledge (Jones and Wallace 2005).

We advocate a shift of emphasis from thinking about the coach as a repository of theoretical and applied knowledge that may be limited to physiological, psychological, biomechanical or pedagogical ingredients, to one that emphasizes a person's behavioural qualities. It suggest a more humanistic approach to coaching in which what gains in importance is how persons define themselves by their values, integrity and character (Cassidy *et al.* 2004).

In practical terms, this humanistic approach to coaching also suggests that employers may need to develop more eclectic appointment criteria in order to get the right person for the job. A commonplace notion of what makes a good coach often involves two primary considerations: (1) that they have expertise because of their past sporting achievements or their coaching badges; and (2) that what they demand in terms of financial numeration is acceptable. Our view, however, is that employment based on won/lost records or champion performers 'produced' is misdirected. Instead, we argue that there should be greater scope for evaluation, which should focus primarily on who the coach 'is'. This of course leads us to the second issue and the question of how coaches should act and behave.

Coaching conduct

We see who the coach is as a person through their interaction with others in both sporting and non-sporting contexts. How they act and behave towards others (all persons as well as their athletes) reveals aspects of personality, idiosyncrasies of mood and disposition, and, in particular, what it is they value.

In the coaching environment, qualities of character are revealed – is the coach patient or impatient with a performer struggling with a new routine? Do they exhibit self-control or rage profusely when officials make a mistake? Do they persevere with diligent practice or seek to use questionable means when competitive success is in doubt? In such a way, not only does the coach reveal what it is they value within and through sport themselves, but by expressing their sport values they also invite and initiate others to value them in a similar way (Kristjansson 2006).

Through caring about sports and demonstrating personal interest, the coach is more likely to influence athletes to value the pursuit of particular kinds of goods and virtues of sport. The coach, therefore, has an important role in identifying and clarifying what kinds of values, aims and objectives ought to be pursued by athletes, as well as embodying how they are to be achieved by them. When athletes also appreciate and value the same core qualities of the practice, they also take responsibility for developing a 'thick' understanding of the practice, its goods and its particular traditions (Spiecker 1999).

If the coach is to inculcate and induct athletes appropriately and effectively, he or she will need to develop skills capable of seeing and responding to the make-up of each individual athlete's character and moral disposition. For example, the coach needs to know how to deal with the selfishness of a team player or the loss of sporting appetite from an emerging talent. It suggests their role in such instances is more than that of a movement and tactical technician. The coach should be capable of and interested in doing more than deferring to experts (e.g. psychologists, biomechanists, physiologists) to supply an appropriate 'fix' when faced with difficult cases. A crucial responsibility for the coach is to know how to challenge aspects of problematic moral behaviour in ways that inculcate and develop desirable traits and virtues.

This conception of the coach and coaching focuses more on the athlete as a person than on the end performance itself. It starts from the perspective that each athlete is a unique individual. It aims towards understanding their character and requires getting to know things such as their hopes and fears, their aptitudes, and their skills and abilities. In addition to attending to a list of mechanistic motor performance requirements, the coach now also should explore and examine those qualities within athletes that have to do with their character and personality. Our view is that a core coaching quality or disposition involves being interested in the athlete as a person through listening, and engaging with their attempt at self-construction and representation. Though we are sensitive to Burke's (2001) view that 'distrust' rather than 'trust' ought to pervade children's sport, the virtue-based approach to coaching we are advocating must involve coaching persons rather than athletes primarily because such a view prioritizes persons as ends in themselves and not just as a means to a (sporting) end.

The account of coaching we are suggesting argues that though there are practical, temporal and spatial boundaries to coaching practice, the coach is never 'off duty'. The upshot for coaches is that how they behave and what they say outside immediate coaching contexts may be just as influential as technical and tactical information imparted during a coaching session. Coaches need to be aware that the impact they may have on athletes extends into a much greater range of situations than they anticipate. Informal interactions with parents, players and officials all contribute to the panorama that develops about them.

Meaning, joy and coaching

The third and final issue focuses on matters of ultimate significance for the coach. If the development of moral character and cultivation of virtue are central to sport, sound reasons are needed as to why such ends should constitute the coach's ultimate goal. Other goals clearly have merit and more often than not are the preferred choice for most. In particular, the significance of winning, and the attendant rewards, tend to harness the personal and collective resources of those who invest effort into coaching competitively. Arguably, such values tend to eclipse all other possibilities for sport – for both coaches and athletes. In practical terms, the coach will be tempted continuously to use morally dubious means to win at all costs.

The coach alone should not have to face down such tensions. Sporting organizations and their administrators ought to consider how they can contribute to creating a competitive sporting environment where there is an absence, or minimization, of what Kretchmar (2004) calls 'necessity'. Healthy sport produces a motivational mindset that downplays the significance of contest outcomes in terms of consequences that are both extrinsic and immediate. Such a sporting context may deter the oppressive instrumentality that may drive a coach too far.

Kretchmar's (2004, 2007) view is supported by an anthropological argument. He champions the experiences of what has been called 'deep play' because it captures a way of engaging and a way of doing that is more in accord with our embodiment, with who we fundamentally are. 'Deep play', he suggests, becomes a part of who we are and, perhaps even more important, who we are in the process of becoming. We can have fun experimenting with tennis, for example. It can be enjoyable to hit the ball in the center of the racket, to see it fly over the net and land in the opponent's court, to compete, and to win.

(2004: 151)

The means–end coaching relationship, so often separated and a source of moral mischief, becomes radically reconsidered in a 'deep play' environment. The two are now conjoined, and the coach need not work towards any other external thing. 'Deep play' still matters, is seriously undertaken, and is as demanding as any other sporting climate. When pursued rigorously, driven by sobriety rather than hubris, it has the potential for excluding those external influences that can potentially lead to moral misfortune. It is an approach that claims that when sport is given its due gravitas, the ultimate focus of coaching is on internal goods and virtues inherent and unique to a practice, for it is those goods and values that provide such activities with their appeal in the first place. What fades away from the picture is an obsession with the external goods – those goods that are often advanced and capriciously distributed by sports organizations.

That said, contemporary sporting times require coaches to attend to external goods and values. Nevertheless, our view is that, at the same time, promoting 'deep play' may allow coaches the wherewithal to assign an appropriate place to all sporting goods. To do this, coaches should attempt to keep their athletes and themselves away from the corruptive influence of social spheres that are parasitic upon, and potentially distort and skew, sport's enduring appeal (Walzer 1984). Thus, coaches, if they are serious about their sport, should attempt to craft an atmosphere of play where the ultimate goal is the shared pursuit of those standards of excellence that are definitive of the sport itself.

Such a view of excellence requires all to appreciate that the pursuit of 'deep play' is a mutually dependent activity. It will make us consider our competitors, for example, as persons who make possible, rather than deny us, our sporting desires. At the core of coaching practice, then, is the notion that those we encounter and share time and space with in sport are fellow playmates. Like ourselves, they demand to be respected and treated first and foremost as moral beings, as ends in themselves, rather than means to our exclusive ends.

Conclusion

The preceding account of virtue ethics suggests that coaching entails, or ought to entail, an outlook that embraces sensitivity towards moral obligations. In adopting such a stance, we have argued for a multi-dimensional and highly nuanced understanding of coaching as a process of moral development of persons. Our case has been that the development and cultivation of morality in sport, set within the philosophical framework of virtue ethics, transcend divisions between the structures of sport and the individual agents who are engaged in its practices. We have argued that sport practices require attention to the pursuit of particular kinds of goods that necessarily demand the exercise of judgements that are of a moral nature and, thereby, provide sport's practitioners with the opportunity to cultivate particular kinds of moral virtues. When such behaviours are habituated over time through repetition, and refined and adjusted through reflection, the formation of one's sporting character is likely to take shape. Emulation of moral exemplars play a crucial role in this process and, as coaches are central to the contemporary sporting experience, they have a pivotal role to play in the moral education of those who come under their care.

Finally, the focus on character development as a core goal for sport may prompt greater scrutiny as to how coaches can do 'ethics' better. It will require coach education programmes to give such matters much greater priority in their coaching awards and greater prominence within performance programmes such as long-term athlete development pathways. Indeed, if our argument is to be fully accepted, it suggests that such a moral outlook infuses and prescribes a framework from which the coaching of other psychomotor performance matters takes its cue.

References

BBC (2006) 'Sweetenham is cleared of bullying', online. Available HTTP: http://news.bbc.co.uk/sport1/hi/other_sports/swimming/4580822.stm (accessed 11 March 2010).

Brackenridge, C. (2001) *Spoilsports*, London: Routledge.

Burke, M. (2001) 'Obeying until it hurts: coach–athlete relationships', *Journal of the Philosophy of Sport*, 28(2): 227–240.

Carr, D. (1991) 'Educational philosophy, theory and research: a psychiatric autobiography', *Journal of Philosophy of Education*, 35(1): 461–476.

Carr, D. (1998) 'What moral educational significance has physical education? A question in need of disambiguation', in M. McNamee and S.J. Parry (eds) *Ethics and Sport*, London: Routledge.

Cassidy, T., Jones, R.L. and Potrac, P. (2004) *Understanding Sports Coaching: The Social, Cultural and Pedagogical Foundations of Coaching Practice*, London: Routledge.

Clarkson, I. (2007) 'Bobby Moore Award: Dario's fair play policy sees Crewe chalk up a perfect ten', *Givemefootball.com*, Online. Available HTTP: http://www.givemefootball.com/pfa/pfa-news/bobby-moore-award-darios-fair-play-policy-sees-cre (accessed 11 March 2010).

Fraleigh, W. (1984) *Right Action in Sport: Ethics for Contestants*, Champaign, IL: Human Kinetics.

Jones, C. (2001) 'Towards an understanding of ethical action in professional football', *Journal of Professional Ethics*, 9(3/4): 97–119.

Jones, C. (2003) 'The traditional football fan: an ethical critique of a selective construction', *Journal of the Philosophy of Sport*, 30(1): 37–50.

Jones, C. (2005) 'Character, virtue and physical education', *European Physical Education Review*, 11(2): 139–151.

Jones, R.L. (2000) 'Toward a sociology of coaching', in R.L. Jones and K.M. Armour (eds) *The Sociology of Sport: Theory and Practice*, London: Addison-Wesley Longman.

Jones, R.L. (2007) 'Coaching redefined: an everyday pedagogical endeavour', *Sport, Education and Society*, 12(2): 159–174.

Jones, R.L. and Wallace, M. (2005) 'Another bad day at the training ground: coping with ambiguity in the coaching context', *Sport, Education and Society*, 10(1): 119–134.

Jones, R.L., Armour, K.M. and Potrac, P. (2004) *Sports Coaching Cultures: From Practice to Theory*, London: Routledge.

Kretchmar, R.S. (2004) *Practical Philosophy of Sport and Physical Activity*, Champaign, IL: Human Kinetics.

Kretchmar, R.S. (2007) 'What to do with meaning? A research conundrum for the 21st century', *Quest*, 59(4): 373–383.

Kristjansson, K. (2006) 'Emulation and the use of role models in moral education', *Journal of Moral Education*, 35(1): 37–49.

Ley, J. (2008) 'Joe Kinnear rails at "Mickey Mouse" referee after Fulham penalty defeats Newcastle', *Daily Telegraph*, online. Available HTTP: http://www.telegraph.co.uk/sport/football/leagues/premierleague/3406122/html (accessed 11 November 2008).

Lyle, J. (2002) *Sports Coaching Concepts: A Framework for Coaches' Behaviour*, London: Routledge.

MacIntyre, A. (1985) *After Virtue*, London: Duckworth.

McFee, G. (2004) *Sport, Rules and Values: Philosophical Investigations into the Nature of Sport*, London: Routledge.

McNamee, M.J. (1995) 'Sporting practices, institutions, and virtues: a critique and restatement', *Journal of the Philosophy of Sport*, 22: 61–82.

Morgan, W.J. (1994) *Leftist Theories of Sport: A Critique and Reconstruction*, Champaign, IL: University of Illinois Press.

Pincoffs, E. (1986) *Quandaries and Virtues: Against Reductivism in Ethics*, Kansas: University of Kansas Press.

Simon, R.L. (1999) 'Internalism and internal values in sport', *Journal of the Philosophy of Sport*, 27: 1–16.

Slote, M. (1997) 'Agent-based virtue ethics', in R. Crisp and M. Slote (eds) *Virtue Ethics*, Oxford: Oxford University Press.

Spiecker, B. (1999) 'Habituation and training in early moral upbringing', in D. Carr and J. Steutel (eds) *Virtue Ethics and Moral Education*, London: Routledge.

Walzer, M. (1984) 'Liberalism and the art of separation', *Political Theory*, 12(3): 315–330.

PART III

Coaching specific populations

6

THE MORAL AMBIGUITY OF COACHING YOUTH SPORT

John S. Russell

Introduction

Anyone who has coached children's sport knows it is fraught with moral problems and dilemmas, many of which defy straightforward resolution. The familiar aspects of this have to do with encouraging teamwork, commitment, fair play, sportspersonship, and balancing obligations to individual team members and to the team as a whole. But while these represent substantial coaching challenges, they fail to convey the depth of moral complexity that surrounds youth sport and being a youth coach. In fact, youth sport is an arena of vexing moral ambiguity and regret. This is reflected in the flawed moral character of sport itself and in uncertainties surrounding the status of children and our obligations to them – or so I shall argue. There is, I think, a hopeful expectation among parents and lovers of sport generally that children's sport is, or should be, an innocent source of play and fun and a robust opportunity for moral education and development. In fact, the truth is more complex and troubling. Despite the many positive contributions sport can make to a child's life, sport also exposes young persons to certain moral and other hazards. Many of these should be better recognized and understood.

My focus in this chapter will be mainly on competitive sport involving children who are gifted or elite athletes for their age (including, for example, participants on 'rep' or 'all-star' teams), since these are the contexts where the moral problems of youth sport are most evident and the moral demands on a coach are most severe. However, many of my comments will apply to all spheres of youth sport and will have relevance to sport and coaching more generally. I shall leave aside questions about the age at which gifted or elite athletic programmes or teams should be created (cf. Dixon 2007). As a rough approximation, I suspect that this chapter is directed at competitive sport involving children who are aged 10–18. I will assume that in referring to 'children's' or 'youth' sport, I will be referring to athletes who lack full adult capacities for decision-making (though they may have full capacities for some decisions within sport and elsewhere).

A moral dilemma

Coaches have special fiduciary-like obligations to youth athletes under their supervision in virtue of the fact that they are children and not yet full adults. As such, coaches have duties to consider and act in a child's best interests. Just what this means is contested, but perhaps the most familiar view is the Kantian position that we have duties to children to do the most we can to ensure that they become functioning autonomous adults. Paternalistic interference in children's lives is therefore warranted whenever there are impediments to the most efficient acquisition of adult autonomy (Schapiro 1999). Another influential interpretation of the fiduciary obligation to children is Joel Feinberg's (1980) idea that children have a right to an open future. This mandates adult duties to develop children's capacities for autonomous choice so that they have opportunities to pursue a maximal array of life plans when they reach adulthood. Arguably, ideas like Feinberg's are reflected in documents like the United Nations Convention on the Rights of the Child (1989) which require governments to ensure 'the maximal development of the child'.

These positions have appeared plausible to some, but they have also been subject to much criticism. One compelling objection is that the paternalism they mandate is too severe. It gives too much priority to the rights and interests of the adults the children will become and fails to respect the rights and interests of children as the individuals they are *now*. Gareth Matthews (2005) has observed that on these sorts of views, 'Childhood is essentially a prospective state . . . the goods of childhood will be, on the whole, derivative of the goods of adulthood.' But Matthews and others argue that not all goods of childhood are derivative in this sense. Some goods are only available, or are only readily available, to children, and so should not necessarily be denied to children on the grounds that they may interfere with or limit access to adult goods or opportunities. Matthews gives the example of art and artistic development, but sport is at least as compelling an example. Thus, it is evident that competitive youth sport, especially rep or all-star sport, can involve onerous time commitments and commitments to develop a narrow range of mainly gratuitous physical skills that can be at odds with the development of other capacities that may turn out to be important from childhood through the end of life. Dangerous sports, like hockey, rugby, gymnastics, American football, and so on, add another dimension, since they arguably pose unnecessary physical risks to the development of basic adult bodily and mental capacities.

If we viewed childhood as Schapiro, Feinberg and the UN Convention propose, we would have to severely restrict such activities because of the various unnecessary threats they represent to the autonomous adult the child will become (Russell 2007b). But this would involve a remarkable upheaval of current social practices, which arguably recognize the need to respect the child for who he or she is now, including recognition that certain life goods, including realization of some physical skills, are only readily accessible to children. Social practice and compelling philosophical treatments of childhood recognize, then, that proper respect for children includes providing meaningful opportunities for self-affirmation and avoiding 'culpable squandering' of special talents despite the fact that they may close options or represent other threats to the adult the child will become (Archard 2004: 83; Russell 2007b).

A youth coach is at the centre of these conflicts. A heavy schedule of intensive practices, travel, and regular season and tournament games can clearly interfere with development of important adult capacities, including literacy, communication skills, general knowledge, and analytical and critical thinking abilities. Of course, modern knowledge-based economies require that such skills be developed more widely, over a longer period, and to a higher level than before. Arguably, then, the inevitable 'trade-offs' that young athletes face are becoming more significant and difficult as general educational requirements increase and as youth sport becomes increasingly competitive and demanding of children's time and energy. This conflict has long been recognized, however. Plato recommended that the future guardians and rulers of the republic go through a period devoted exclusively to athletic training, in part because arduous physical activities and the time needed to recuperate from them 'are the enemies of study' (2004: 537b4).

One obvious solution is to leave these choices up to the child and his/her parent. But coaches have power to impose undue time and competitive commitments. When is that boundary crossed? Some answers appear obvious. If the requirements are so demanding that a child will fail or drop out of high school, this seems unreasonable. Of course, it is not uncommon for some teens to make this choice in some professional sports (hockey is an example). Even if we say that minimum requirements for a high school education should be met, this is so relatively undemanding that it potentially closes off many options. Is that acceptable? Shall we say that players should be prepared to enter post-secondary education? This is likely to be supported by the readers of this article, but many children and their parents do not have this ambition or expectation. A relevant comparison here may be the latitude that is given parents to inculcate religious values in their offspring, including fundamentalist values and ways of life. This may have regrettable consequences for the adult the child will become, including restricting educational opportunities and closing off many options. If this is a minimum test, competitive sport appears to pass it at least as well. Nevertheless, it is reasonable to feel unease about the consequences for children of religious or sporting commitments that prevent or interfere with access to a wide range of adult life options.

Frankly, I see no solution to this dilemma, and it seems to me that a sense of moral unease is entirely appropriate. Programmes for gifted athletic children are bound to produce adult casualties, including lifelong ones, particularly given the increasingly training-intensive nature of higher-level or elite youth sport and the educational demands of modern societies. The question is not just whether we can minimize those casualties. The deeper problem is that we have no conception of what minimizing them would look like, given that the Kantian/open-options position is subject to severe criticism and we cannot draw clear boundaries between duties to respect the child as a child and as the adult he/she will become.

What should a coach (or parent) do? One minimalist proposal is to say that participation in sport should not interfere with development of minimum capacities of being an autonomous moral agent, namely, the capacity to know right from wrong and to function productively in society. This is a position that cannot be gainsaid. But it is a truly minimalist position. It is far from Feinberg's open-options idea or the UN Convention requirement that governments maximally develop a child's capacities. It is difficult to be confident that this is the right position to take, and there should be more inquiry and debate about this, including empirical investigation into the effects of high-level youth competitive sport on adult life prospects and dissemination of results to parents, educators, sports officials and coaches. Moreover, there are ways in which competitive sport is arguably in conflict even with these minimal goals. For example, dangerous sports can pose unnecessary risks to the realization and exercise of adult autonomy. In the next section, I will argue that there are features inherent in sport and human psychology that interfere with the capacity of sport to contribute to moral education. They do not mean that sport cannot fulfil certain minimum requirements of morality, but rather that sport is in significant and troubling tension with morality nevertheless.

Sport and moral development

One way to play sports would be simply not to keep score and allow whoever shows up, regardless of age or ability, to play. In this context, winning is irrelevant and competition is therefore 'not serious'. There are of course real-world examples of this. The best one I know of is pick-up ice hockey or 'shinny' games on outdoor ice hockey arenas in Canada. No one keeps score, anyone can play, and the rules are adjusted accordingly (no lifting the puck or slapshots, for example). But there are analogues in soccer and basketball and other sports. Not surprisingly, these types of game-playing tend to be friendly affairs, marked by good sportspersonship, good humour and respect for others. However, they have obvious drawbacks from the perspective of sport and games. The main one is that they are not conducive to the development and display of sporting excellence. There is no expectation that players will play at their highest level of exertion and ability, and play will not reflect a sophisticated understanding and execution of game strategy and teamwork. All this, of course, changes when competition is formally added and the goal is to try to win. Then there is a need to develop and display individual skills and to compete with a sophisticated understanding of the game itself. In these circumstances, individuals with specialized knowledge of game skills and strategy and the ability to teach them are required. Coaches are a practical necessity in this context.

But the formal addition of competition also clearly changes the moral landscape of sport. Sportspersonship and friendliness and respect for opponents are no longer givens in this context. They have to be taught and reinforced. The explanation for this is not difficult. Once sport becomes competitive, it is not evident that familiar moral virtues of friendliness, sportspersonship, and respect for others will be conducive to the highest level of competition and sporting excellence. In fact, the available evidence suggests the contrary (discussed below). Much of the blame for this is often placed on the emphasis on winning, but even other approaches to competition in sport cannot avoid straining moral virtue. Robert Simon (2004: 27) has persuasively argued that sport is best understood as a 'mutually acceptable quest for excellence through challenge'. However, the *competitive* element in this quest for excellence means that opponents have something important at stake in competition, namely, their interest in displaying *superior* excellence. Moreover, winning in competition is generally the best, even if it is a far from perfect, mechanism for identifying superior displays of excellence (Dixon 1999). If so, an opponent is also an obstacle to realizing a cherished end, one requiring a great deal of commitment and energy. Friendliness, good humour towards others, and good sportspersonship are anything but givens in these contexts.

There is no straightforward natural alliance with sportspersonship and competitive sport in the way that there is for non-competitive sporting activities like shinny. Indeed, moral virtue and competitive sport seem to be in uneasy tension. It is natural and expected, then, that coaches in children's sport will also have to be moral educators in this context to ensure that standards of sportspersonship and respect for others (including team-mates, opponents and officials) are maintained. I suspect that one reason that parents and others look to sport and coaches to teach moral virtue is that their acquisition is *hard* in this context. This is something that has not escaped the attention of philosophers from the earliest times. Plato (2004: 537b–d) thought that those training to be rulers should spend long parts of their late adolescence devoted exclusively to sport. Those who were most suited to move on to become rulers would be identified through how they performed in competition, both physically and morally (Reid 2007). Whether or not Plato is right that this is the best way to identify political rulers, he was assuredly right that competitive sport is a sort of moral testing ground.

But the moral problem with competitive sport is not just that moral training is difficult in this context. There is again a deeper moral problem and dilemma, for there is good reason to believe that striving for excellence or playing one's best can for some individuals, and perhaps for most individuals at least some of the time, require motives that are morally disturbing or even destructive of personal character. In a thoughtful discussion of the costs of competition, Thomas Hurka puts the matter this way:

> It would be nice if we could always do the best thing from the best motive, playing the most skilful hockey without wanting anyone to lose. But we aren't like that. Often we need extra motives for excellence, and what comes with these motives isn't always attractive.
>
> *(1994: 271)*

Hurka is thinking of dislike of opponents as providing an edge in competitive sport, especially contact sports, but there is no doubt that many competitors in all sport find this essential to motivation. Coaches also look for it in their players. Perhaps the most extreme (and frank) example was baseball coach/manager Leo Durocher, who was famous for the line 'nice guys finish last'. Here is what Durocher (1975: 5–6) looks for in a team-mate: 'Give me some scratching, diving, hungry ball players who come to kill you . . . That's the kind of guy I want playing for me.' Durocher admits his attitude is shocking, but it is only so because it is so extremely stated. Hurka's point remains well taken. Even if some players can perform at the highest level from the best motives, it does not follow that all can. Often we need extra motives for excellence. As well, I suspect that even the best moral characters found in sport use questionable motives in an effort to enhance performance from time to time. What player has not wanted 'to avenge' a loss or exact some 'payback'? What coach has not used this sort of tool? And the strategy also works for winners as well. 'Don't let them get back up when they are down.' The most colourful example I know was a coach who asked his team of 14–15-year-olds to mark 'BOHICA day' on the calendar for a rematch against a team that they had beaten handily in a previous contest. The players were naturally curious about what 'BOHICA' meant, and with a little informal research were able to find out: BOHICA = bend over, here it comes again. The players were delighted at solving the puzzle, and this added pedagogic force to the 'lesson' – as it was meant to. This may seem shocking to some, and some unease is appropriate. But one does not have to look hard to find similar ideas expressed by almost any elite athlete. Tiger Woods once admitted in a *60 Minute* 'Up Close and Personal' television interview with Ed Bradley that for him the desire to compete, in anything from cards to golf, was fundamentally about wanting 'to kick your butt' (Schom 2006). His mother, in the same interview, went further: 'That's sport. You have to. No matter how close friend [*sic*] you are, you must kill that person.'

These are all morally offensive metaphors. One might respond that they are just metaphors that are meant ironically and are not to be taken seriously. There is truth to this, but the problem is that it cannot be denied either that their purpose is to enliven morally doubtful emotions as motivation – vengeance or revenge or desires for domination and even annihilation being the main ones. We can therefore be rightly concerned about their effect on moral character, particularly for those who are in the process of moral development.

It is false that nice guys always finish last. But the simple, and regrettable, fact is that these sorts of motivations have a place in human psychology precisely because they wonderfully focus the mind and are highly effective as motivational tools. Perhaps those who are fitted to be philosopher kings can attain the highest level of performance and be motivated only by the best moral character. There is no reason to think that this is true of all of us, or even most of us. The empirical evidence suggests this must be taken seriously. Studies of youth and college-age athletes over the past 40 years uniformly support the view that elite athletic performance tends to be correlated with lower levels of moral development (Ogilvie and Tutko 1971; Kleiber and Roberts 1981; Bredemeier and Shields 1995; Shields and Bredemeier 2009; Stoll and Beller 2009). One plausible explanation for this is that sport has not lived up to its obligations to provide moral instruction to athletes. But another, equally plausible explanation is that elite-level athletic performance is assisted by lower levels of moral development. It is possible of course that both are true and that the two claims are in tension with each other. (In the next section, I will argue that there is a more direct way that sport can interfere with moral development which may also help to explain these empirical results.)

The use of morally problematic motivational devices is of course particularly disturbing where children are involved, since coaches have duties to act in their best interests, and this includes contributing to their moral education. But we seem to face the dilemma then, as Hurka points out, of whether we want to do the most we can to perform at the highest level of sporting skill or of moral excellence. Contra Durocher and others, there is no necessary contradiction here, but there is good evidence that there is a profound psychological tension. Moralists will say that we should resolve the tension in favour of moral education, because of our obligation to train children to be morally autonomous adults. But it is not a given or a necessary truth that morality should win out. This requires *argument*. As well, there are important considerations that can be raised on the other side. We have canvassed one already. It says that we should respect the child for who he/she is now as well as for the adult he/she will become. The most important thing for the child now may be to develop his/her athletic skills. Another question is more straightforwardly empirical in nature. Will the morally problematic aspects of sport undermine minimum abilities to function morally? There is no evidence that this is the case, but this does not mean that sport is in the clear morally. Competitive sport may have costs in the development of good moral character. Once more I think we are forced to acknowledge that genuine moral ambiguity and uncertainties are associated with competitive sport generally, and children's participation in it in particular. These may be permissible but is also regrettable, in the same way that some types of religious instruction may be permissible but have regrettable moral and other costs associated with them.

A corrupt ideal of value

There is a yet more basic morally problematic aspect of children's competitive sport. It has to do mainly with the connection between sport and what Kant (1963: 215) calls 'jealousy in emulation' and is related to Kant's rather dark assessment of how personal ambition – the desire to be superior to and to dominate others and to be recognized for this – is both a basic element of human nature and its most fundamentally corrupting feature (Wood 1999). I shall argue that these ideas are reflected and expressed in fundamental features of competitive sport.

Kant argues that jealousy arises, and contributes to the vices associated with personal ambition, through certain incorrect ways of measuring perfection. Kant is of course thinking primarily of moral perfection, but that is not his only concern. If I compare myself to an ideal of perfection, there can be no jealousy, and this is the proper way therefore of measuring one's worth. By contrast, if I measure my worth or ability against someone who is better than me, jealousy is the inevitable result. There are two types of jealousy: 'grudge' and 'jealousy in emulation'. Grudge is expressed in the deprecation of another's good points so that the jealous party does not feel inferior. 'Jealousy in emulation' exists where we try to add to our worth or value in order to compare well with another (or others). Grudge is of course a familiar human vice and is found wherever human achievement is taken seriously. Children's sport is no exception. Jealousy in emulation is perhaps less familiar and its vicious nature may appear puzzling. It is noteworthy that Kant thinks its vicious character is most likely to affect children. One point he makes is that jealousy in emulation is likely to resolve into grudge. If one finds it difficult or impossible to be as good as the person one aims to emulate, deprecating their abilities to give oneself a false sense of equality or superiority is a natural response. But there are more distinctive and arguably more serious vices that are associated with jealousy in emulation.

Kant says that choosing to pursue an ideal of perfection and to be good for its own sake is commendable, but aiming to be better than another is not. Why? Kant does not develop a systematic answer in his discussion of jealousy, but it is fairly easy to see what he finds problematic about this. What is there that is good or commendable about having as a goal being as good as or better than others? There is nothing that is valuable *per se* about that. Being in the grip of jealousy of emulation thus mistakes what is truly valuable, which it takes to be comparative or relative worth rather than perfection itself. It mistakes something trivial and of no intrinsic value on its own as an end. Of course, since it replaces an ideal standard with comparative worth as a goal, it tells me nothing at all that is necessarily reliable about my own (or another's) value or worth. If I aim to be better than Jack, that may be no accomplishment at all. Jealousy in emulation not only fails to have something intrinsically worthwhile as a goal, but has a fundamentally mistaken conception of personal worth, both my own and my competitor's. Thus, it fundamentally misunderstands individual value. As such, it replaces perfection with superiority or dominance over others as an end. Moreover, to the extent that I regard personal worth in comparative or relative terms, I will regard myself as worth more (or less) than others, and so fail to see the absolute worth of individuals (including myself). In the extreme case, I will not be able to recognize their absolute worth at all.

Kant is onto something important here. Imagine a sport philosopher whose career ambition is to be recognized as a better sport philosopher than Robert Simon. There is something seriously flawed and even absurd about identifying one's academic or intellectual worth or value in this way. This is not what sport philosophy is for, and it misunderstands its value, treating as an end something that is not and bringing into view all the morally suspect aspects just reviewed. Moreover, it is reasonable to think, as Kant does, that children will be particularly susceptible to this type of jealousy (although to be fair this is often encouraged by parents and also represents a failure of good parenting, as Kant (1963) explicitly recognizes). Common examples of jealousy in emulation are on display every time report cards are handed out in school. Consider Jack, whose goal is to get better grades than his friend Jill (who let us say is the best student in Jack's grade). Jack is clearly in the grip of jealousy of emulation. He has failed to identify the purpose and value of education. Jack's ambition is inappropriate, therefore. Moreover, by seeing value in comparative or relative personal terms, Jill's own worth is not judged on its intrinsic merit simply because of a relative superiority. This wrongly implies that her worth and accomplishments are lessened when someone exceeds them. Thus, Jill will rightly think then that Jack's goal of exceeding her not only is based on a mistaken conception of value, but also threatens to belittle her own worth and achievements. It is difficult to see how Jack and Jill can be friends in these circumstances. Finally, if Jack is so hyper-competitive that he sees all his relations with others in this way, he fails to recognize the absolute value of others. It is no wonder that students who have this sort of competitive approach to grades are generally not liked by others.

It is not difficult to see the relevance of this to sport. Indeed, we can see jealousy in emulation at work in any genuinely competitive sport activity, from a cross-town Little League rivalry to Olympic and professional sport. Competitive sport *institutionalizes* the aim of seeking superiority over others, and the greater and more public the superiority, the better. Competition *requires* the assessment of excellence against *opponents*. Even if one is trying to run farther or faster, jump higher, or be stronger, *victory* is still a relative comparison between individuals. Winning over others is, whatever else it may be, a statement of superiority or dominance over others. Thus, the cross-town Little League winner has earned 'bragging rights' over its opponents for the coming year; a reigning Olympic champion national hockey team has that for four years, and so on.

Of course, assessment of any important individual human achievement inevitably requires comparison with others, but competitive sport is importantly different from many other types of comparative assessments. When we assess Jill's achievements as a student, we may count the numbers of 'A's she received as compared to other students. Or if we assess Simon's achievements in philosophy of sport, we might count the number of his published works or references to his work compared to others. Such evaluation is not clearly an instance of jealousy of emulation, however, since no motive to be better than, or superior to, or to dominate another is involved. Nevertheless, that motive is always present in *competitive* sport, even as a mutual quest for excellence, since victory is sought as a comparative measure of excellence and its pursuit is an inherent aspect of the activity. Less abstractly, if the Boston Red Sox compete with the New York Yankees for the right to play in the World Series, their goal is to be *better than* the Yankees (just as Jack wants to be a better student than Jill). If the Red Sox want to finish first in their division ahead of the Yankees, their goal is *to win more games than* the Yankees (just as Jack wants to get more 'A's than Jill). There is something regrettable and flawed about this. It is not the best approach to excellence, and it may interfere with a proper understanding and appreciation of excellence and of value generally. The evidence of this is everywhere in sport.

It is reasonable to ask why, then, does competition in sport seem so much more acceptable than Jack's competition with Jill? A Kantian response would be that we are so much in the grip of human ambition, which is a sort of innate compulsion to see our relations with others in terms of comparative worth and to desire being regarded as superior to others (Wood 1999), that we will find it difficult to recognize the moral flaws that come with it, such as jealousy in its various forms. I suspect, then, that it is because competitive sport buys into comparative worth from the beginning that it seems more acceptable. To accept competitive sport is just to accept the validity of assessments of comparative worth. But arguably, then, we should be vigilant and more critical of the moral limitations of competitive sport in light of arguments like the ones given in this essay. Still, there are at least two answers one might give to this position.

The first is to respond that while winning is a necessary aim of competitive sport, the goal is (should be?) to demonstrate personal excellence *through* this. Tiger Woods wants to exercise and demonstrate his mastery of golf and he requires competition to do this. The goal is personal excellence, and competition is only a means – perhaps a means to mutual pursuit of excellence, as Simon argues. From a moral perspective, this is an attitude that should be encouraged. The problem, however, is that it simply ignores the fact that the pursuit of personal excellence in competitive sport cannot be separated from the aim to be superior to, and indeed to try to dominate, others. Having personal excellence as the ultimate goal of participating in competitive sport is not something that is an intrinsic feature of sport. We can choose to have that goal or not. The goal that is always there, that is intrinsic to competitive sport, and that is troubling, is to *win over others*. Indeed, this need not even involve a belief in, or having as a goal, superiority over others. It could just be about seeking public recognition of dominance (e.g. by winning any way you can). Of course, we can encourage people to take a higher-minded approach, but this will always be in tension with aspects that are intrinsic to sport itself. And to hark back to the argument of the previous section, it is a further contingent empirical question whether taking the higher-minded approach will be most conducive to producing athletic excellence. The existing evidence about this is not encouraging. This represents a further potential tension for the moralists' position.

A second response might be to argue that because sport is undertaken by voluntary agreement, part of that agreement is to accept relative comparisons of worth. Thus, competitors cannot complain if competition involves the goal of bettering others, since all have agreed to that. Let us suppose this is true. It does not address the problem that there may be something morally troubling about being motivated by such comparisons to begin with. The fact that two people agree to a duel does not mean that duelling is not morally problematic at all, though it does arguably make it less morally problematic than a defenceless, cold-blooded assassination. In the case of sport, the moral problem remains, and is evident everywhere. Are the achievements of all sporting competitors recognized on their merits? Almost never, if ever. What sort of respect does a second (or third or fourth) place finisher receive in sport? Are their achievements properly recognized by others or themselves for what they are in themselves? If we recognize jealousy of emulation as a vice, we can trace these failures to the fact that sport achievement and worth are ineluctably grounded in the goal of comparative achievement and success among individuals. If this is right, it is not an accident that attitudes prevail like the one that to finish in second place is to be a loser, or that only losers can be satisfied with second place, and winners will only find a gold medal or first place acceptable.

Of course, a familiar response to the moral perils that are associated with competition is to say that athletes should be trained to focus on the process of their activities, the striving for excellence and its execution, rather than on winning or losing. Thus, Stanley Eitzen (2002: 239) has argued that a solution to the hyper-competitiveness of modern sport is to recognize that 'it's the process that is primary, not the outcome. White water rafters and mountain climbers understand this. So, too, do players in a pick-up touch football game. Why can't the rest of us figure out this fundamental truth?' But the reason we have so much trouble figuring this out should be evident by now. The examples of sport that Eitzen gives are all fundamentally non-competitive, or at least not seriously competitive. Eitzen's hope that the rest of us might adopt a different attitude to competitive sport is a vain one. Once competition is introduced and accepted by the participants, the process becomes competitive (as Grant's tomb is the tomb of Grant) and thus aims to identify the comparative worth of the participants. A comparative assessment of value is intrinsic to the whole enterprise of competitive sport. In a race of 100 individuals, there will be 1 winner (excluding ties) and 99 losers or also-rans. This is true, to a certain degree, even for a friendly pick-up game of touch football. As the competition becomes more serious, so does the emphasis on comparative worth or achievement.

Jealousy of emulation also explains the familiar saying that 'everyone loves a loser' (and its corollary 'no one likes a winner'). The easy but false friendliness that competitors often express towards losing or struggling or inept opponents is a product of a feeling of relative superiority. The contrasting distaste or hostility towards successful opponents flows from an awareness or concern about being inferior. Kant is certainly right that jealousy of emulation leads directly to grudge, particularly for children and children's sport, but it is there in all sport. (As a coach of youth athletes for many years now, I report that I doubt that any participant, player or coach, is immune completely from these feelings. More evidence here, if any were needed, that nothing straight was ever made from the crooked timber of humanity.)

Of course, it barely requires mention that coaches are particularly susceptible to jealousy of emulation. Coaches who judge their performance as coaches not in terms of development of athletic talent and competitive skills, but solely in terms of competitive success, are ubiquitous and probably the rule in all competitive sport, including children's sport. This is of course a profound error on many levels, all of which stem from regarding individual worth in comparative terms as based on whether one wins or loses. The basic error is evident in the fact that one can do a better job of coaching a less talented team/individual that does not have competitive success than of coaching a talented/individual team that does. It follows that regarding one's own value as a coach in comparative competitive terms can lead to improper devaluing or overvaluing one's own (or others') worth and abilities as a coach. It can lead to failure to recognize the athletic progress (or lack of progress) that individual athletes have made. It can lead to neglect of duties to develop the talent of individual athletes. These are such familiar failures of youth sport that they hardly need mentioning, though they are explained and put in context here. Even more troublingly, such approaches to coaching produce false opinions about self-worth and the worth of others. If I regard my worth as a coach as a matter of competitive success, opponents are a constant threat to my worth. This is false for reasons that have just been given. As well, Kant is surely right that since such ideas of personal value are so seriously mistaken in themselves and yet so passionately sought, they are likely to supplant a clear conception of absolute worth of individuals, at least within this context but perhaps elsewhere as well. Indeed, Kant's claim of a connection between measuring personal worth in comparative terms and neglect of absolute worth of individuals, gains further support by coaches' use of dehumanizing 'extra' motivations discussed in the previous section. (I do not imagine any coach would tell an opponent to mark 'BOHICA day' on *their* calendar.) Thus, the Kantian account of jealousy and ambition gives a thoughtful account of the sources of the morally problematic motivational devices discussed earlier. As well, it provides a plausible and deeply troubling explanation of why a lower level of moral development has been correlated with participation in higher-level youth sport. The problem can be said to lie significantly within sport itself. Sport begins with a flawed conception of value and personal worth, it enlists a corrupt form of motivation for excellence (the desire to be better than others and to be regarded as such), and these factors work together to encourage other corrupt forms of motivation.

Finally, the tribalism or exaltation of one's own team or group or nation over others that is found everywhere in sport, from the Olympics to the cross-town Little League rivalry, is itself an expression of jealousy of emulation, though on a collective level. The sense of superiority felt by the 'Red Sox Nation' by *its* defeat of the 'Yankees Nation' when the Red Sox beat the Yankees, or the sense of national superiority felt by Canadians for the defeat of the Russians in a gold medal hockey game, reflects a vicarious collective form of jealousy of emulation that is utterly absurd. Indeed, tribalism in general is a vice precisely because, like sport, it is grounded fundamentally in jealousy of emulation, that is, of regarding one's worth or achievement in comparative terms and desiring to be regarded as better than others. It is no accident either, then, that tribalism and sport are familiar partners.

These attitudes all represent profound and troubling examples of jealousy of emulation. An important point is that it is not just our culture or expectations that create or motivate the attitude of jealousy of emulation, though these often get the blame for any moral failures in sport. The deeper problem is that the motives and attitudes that go along with jealousy of emulation are fundamental to competitive sport itself. Competitive sport directly contributes to and reinforces this culture by being ineluctably a sphere of jealousy of emulation and corrupt human ambition. In this sense, we need to be concerned about its impact on children's moral development. More generally, the dominance of sport in our culture is also problematic, because its competitive model does not set a good example for other contexts which lend themselves to competition.

We might hope to resolve the problem here by encouraging children and coaches to pursue absolute standards of perfection in sport. This is what is suggested by the Kantian discussion of jealousy. Undoubtedly, this is what is hoped for, in part, when we talk about playing for the love of the game. However, this cannot eliminate the focus on comparative worth which is intrinsic to competition. Even more bleakly, however, it is quite unclear that there are any meaningful absolute objective standards of perfection in sport. Rather, whatever value there is in the mostly gratuitous activities of sport seems trivial and personal at best. As well, it is particularly difficult to assign merit to individuals for their sporting achievements, since they are bound to be a function of circumstances for which the athlete is not responsible – natural endowments, social context and upbringing, and the assistance of others (Carr 1999). If so, this undermines meaningful comparative assessments of merit, which of course makes jealousy of emulation (and grudge) even more problematic. David Carr suggests that the only interesting standard for judging athletic performance and achievement may be moral, because this appears to be something that is genuinely praiseworthy and blameworthy. But, as he notes, we are then no longer judging such individuals for their athletic achievements, but for their realization of general moral virtues. More importantly and troublingly, if the argument that has been presented here is right, sport is fundamentally and significantly at odds with the development of exactly those virtues.

Undoubtedly, a hard-nosed response to the above would be to say that the competitive nature of sport has the important virtue of preparing young persons for the harsh competitive environment of modern everyday life, which is indeed real and important and which children will inevitably face as adults. This may be true. However, it does not address the moral critique of competition, which applies outside sport as well. If we are interested in moral development, then we should still be concerned about the influence of sport on children and justice generally.

Let me conclude this part of the discussion by noting that the jealousy of emulation evident in sport not only yields a corrupt conception of value, achievement and personal worth, but can also be one of the morally suspect 'extra' motives that Hurka refers to. Indeed, despite its flaws, the desire to be better and to be judged better than others is deeply ingrained in humanity. It is no accident that it is institutionalized in many ways, including in sport. The following remarks, again from Leo Durocher, reflect both the general motivation and its specific application in sport. They are useful for the way they reflect all the failures associated with jealousy of emulation:

> I never did anything I did not want to beat you at. If I pitch pennies, I want to beat you. If I'm spitting at a crack in the sidewalk I want to beat you. I would make the loser's trip to the opposing dressing room to congratulate the other manager because that was the proper thing to do. But I am honest enough to admit that I didn't like it. You think I liked it when I had to go to

see Mr. Stengel and say, 'Congratulations, Casey, you played great'? I'd have liked to stick a knife in his chest and twist it inside him. I come to play! I come to beat you! I come to kill you!

(1975: 6)

And Durocher goes on immediately to demonstrate, as Kant predicts, that his jealousy of emulation naturally resolves into grudge. Thus, he says of Stengel, '*I'm just a little bit smarter than you are, buddy, and so why the hell aren't you over here congratulating me?*' (Durocher 1975: 7, original emphasis). These remarks reflect jealousy of emulation and grudge raised to its highest form, to the point of pathology one might think. It is no accident, I suspect, that they are expressed by a competitive athlete. Indeed, the real-life sportsman and baseball hall-of-famer Durocher has precisely the same failings and is as morally repulsive as the hypothetical student Jack who sees all his relations with others in terms of comparative worth and desires only to excel others. They are fundamentally the same person. The only difference is one of context: competitive sport, unlike pursuit of intellectual excellence, requires the pursuit of comparative worth and the related desire to excel others. We should not be surprised, then, that competitive athletes have these attitudes – and to hear slightly more muted expressions of them, like Tiger Woods' wanting 'to kick your butt' in any competition, or his saying 'I want to be what I've always wanted to be – dominant' (Verdi 2000). Regrettably, perhaps, Jack, Durocher and Woods might succeed, and even succeed spectacularly, because they have these competitive motives.

What is a coach to do?

So far, I have presented what might appear to be a morally bleak picture of competitive sport. But competitive sport is no moral abyss. Whatever its moral failings – and they are significant – it is an institution that also embodies important moral ideals (Simon 2003, 2004; Russell 2004, 2007a). Competitive sport is grounded in the consent of its participants, and so it contains a commitment to equal concern and respect for each participant. Such consent incorporates an agreement to play fairly within the rules and practices of a sport. It requires willingness to cooperate with and be fair to adversaries as well as allies. These are important life skills. Moreover, sport regarded as a mutual quest for excellence encourages us to expand the limits of our abilities and therefore requires us to seek and accept meaningful challenges. It reminds us, then, of the importance of seeking excellence and that personal challenge is necessary to developing excellence. It follows from this that sport is fundamentally colour- or culture-blind and promotes broad ideals of equal opportunity. (Thus, sport requires something like the Olympic Movement and the lifting of the colour barrier in baseball.) The quest for excellence also requires the courage to take risks, perseverance, and the ability to be self-critical and to learn from failure without being overwhelmed by it. And, of course, sport contributes to personal health and can be an immense source of satisfaction and pleasure.

In all these ways, competitive sport is broadly continuous with cherished human values and virtues. But as we have seen, there are unavoidable tensions with many of those values, and these need to be recognized. They need to be recognized in particular by coaches of child athletes, because of all coaches they have special responsibilities for the moral growth and development of their players. From a moral perspective, one of the best things that these coaches can do is to recognize, acknowledge and talk openly about the moral tensions and ambiguities that sport poses, as well as its moral virtues. This is itself an important source of moral training and understanding for children, for human institutions tend to be morally flawed, and sport is no exception. Plato's and Hume's critiques of democracy have never been fully refuted. Indeed, democratic government might well be the worst form of government – except for all the rest. Adversarial systems of justice have obvious moral flaws. So does the institution of the family. The optimistic view is that all these institutions are better than the alternatives. Let us hope this is true for competitive sport. Coaches in their role as moral leaders will nevertheless have a moral responsibility to alert their players, particularly children, to the moral perils of sport, to help them recognize them and to hope that they can be contained as much as possible within and outside sport. Coaches might be encouraged to focus on the process of sport (the execution of skill and striving for excellence) and not on the outcomes of competition.

But of course it may be the case that focusing merely on process, and maybe even acknowledging the moral ambiguity of sport, will not be as likely to contribute to athletic achievement as a more overtly competitive, single-minded approach. Faced with such a quandary, it is clear what a moral perspective would prescribe. But it is not a given that the moral approach should take precedence. 'Bad but permissible' is an option too, particularly if jealousy in emulation and other vices can be effective motivational tools and are perhaps even necessary to the highest level of sport achievement, at least for some athletes. Then coaches face a genuine dilemma. The question becomes what should we value more: morality or excellence in sport? For moralists the answer will seem just as obvious as to some of those who are fully devoted to sport and athletic excellence. I suspect there is no straightforward resolution to the dilemma. But this is a suspicion, albeit one that is supported well by the available evidence. We do not yet have either the philosophical or the empirical evidence to know whether the dilemma can be resolved, in part because it has not been that well understood. We need to think more carefully about all these matters. To take on the mantle of moral educator in the midst of such moral ambiguity should be an unsettling task for any coach of youth sport. Perhaps a further lesson to be learned is that youth coaches are entitled to a measure of tolerance from the rest of us as they struggle to navigate a path through the moral vagaries of sport itself.

Acknowledgements

I am indebted to Ted Palys and Alister Browne for comments on an earlier draft of this chapter. The chapter draws on ideas in my paper 'The moral ambiguity of sport'

(Russell 2009), which was presented at the International Association for Philosophy of Sport annual meeting at Seattle University in August 2009.

References

Archard, D. (2004) *Children, Rights, and Childhood*, 2nd edn, Oxford: Routledge.

Bredemeier, B.J. and Shields, D. (1995) *Character Development and Physical Activity*, Champaign, IL: Human Kinetics.

Carr, D. (1999) 'Where's the merit if the best man wins?' *Journal of the Philosophy of Sport*, 26: 1–9.

Dixon, N. (1999) 'Winning and athletic superiority', *Journal of the Philosophy of Sport*, 26: 10–26.

Dixon, N. (2007) 'Sport, parental autonomy, and children's right to an open future', *Journal of the Philosophy of Sport*, 34: 147–159.

Durocher, L. (with Linn, E.) (1975) *Nice Guys Finish Last*, New York: Simon and Schuster.

Eitzen, D.S. (2002) 'The dark side of competition', in M.A. Holowchak (ed.) *Philosophy of Sport: Critical Readings, Crucial Issues*, Upper Saddle River, NJ: Pearson Hall.

Feinberg, J. (1980) 'A child's right to an open future', in W. Aiken and H. LaFollette (eds) *Whose Child? Parental Rights, Parental Authority and State Power*, Totowa, NJ: Littlefield, Adams.

Hurka, T. (1994) *Principles: Short Essays on Ethics*, Toronto: Harcourt Brace.

Kant, I. (1963) *Lectures on Ethics*, trans. L. Infield, New York: Harper Row Torchbooks.

Kleiber, D.A. and Roberts, G.C. (1981) 'The effects of sport experience on the development of social character: an exploratory investigation', *Journal of Sport Psychology*, 3: 114–122.

Matthews, G. (2005) 'The philosophy of childhood', in *Stanford Encyclopedia of Philosophy*, online. Available HTTP: http://plato.stanford.edu/entries/childhood/ (accessed 27 May 2007).

Ogilvie, B.C. and Tutko, T.A. (1971) 'Sport: if you want to build character try something else', *Psychology Today*, October: 61–3.

Plato (2004) *The Republic*, 3rd edn, trans. C.D.C. Reeve, Indianapolis: Hackett Publishing.

Reid, H. (2007) 'Sport and moral education in Plato's *Republic*', *Journal of the Philosophy of Sport*, 34: 160–175.

Russell, J.S. (2004) 'Moral realism in sport', *Journal of the Philosophy of Sport*, 31: 142–160.

Russell, J.S. (2007a) 'Broad internalism and the moral foundations of sport', in W.J. Morgan (ed.) *Ethics in Sport*, 2nd edn, Champaign IL: Human Kinetics.

Russell, J.S. (2007b) 'Children and dangerous sport and recreation', *Journal of the Philosophy of Sport*, 34: 176–193.

Russell, J.S. (2009) 'The moral ambiguity of sport', paper presented at the International Association for the Philosophy of Sport conference, Seattle University, 27–30 August 2009.

Schapiro, T. (1999) 'What is a child?' *Ethics*, 106: 715–738.

Schom, D. (2006) 'Tiger Woods up close and personal: golf superstar talks to Ed Bradley about planning a family', *60 Minutes*, Online. Available HTTP: http://www.cbsnews.com/stories/2006/03/23/60minutes/main1433767.shtml?tag=content Main; contentBody (accessed 1 October 2009).

Shields, D.L. and Bredemeier, B.L. (2009) 'Moral reasoning in the context of sport', Online. Available HTTP: http://tigger.uic.edu/~lnucci/MoralEd/articles/shieldssport.html (accessed 20 June 2009).

Simon, R.L. (2003) 'Sport, relativism, and moral education', in J. Boxill (ed.) *Sports Ethics*, Malden, MA: Blackwell Publishing.

Simon, R.L. (2004) *Fair Play: The Ethics of Sport*, 2nd edn, Boulder, CO: Westview Press.

Stoll, S.K. and Beller, J. (2009) 'Moral reasoning in athlete populations – a 20 year review', Center for Ethics, University of Idaho. Online. Available HTTP: http://www.edu_c.uidaho.edu/center_for_ethics/research_fact_sheet.htm (accessed 20 June 2009).

United Nations (1989) Convention on the Rights of the Child, Online. Available HTTP: http://www.unhchr.ch/html/menu3/b/k2crc.htm (accessed 19 June 2009).

Verdi, B. (2000) 'The Grillroom: Tiger Woods – brief article – interview', *Golf Digest*, online. Available HTTP: http://findarticles.com/p/articles/mi_m0HFI/is_1_51/ai_5831 4355/ (accessed 1 October 2009).

Wood, A.W. (1999) *Kant's Ethical Thought*, Cambridge: Cambridge University Press.

7

SPORT-SMART PERSONS

A practical ethics for coaching young athletes

Dennis Hemphill

Introduction

Sport can be thought of as a form of embodied intelligence that is acquired and refined in the context of relations with coaches and parents. Sporting intelligence is not simply athleticism, nor is it simply a conceptual understanding of tactics and strategies. Rather, it is also 'game sense', the ability to adapt readily and perform creatively and effectively to solve game problems. Coaches and parents can be facilitators of learning by encouraging athletes to step outside their comfort zones and test their abilities in novel ways.

Sport also provides an opportunity for young athletes to develop as persons. To be a person, especially in Western accounts, is to be capable of self-determination and valued life plans. Coaches and parents have a duty of care to ensure the safety and well-being of young athletes, which may entail the imposition of certain restraints on their behaviour. However, coaches and parents can contribute to the development of personhood by gradually expanding and supporting opportunities for athletes to develop decision-making abilities and commitments to meaningful engagement.

This chapter explores how athletes can be treated as sport-smart persons. It will include several practical examples and cases to illustrate dubious coaching practices and also those that are more ethically sensitive and responsive to young athletes. Both types are instructive in terms of how to coach and provide parental support to young athletes in an educationally valuable and respectful manner.

Sport-smart

Research in educational psychology and sport philosophy suggests that sporting prowess can be considered a unique form of intelligence. For example, Howard Gardner (Gardner and Hatch 1989: 5) views intelligence as 'the capacity to solve problems or to fashion products that are valued in one or more cultural settings'. In Gardner's theory of multiple intelligences (1983), bodily-kinaesthetic intelligence stands alongside literacy and numeracy, as well as musical, spatial, personal and interpersonal intelligence. On this account, an individual can be musically articulate, but so-so at auto mechanics; likewise, scientifically brilliant, but socially inept. The application of this theory has seen school curricula designed to account for a range of intelligences and learning styles.

In sport philosophy, Kretchmar (1994) discusses sport as a form of embodied intelligence. Rather than being seen as a property of mind that directs a mechanical body, intelligence is person–sport-specific proficiency. That is, it is not the type of activity that makes it intelligent, but rather how adept one is doing it. For Kretchmar (1994), sporting actions exhibiting 'unimpressive' or 'low' intelligence are characterized as simple, rigid and repetitive, and the athlete experiences difficulty adapting to new situations. Compared to this, 'impressive' or 'high' intelligent action is characterized as free, creative, adaptable, complex and flexible. The development of sporting intelligence from novice to expert marks the gradual improvement of the capacity to interpret tactics and strategies, adapt readily to challenges, manoeuvre fluently and deftly in game situations, and create opportunities for self and teammates.

Similarly, Whitehead (2007) refers to 'physical literacy', in part, as the person's ability to 'read' the environment, anticipate movement needs or possibilities, and respond appropriately with poise, economy, confidence, intelligence and imagination. Roberts (1997: 69) refers to a sport practice as a coherent set of beliefs that are manifested as 'highly specific actions designed to cope effectively with environmental demands' to get more of what the sportsperson wants and/or to get less of what the sportsperson wants to avoid'. Taken together, sport-smart can be regarded as the embodied knowledge and skills to interpret situations and creatively solve problems to fulfil individual or team goals.

The view of sport as a form of embodied intelligence can go some way to breaking down unjust stereotypes, such as athletes being 'all brawn and no brain'. It could also help prevent demeaning coaching practices, similar to the one captured in the following scenario:

> A young athlete walks dejectedly from the playing field, head hung low. His body language betrays the tactical error that just cost his team a touchdown. The coach is heard to say 'What happened?' Before the boy can get beyond 'Coach, I thought . . .', the coach interrupts, admonishing the boy with the words 'Son, that's your first mistake; I do the thinking, you just do what you are told!'

This 'don't think, just do (what I say)' attitude is prevalent where coaches have unquestioned authority, which is often the case in youth sport.

The notion of sport-smart may also encourage us to think differently about the relation between intelligence and instinct, intuition and magic. Spectators marvel at exceptional sporting feats, and commentators often put superb performances down to natural instinct, intuition or even magic. While descriptions such as these can be appealing at times, they can conceal or diminish the significance of the sport-specific reasoning (i.e. tactical, strategic), skills and disciplined effort that go into the well-played game.[1]

A former student of mine, an Australian Football League legend and now a professional coach, referred to sporting intuition as a learned habit. Immersion in a particular sport, and interaction with team-mates and opponents intensely enough over an extended period of time, improves an athlete's ability to predict the movements of team-mates and opponents. This can give an athlete a decided advantage in terms of performing effectively. On this account, uncanny sporting prowess can be attributed, at least in part, to acquired or refined knowledge in a specific sport context over time.

Once sporting prowess is recognized as a unique form of embodied intelligence, a more critical view can be taken of coaching approaches that are authoritarian, mechanistic, or demeaning to young athletes. It also means that, regardless of initial ability, steps can be taken to improve the sporting intelligence and meaningful engagement of young athletes. This is where coaches and parents can have an important role to play in the creation of good learning environments in sport.

Respect for sportpersons

A prominent feature of personhood, especially in Western cultures, is self-determination – the opportunity and ability to weigh up the pros and cons of alternative courses of action, make decisions without undue reliance on the help of others (Downey and Telfer 1969), and accept responsibility for one's choices. In popular terms, personhood refers to the ability to 'stand on your own two feet', 'make up your own mind' or 'be your own person'. The legal system, plus social praise and blame, would be unintelligible without the attribution of choice and responsibility to persons. The dim view often taken of those who endlessly procrastinate and make excuses, or for those who are overly dependent on others, also indicates the embeddedness of this notion of personhood in Western culture.

For McNamee (1992, 2005, 2008), following Charles Taylor, personhood is more than the capacity to make informed choices. It also can be conceptualized as the capacity for emotional attachment and commitment to ways of life that matter; that have significance. For McNamee (2005: 16), 'Persons . . . are beings who have the capacity to develop, evaluate and carry out life-plans based upon a combination of projects, relationships and commitments.' Unlike machines, humans have the capacity to live out ways of life, including those in sport, which are meaningful and can create an enduring sense of identity and purpose.

Accordingly, respect for persons can mean treating others in ways that promote the development of self-determined action and meaningful ways of life. This can be done by creating opportunities, pointing out options, and clarifying consequences for individuals such that they can make informed and voluntary decisions. It can also be promoted by providing opportunities to model and reinforce exemplary or desirable practices as part of a committed and meaningful sporting way of life.

However, in some cases, adults can undermine personhood. For example, they can do so by helping too much. Well-meaning parents may mollycoddle their children and thus undermine independence and responsibility. In other cases, they can help too little, especially in situations when there is a legal duty of care. That is, there are times when the risk to a person is such that it is inappropriate to let children simply 'learn from their mistakes' or rely exclusively on experience as the best teacher.

There are situations where a person lacks the capacity to make an informed or voluntary choice, and this can justify stepping in to make a choice for that person. This may be the case where an adult seeks legal authority for parents who, because of severe Alzheimer's disease, can no longer manage their affairs. In the case of children, we assume that they have not yet had sufficient education and life experiences to be able to make voluntary and responsible choices. In each case, though, the decision to intervene is based on what is thought to be in the best interests of the afflicted parents or immature children.

Protective intervention for those who are thought to be incapable of self-care is generally referred to as 'soft paternalism'. For Brown, this has special relevance for the care of children:

> In the case of children . . . restrictions on individual liberty may be justified as preventing significant harm that might not otherwise be recognized and avoided. In such cases it seems clear that paternalistic interference is not only permissible but may indeed be obligatory to prevent harm and allow for a full flourishing of the child's potential development.
>
> *(1995: 215)*

However, Brown is quick to add that '[a]n important part of growing up is making mistakes and learning from them' (ibid.: 215), so paternalism needs to be balanced with the learning opportunities afforded by activities that involve some risk.

On this account, a child or adolescent is not quite a full person. Young athletes may lack certain knowledge, skills and experience to make informed and responsible decisions, so paternalistic interventions may be necessary. For example, it is justifiable for coaches or parents to insist that young athletes wear required protective equipment or sit out of competition due to an injury that, if left unattended, might result in a more serious injury. Similarly, young athletes may not have the knowledge and experience to evaluate and formulate life plans that go beyond their immediate experience of sport.

Yet limitations and prescriptions are justified on the grounds that we expect that children will eventually learn to make informed decisions on their own, provided they have had appropriate instruction, mentoring and experience. For Brown (ibid.: 219), 'Teachers and parents must at some point help facilitate the transition to full autonomy at which earlier limits to freedom can no longer be tolerated.' In other words, paternalism with children is justified on the basis of safety and health concerns, but should taper off as children gradually develop the ability to 'stand on their own two feet' or 'make up their own minds'.

Their not-quite-a-full-person status is no reason to deny young athletes the opportunity to engage in risky, challenging and meaningful learning experiences. For Simon (1995), the ideal of competition is conceptualized as a mutually challenging quest for excellence between persons. This means that competition provides an opportunity for athletes to demonstrate and develop their sporting prowess in response to valuable challenges served up by an opponent. As a test of persons, sport can also provide athletes with the opportunity to 'show their mettle', that is, demonstrate their character (e.g. self-discipline, courage, tenacity, humility in victory, not making excuses in defeat).

MacIntyre's celebrated notion of a social practice (1984) complements this notion of personhood. As a social practice, sport is regarded as a cooperative social activity that promotes the pursuit and achievement of goods internal to the activity. 'Goods internal to a practice' refers to the purpose of the activity and the shared standards of technical, ethical or aesthetic excellence that guide its achievement. For example, in contrast to the game that is 'good' simply because one's preferred team wins, there are performances that are considered commonly 'good' because they are highly skilled, dramatically close, or played fairly.

While the internal goods may evolve, they provide normative force while they are current. Sporting actions, and what it means to be a sportsperson, are made intelligible and deemed legitimate within the context of certain shared purposes and acceptable standards and means in the sport practice community. For MacIntyre:

> [W]hether we are painters or physicists or quarterbacks or indeed lovers of good painting or first-rate experiments or a well-thrown pass – that its good can only be achieved by subordinating ourselves to the best standard so far achieved, and that entails subordinating ourselves within the practice in our relationship to other practitioners.
>
> *(1984: 191)*

'Subordination' in this context refers to the acknowledgement of accepted technical, ethical and aesthetic standards of play and the evaluation of one's performance against them. Yet being a sport practitioner also means having the opportunity and courage to make your own mark on the game by executing distinctive play within existing standards or by devising new methods (e.g. the Fosbury Flop) that may revolutionize the standards of the practice.

'Subordination' can also be understood, in a gentle sense, as socialization. Young newcomers to a sport, who may already be inspired by players considered to be 'legends' and heroes of the game, are gradually introduced, informally and formally, to its rules, standards and styles of play. When Canadian hockey legend Ken Dryden was asked to indicate the 'golden age of hockey', he replied, 'whenever you were 12 years old' (Wilson-Smith 2001: 44). It is during these early years that players may first express their love of the game, emulate star players and live out their heroic fantasies.

From these early involvements, sport may contribute further to the development of sporting personhood. As a social practice, sport can support a way of life which may be characterized by virtues such as hard work, discipline, courage, perseverance and teamwork. For Bloom (1985), young players can move from the 'romance' stage to the 'precision' stage (i.e. technical mastery) through to the 'integration' stage, where sport becomes a central part of their identity and life. While sport performances, youthful or otherwise, often fall short of ideal standards in the social practice, they can still provide a meaningful expression of identity and community.

Coaching practices

The 'transition to full autonomy', the 'full flourishing of a child's potential', and the development of sporting personhood and community may mean that coaches and parents may need to take a step back and assess their motives and interventions. On the notions of personhood discussed above, it is important for coaches or parents to avoid treating young athletes as simply means to adult-defined and adult-valued ends. That is, young athletes are not to be treated simply as machine-like things to fulfil a coach's aspirations or as instruments to satisfy unsatisfied parental needs. Otherwise, youth sport can, and does at times, become a stage monopolized by over-ambitious coaches and over-zealous parents.

The gradual withdrawal of coaching and parental authority does not mean that young athletes will be left entirely to their own devices. Protective interventions may still be necessary at times, but coaching and parental support may need to become more athlete-centred. An athlete-centred approach means that coaches can still facilitate the development of sporting intelligence and sporting personhood. In order to do so, coaches and parents do not teach, *per se*. Rather, they create the conditions and provide support for young athletes to be able to extend their abilities, responsibility and powers of judgement.[2]

Below are several practical cases to examine these notions.

> Tennis coach Clare allocates a substantial amount of training time to decision-making drills. Each drill is structured in such a way as to present at least two strategic or tactical alternatives for the athlete to consider and act on. For example, Clare has the athlete stand on the service line on the opposite end of the court. The coach volleys into the service court, requiring the athlete to reply with either a drop volley or a defensive lob. In the next stage of the drill, the coach adds more 'realism' by moving into the net or retreating to the baseline after each volley. The tennis player must now 'read' the movements of the coach prior to her own body positioning and shot selection.

This approach to coaching is consistent with the development of sport intelligence and personhood, for it provides an opportunity for the development of autonomous decision-making in a sport-specific context. The coach acts as the facilitator of learning by structuring tactical options and providing meaningful feedback. For example, in the above scenario, Clare may query and assist the athlete on how best to 'read' the situation, that is, detect clues in the behaviour of the opponent to better predict the opponent's movements and respond accordingly.

Compare this to the following scenario:

> Coach Paul, who is under pressure to maintain a winning tradition at a community soccer club, tries to increase the likelihood of victory. This coach 'plays not to lose'. Going into the half-time break with a comfortable lead, he instructs athletes to play conservatively, that is, play the odds and avoid making mistakes. The players are harangued with examples of their numerous tactical and skill errors. This is followed by slogans about sticking to the 'tried and true' and 'playing safe'. Somehow the messages are lost on the 10-year-olds, who seem more concerned about comparing grazes and cuts or jostling for an extra orange slice.

This example is instructive for several reasons. From an educational point of view, the players have little opportunity to test and expand their repertoire of skills and tactics, let alone 'show their mettle'. The coach's overly cautious approach, plus the exclusive emphasis on detecting errors, is educationally questionable and less than inspirational. The coach appears to have made some faulty assumptions about what 10-year-olds find important and how much information they can digest and use. It is even debatable whether 'playing not to lose' is an effective strategy to ensure victory; for it is often the case that momentum can shift when a team goes into a shell to protect a lead.

Compare this with Coach Dave, who attempts to inspire a novel and inspired performance in each athlete.

> At the first training session of the year, Dave assigns 'homework' to the 11-year-old boys in his Australian Rules football team. After the groans subside, Dave explains that he wants each boy to bring in a photo of his favourite Australian Football League (AFL) player, plus a description of the player's most admired characteristics. Each and every player returns the following week with a profile of his AFL idol.
>
> Dave works out an individual learning and game plan for each boy based upon the admired characteristics of the role models and what are considered exemplary skills for their respective playing positions. For example, he sets a right-footed full forward the task of attempting at least three kicks for goal with his left foot. Dave challenges a defender to run the ball out of defence before handballing or kicking it, rather than simply kicking the ball away immediately. A boy known also to be a good high jumper is encouraged to attempt at least two 'speckies', that is, two spectacular attempts to launch himself off the back or shoulders of an opponent to take a high-flying mark (i.e. catch of the ball). In one case, a defender and a midfielder are set the task of attempting a 'give and go' manoeuvre.

The individual plans are showcased in the pre-match speech, with parents present in the locker room. Dave stresses aloud the importance of trying something new, even if it proves unsuccessful. The half-time talk provides Dave with an opportunity to highlight examples of novel and creative play and reinforce individual performance plans. Throughout the match, the team's 'runner' is sent out to 'wrap up' in praise players who make attempts to fulfil their respective game plans. In one case, with the opponents watching in stunned disbelief, a right-footed player is spontaneously mobbed by team-mates for kicking a left-footed goal late in the match, even though victory for the team was well out of reach.

There is much to recommend in this approach for player growth and development. Coach Dave attempts to gradually move each player out of his comfort zone in terms of their perceived capabilities, but it is done so in a playful and challenging manner. The challenges are personally relevant, for the players are trying to emulate the skills and tactics of their AFL heroes, but in a way that is applicable to their own playing position. That is, the approach is athlete-centred, but also mindful of standards of excellence to guide improvements for each playing position.

Risk taking is encouraged and celebrated as a group norm. The coach's aim is not to encourage reckless abandon, but to give players licence to experiment and permission to get it wrong. The measure of success lies in the attempts by players to accomplish something novel. This group norm contributes to a strong sense of camaraderie among team members. Parents, too, felt as if attention was being paid to the growth and development of each child on the team, not just to those who would be traditionally looked upon as the star players who contribute most to a winning effort.

Coaching and parent involvement

Much has been said of the 'ugly parent syndrome' and its impact on the sport experience; and none of it is good. Parents who abuse their children, the coaches and officials can undermine the potential of junior sport as a social practice to promote the educational and ethical development of young athletes. Yet there are other aspects of parent involvement in junior sport to be wary of or alert to. The following case study illustrates several of these:

> Much of a junior State-level track and field competition is being conducted in, or interrupted by, rain, sleet and cold winds. On several occasions, events have been suspended temporarily as children in skimpy uniforms huddle together, whipped by the wind and rain, under flimsy canopies at each event venue. On one such occasion during the long jump, a concerned parent leans across the fence and tells his son to put on his track suit to keep warm. Upon noticing this, the event official issues a warning to the parent that he is 'coaching', that is, providing assistance to a competitor against the rules.

Another parent weighs in, reminding the official that, after all, these are 10-year-old children who need protection from the severe weather conditions. Another official is summoned, who in turn issues a stern warning that her child too will be disqualified if she persists with her attempt to assist her child in this manner.

Not long after, when the long jump event resumes, a parent is seen taking his mobile phone out from his jacket to make a call. His son, who is marking out the run-up for the long jump, rummages through his equipment bag to take the call. Instructions follow from the father as to where the starting marker should be placed. He is heard to say 'No, not there; another metre back.' After the warm-up jump, the father calls his son again to have him make an additional adjustment to the run-up starting marker.

The first way to make sense of these events is to refer to the competition rules. In this case, the Assistance to Athletes – rule 2.7 states:

(a) No athlete/team shall give or receive assistance during the progress of an event.
(b) Assistance is the conveying by any means, of advice, information or direct help and includes pacing by persons not currently participating in the event.
(c) An athlete may receive (additional) refreshments during the conduct of a field event with the approval of the Referee or Event Chief Official.

In the first case, the interpretation and enforcement of the rule seems unreasonable. That is, providing protective clothing in adverse weather conditions, when competition is temporarily suspended, seems more about the welfare of the children than it is providing an unfair competitive advantage. This is not a case of 'ugly parent syndrome'. The parents' intervention is clearly paternalistic, but warranted in the circumstances.

One could also argue that the event officials should be taking responsibility, similar to that of the parents, for the safety and welfare of athletes. The provision of protective clothing can be seen as consistent with their duty of care as event officials. It is even implied in section (c) of rule 2.7, where officials have discretion to allow the provision of additional refreshments, presumably in high temperatures when dehydration is a risk.

In the second case, the father's mobile phone call instructions to his son during the event warm-up are clearly in breach of the rule. It is clear that the intervention provides advice intended to improve performance. The advantage provided appears especially insidious given the covert means used by the father to convey the information to his son.

These incidents call out for a clarification of the rule. This is to ensure that there is no confusion over what is meant by coaching/parental assistance; that is, between that which improves performance and that which coaches/parents do to encourage participation and effort. Laying out some clear examples that can guide officials, parents and coaches usually does this. 'C'mon Johnny, go!' is clearly encouragement, while 'C'mon Johnny, lift those knees, you're three seconds off your 400 metre split' sounds more like coaching assistance.

These incidents also raise the question about the need at all for a rule against coaching. After all, many sports permit coaching during an event, and young athletes especially can benefit from feedback in order to improve their skills, abilities and confidence. Using sporting intelligence and personhood as normative criteria, the following defence could be mounted to uphold the no-coaching rule in this case.

In more 'open-skilled' and interactive sports such as football and field hockey, there are many opportunities for athletes to innovate or deal with unpredictable bounces of the ball and actions of opponents. In other words, there are quite a few opportunities for athletes to learn during the action itself. However, in more 'closed-skilled' events in track and field, the actions are more linear, less interactive, with smaller opportunities to innovate or to react directly with opponents. Given the relatively smaller number of learning opportunities in 'closed-skilled' events within track and field, it might be worthwhile to give children more scope to assess their performance and make decisions on their own.

However, a case for limitations on coaching and parental interventions can be made even in open-skilled sports. The emphasis put on success in elite sport means that there is less room and tolerance for experimentation and failure. The increasing scientific management of athletes means that sport performances are more scripted and subject to increasing surveillance in order to ensure the likelihood of success. However, the appeal to the sporting intelligence and personhood may support a case for limiting the extent to which coaches and parents should be involved in direct play calling and performance feedback during a sport event.

Conclusion

There is no question that coaches and parents have a duty of care to ensure the safety and well-being of young athletes. This can be shown when coaches schedule regular water breaks during training sessions or parents ensure that their children eat the right foods for sport. Moreover, sport officials often justify sun-smart and bad weather policies, as well as smoking and alcohol consumption bans at junior sport venues, with appeals to good role modelling, health and player welfare. Protectionism of this type is a short-term measure, for we expect and hope that as adolescents move into their later teens, they will make (good) choices of their own.

Junior sport can be a relatively safe environment where children learn a number of lessons about participation, skill development, fair play, teamwork and other benefits of competition. Sport can also provide an opportunity for risk-taking behaviour that can contribute to personal growth and development. However, over-protective, overbearing or over-zealous coaches and parents, whether for paternalistic or selfish reasons, may undermine these lessons and stifle the ability of young athletes to take responsibility for their learning and valued commitments.

Sport knowledge is oftentimes thought of as the exclusive possession of coaches, who then use it as power 'over' athletes. This is the case with over-coached athletes who are expected to 'not think, just do'. However, sport knowledge can be seen as power 'for' others. It means that coaches and parents create more room in sport for experimentation, novelty, challenge and risk-taking, but guided in such a way that young athletes learn to make informed, creative and meaningful decisions of their own.

This chapter has demonstrated how sport can be considered a form of embodied knowledge in its own right, and how it can contribute to the development of personhood. The notion of athletes as 'sport-smart persons' shifts the understanding of what it means to be good at sport and to be good at coaching young athletes. Coaching has an important role to play in junior sport, and this chapter has attempted to demonstrate that it is justified on educational and ethical grounds to the extent that it supports a community of practice where young athletes become more skilful, expressive and self-determined.

Notes

1 Contrary to the popular myth that 'game intelligence' is simply innate, intuitive or 'gifted', Williams and Hodges (2005) cite empirical research to support the view that the development of sporting expertise is dependent on a complex recipe of hereditary factors, environment (including influence of parents and coaches) and the athlete's commitment and motivation to practice. The research evidence cited supports the view that 'game intelligence' is amenable to practice and instruction.
2 Williams and Hodges (2005) cite a number of empirical research studies in order to debunk long-standing beliefs about the coach as sole authority, whose 'hands-on' role it is to pass on all necessary information and provide continuous feedback to guide sport skill acquisition and performance. The research evidence cited points to the value and effectiveness of 'constraints-based', 'guided discovery' and 'problem-based' methods of learning, where athletes are expected to take more responsibility for their learning. In these athlete-centred approaches, a premium is put on the ability of athletes to develop flexible and adaptable movement patterns in order to find innovative solutions to game problems.

References

Bloom, B. (1985) *Developing Talent in Young People*, New York: Ballantine Books.
Brown, W. (1995) 'Paternalism, drugs, and the nature of sports', in W. Morgan and K. Meier (eds) *Philosophic Inquiry in Sport*, 2nd edn, Champaign, IL: Human Kinetics.
Downey, R. and Telfer, E. (1969) *Respect for Persons*, London: George Allen and Unwin.
Gardner, H. (1983) *Frames of Mind*, New York: Basic Books.
Gardner, H. and Hatch, T. (1989) 'Multiple intelligences go to school: educational implications of the theory of multiple intelligences', *Educational Researcher*, 18(8): 4–9.
Kretchmar, R.S. (1994) *Practical Philosophy of Sport*, Champaign, IL: Human Kinetics.
MacIntyre, A. (1984) *After Virtue*, 2nd edn, Notre Dame, IN: University of Notre Dame Press.
McNamee, M. (1992) 'Physical education and the development of personhood', *Physical Education Review*, 15(1): 13–28.
McNamee, M. (2005) 'The nature and values of physical education', in K. Green and K. Hardman (eds) *Physical Education: Essential Issues*, London: Sage.
McNamee, M. (2008) *Sports, Virtues and Vices: Morality Plays*, London: Routledge.

Roberts, T. (1997) ' "It's just not cricket": Rorty and unfamiliar movements: history of metaphors in a sporting context', *Journal of the Philosophy of Sport*, 24: 67–78.

Simon, R. (1995) 'Good competition and drug-enhanced performance', in W. Morgan and K. Meier (eds) *Philosophic Inquiry in Sport*, 2nd edn, Champaign, IL: Human Kinetics.

Whitehead, M. (2007) 'Physical literacy: philosophical considerations in relation to developing a sense of self, universality and propositional knowledge', *Sport, Ethics and Philosophy*, 1(3): 281–298.

Williams, A. and Hodges, N. (2005) 'Practice, instruction and skill acquisition: challenging tradition', *Journal of Sport Sciences*, 23(6): 637–650.

Wilson-Smith, A. (2001) 'The good old days: hockey's golden era, Ken Dryden says, was whenever you were 12 years old', *MacLean's*, 5 February, p. 44.

8

MALES COACHING FEMALE ATHLETES

Michael Burke

Introduction

The author Mariah Burton-Nelson (2002) revealed that, as an adolescent athlete, she was the victim of sexual harassment and statutory rape perpetrated by her coach. This criminal behaviour by the coach lasted three years, and the behaviour only ceased when Burton-Nelson's family moved across the country. Her description of her response to the harassment is revealing:

> I felt deeply flattered, horribly ashamed, guilty, infatuated, scared, and, because he was married, brokenhearted. Bruce called the behavior 'an affair' and complimented me on being 'mature enough to handle it.' He explained that 'other people wouldn't understand especially your parents,' and warned me that if I told anyone, he would go to prison . . . I did not tell because I didn't want the affectionate and exciting contact to stop . . . In my case, I adored this man, and wanted him to love me. I also wanted desperately to believe that his sexual behavior proved that he did love me.
>
> *(2002: 7)*

Burton-Nelson's honesty provides a launching pad for this chapter, because it exhibits two important factors about the male coach–female athlete relationship. The first, that male coaches have been perpetrators of sexual harassment and abuse against female athletes of all ages, has been widely researched. The second, that consensual sexual relationships have occurred between adult coaches and adult athletes, has largely been ignored in the sports ethics literature.[1]

This chapter will commence with a brief overview of the contemporary literature on sexual harassment and abuse in sport/coaching. It will agree with several authors who have argued that the sports environment is a fertile place for (mostly male) predatory coaches to engage in harassing or abusive behaviour (Brackenridge 1997; Fejgin and Hanegby 2001; Fasting *et al.* 2003). The ignorance of this possibility by sporting organizations, and the failure to take any preventative action (Brackenridge 1997), may allow for successful claims to be made against the organizations by victims of the harassment and/or abuse. While this should not be the primary motivation for greater coach education and monitoring, it may be the most effective force to get sporting organizations to understand the breadth of their responsibilities in providing harassment-free environments for athletes.

The chapter will then discuss the reasonably common occurrence of coaches forming consensual sexual or other relationships with their adult athletes. Burton-Nelson (2002: 7) describes her harassment as 'a subtle, insidious kind that masquerades as innocent seduction, or mutual attraction, or dating, or an affair, and occasionally even leads to marriage, which further validates the behavior and distorts the inherent power imbalance'. There is a body of literature that discusses sexual relationships across the power imbalances of supervisor/student and therapist/client and suggests that age is only partly relevant to any ethical analysis of the relationship. Likewise, the difference in power between coach and athlete exists regardless of the age of the athlete, and while coping or resistant mechanisms may be more developed in older athletes, the 'consent' of older athletes is not the trump card in deciding the ethical nature of the relationship. This chapter will conclude with an application of the body of literature that deals with the ethics of consensual sexual relations in a therapeutic and educational setting to the sporting environment, and a suggestion of some modifications to coach education and accreditation that have seemed to be successful, particularly in the therapeutic professions.

Sexual harassment and abuse

Brackenridge (1997) locates sexual harassment along a continuum of behaviours from sexual discrimination to sexual abuse. Rarely is sexual harassment based on romantic attraction. It is, like sexual discrimination and abuse, based on a restatement of one person's power over another (Dalmiya 1999). The personal and social costs of all three behaviours are devastating for the victim (Volkwein-Caplan and Sankaran 2002).[2]

Sexual harassment is understood as 'unwelcome and/or unwanted behaviour involving sexual overtures, innuendo or propositions' (Tomlinson and Yorganci 1997: 134) that cause a person to feel offended, humiliated or intimidated. While perceptions of sexual harassment are age, gender and context-specific, it is the unwelcome and unwanted nature of the act that makes something sexually harassing behaviour. But self-perception is not the entire story (Dalmiya 1999), as morally and legally we must look at the way self-perceptions are tainted by traditional beliefs and power imbalances.[3] For example, massaging a junior athlete in a sexual way may not be perceived by that athlete as harassing, but the standard of reasonableness will make it harassment. Sexual harassment is often the precursor to sexual abuse and assault, defined as 'groomed or coerced collaboration in sexual or genital acts where the perpetrator has entrapped the victim' (Brackenridge 1997: 117).

Harassment and abuse are most likely to occur when either men or women deviate from traditional role expectations, but particularly when women enter a male-dominated environment, and harassment is used as a method of demonstrating female incompetence (Krauchek and Ranson 1999; Thornton 2002). The existence of women as athletes may still be a deviation for some professionals working in the sporting field, such that they use harassment to intimidate the women who participate, into accepting less powerful, more traditional roles (Tomlinson and Yorganci 1997; Fasting *et al.* 2003).

Brackenridge (2003) has explained several normative and constitutive factors of sport that specific sporting organizations should analyse and deal with in managing or reducing the risk of sexual abuse and harassment in their own sports. She has also explained a number of high-risk locations for the sexual harassment and abuse of athletes (2003; see also Cense and Brackenridge 2001). In this chapter, I will focus on the athlete and coach variables that sporting organizations can impact on, and largely ignore these situational variables and high-risk locations. That is not to deny the relationship between these situational variables and the opportunities provided by these variables for coaches to harass and abuse their athletes; for example, some sports offer greater opportunities for physical and social isolation, greater requirements for the athletes to be in a state of relative undress, greater needs for dependence on the coach, and greater needs for physical touch between coaches and athletes, and so on, than other sports.

Research suggests that almost one in four female athletes experience some form of unwelcome behaviour by a coach that would normally be defined as sexual harassment (Kirby and Greaves 1996, cited in Fasting *et al.* 2003).[4] At the same time, Tomlinson and Yorganci (1997) report that half of the athletes who reported experiencing unwanted behaviour of a sexual/sexist nature by their coaches did not consider these actions as sexual harassment (see also Lackey 1990; Krauchek and Ranson 1999; Fejgin and Hanegby 2001). Why is it that the victim-athletes do not report forms of unwelcome behaviour experienced in sport as sexual harassment? The answer lies somewhere in between the coping strategies adopted by the victims of harassment, fired by a blend of pragmatism and ambition (Brackenridge 1997; Tomlinson and Yorganci 1997; Krauchek and Ranson 1999), and an environment of sport that imposes weak organizational controls over coaches in positions of great power (Heywood 1999; Cense and Brackenridge 2001).

The athlete may lack the conceptual apparatus to put the crime into words, to explain that such behaviour is unwelcome and/or sexual, and the athlete may also not want to threaten either the existing coach–athlete relationship or her position in the sporting community. The athlete may have been socialized into a community which condones and tolerates such behaviours (Lackey 1990; Fasting *et al.* 2003). The athlete may be ashamed to talk about the incident, or may be frightened of the claim that she made a false accusation (Heywood 1999; Leahy *et al.* 2002). Or, as Mariah Burton-Nelson (2002) explains, the athlete may be enchanted by both the harassing behaviour and the charismatic coach/harasser. However, neither resignation nor enchantment may prevent the many harms that accumulate with harassment, suffered both by the victim of harassment and, potentially, by the sporting organization and its directors.

Following on from Finkelhor's model of sexual abuse (1984, cited in Brackenridge 1997: 120), Cense and Brackenridge (2001) have elaborated on a series of temporal and developmental risk factors that administrators can use to judge the risk for sexual abuse and harassment in their own sports. These factors are sequentially linked:

1. motivation of the potential abuser to abuse sexually;
2. the overcoming of the abuser's internal inhibitions;
3. the overcoming of external inhibitors in the sports environment;
4. the overcoming of the child's resistance.

Overcoming the abuser's internal inhibitors is more likely if the abuser is in a position where he is not easily monitored and if the sporting organization has 'a lack of clear sanctions and punitive measures' for harassment and abuse (Cense and Brackenridge 2001). Overcoming external inhibitors is made more possible by the social and physical isolation of the athlete by the coach, by the degree of physical intimacy that is permitted within the coaching process, and the creation of conditions conducive to athlete secrecy (Krauchek and Ranson 1999). Victim selection and grooming, including grooming of the athlete's family, also ensure athletic secrecy and isolation (Brackenridge 1997; see also Toftegaard Nielsen 2001). Overcoming resistance is more likely to occur with the social and emotional isolation of the athlete, where the athlete has low self-esteem but high dependence, and where the young athlete lacks the conceptual resources and judgement to understand harassment or abuse (Cense and Brackenridge 2001). In addition, the athlete who seeks physical/emotional attention and who has poor family support will more likely be targeted for abuse (ibid.).

There is also a higher risk of abuse when the athlete is at the stage of imminent achievement (near elite level) and especially if this coincides with the onset of puberty; that is, with 'early-peaking sports' (Cense and Brackenridge 2001; Brackenridge 1997, 2003: 7). The reasoning is that athletes at this level of sport are less likely to resist or leave a coach and more likely to have developed a relationship where inhibitors are overlooked (Cense and Brackenridge 2001)

Patriarchal sport provides the coach with almost unquestioned authority over the athlete (Brackenridge 1994). Coaching female athletes is also a rare activity where adult males are allowed to practise control over the bodies of adolescent and adult females (Krauchek and Ranson 1999). Coaches can also be positioned with power over both parents, who want their children to improve, and organizations, which have employed the coach. In situations of conflict, organizations can remain silent about suspicions of abuse or harassment (Brackenridge 1997). Coaches may enact any number of restrictions on their charges – restrictions which could normally only be placed by parents. But in sport, loyalty and obedience to coaches are considered the norm, so athletes and their parents willingly embrace the imposition of these restrictions. This possessiveness may extend to a coach having a far more liberal attitude towards the right to touch, caress or hug the athlete, to interfere with the athlete's personal life, and to initiate a personal and/or sexual relationship with the athlete, than any other adult in a professional position of authority over adolescents (Tomlinson and Yorganci 1997).

Toftegaard Nielsen's (2001) research with Norwegian coaches revealed that among the 186 coaches surveyed, there was a subgroup of male coaches, aged 30–45, who had far more liberal attitudes towards intimacy with athletes than the other coaches. These coaches also found it legitimate to give massages and hugs to athletes, give athletes lifts to and from sporting events and training, sleep in the same room as athletes on away trips, and shower with athletes of the same sex, all high-risk activities for sexual harassment and abuse. A number of these coaches also found it acceptable to flirt, call athletes by pet names, tell dirty jokes, attend parties with players, accept athletes drinking alcohol, go dancing with players, and engage in 'horseplay' with athletes, all of which create an acceptance of the sexualized culture of sport, which is a high-risk situational variable associated with sporting sexual harassment and abuse.

Autocratic authority systems that give coaches absolute and unfettered control over athletes also provide conditions to reduce the athlete's resistance (Tomlinson and Yorganci 1997; Toftegaard Nielsen 2001). In many situations, the imposition of control by the coach over the athlete does result in some type of short-term performance benefit for the athlete. Yet in some situations, the dependent relationship can result in other exploitations, such as verbal harassment or intimidation of the athlete being condoned by the athletes, their parents and the sporting community (Lackey 1990). Fejgin and Hanegby (2001: 475) suggest that the institutional support for the coach may mean that coaches 'think they may use the power granted to them . . . to control and abuse, and they don't define this behaviour as abuse, but rather view it as part of the accepted role behaviour'.

This recognition of athletic dependence is an important starting point for understanding and combating sexual harassment, and other forms of exploitation, in sport. To combat harassment, we should be trying to create dispositions and beliefs in athletes that reduce or eliminate the opportunity for coaches to exploit them. As participants in the experiences of youth athletes, coaches need to find a balance between paternalism, care, safety and the production of empowerment and independence (Brackenridge 1997). As Tymowski (1999) suggests, paternalism, care and safety are not ends that we should aspire to achieve; they should only ever be considered responses to certain shortcomings in the individuals we deal with. The educational ideal that we should be aiming for in children's sport is to address these shortcomings as efficiently as we can, and help to produce young adults who are capable of acting autonomously and with responsibility (ibid.).[5]

Sporting organizations may be held vicariously liable for unlawful acts of sexual harassment and other forms of sex discrimination by employees or agents done in connection with their employment or agency (Parker 1999; Walters 2002). Vicarious liability is where an organization can be found to be responsible for the abuse or harassment that occurred to one of its members, whether or not officials or administrators were aware it was occurring. That can be because the organization had no clear policies, educational programme, or monitoring procedures which would limit the opportunity for harassment to occur. Liability can only be avoided if the employer establishes that it took all reasonable steps to prevent an employee or agent from doing these acts (Parker 1999). Reasonable steps usually include issuing an anti-harassment policy including grievance procedures, communicating management's disapproval of such acts, ensuring that staff members are trained about their responsibilities, and creating a secure workplace environment. 'Ignorance' about the acts of harassment is not a defence unless reasonable steps have been undertaken by management.

Recent case law judgments concerning male-dominated workplaces suggest that obligations on employers are demanding and would not be dispensed with by the implementation of tokenistic policies and practices (Walters 2002). The 1997 decision of the Queensland Anti-Discrimination Tribunal in the case of *Hopper v. MIM and others* found that even though Mount Isa Mines (MIM) had an educational programme in place about sexual harassment, the failure of the company to monitor the high attrition rate of female apprentices recruited to work in the mine, or follow up on their reasons for departure, contributed to the company and the directors being found vicariously liable for the sexual harassment suffered by Narelle Hopper (Parker 1999). A second reason expressed by the tribunal in its judgment concerning the Hopper claim was that the employer, MIM, failed to ensure that the information about sexual harassment that it disseminated to its middle managers and supervisors had reached the crews who were to work with Narelle Hopper (Parker 1999; Thornton 2002; Walters 2002). No training was given to men who were going to be working with a female beside them for the first time in their career with MIM.[6]

It is widely reported that female athletes have a high attrition rate during adolescence, a time that coincides with several risk factors for sporting sexual harassment (Brackenridge and Kirby 1997). Have sporting organizations monitored and followed up on the high attrition rates of female athletes from their sports programmes? Given that some sporting environments are both hyper-masculine and excessively heterosexual (Fasting *et al.* 2003), it is also imperative, both legally and ethically, that the information regarding sexual harassment gets to the often young and inexperienced coaches who are employed by sporting organizations.[7]

Unfortunately, many sporting organizations lack the political will to deal with harassment and abuse, and sometimes deny the existence of these practices and turn a blind eye to deviant coaches (Brackenridge 1997; Heywood 1999).[8] Many sporting organizations have neither a clear-cut anti-harassment policy nor educational training programmes (Brackenridge 1994). This leaves them open to litigation and liability. Where programmes do exist, they are sometimes tokenistic attempts to avoid liability that are captured as codes of behaviour, and are rarely usefully passed on to existing coaches through in-depth educational programmes oriented towards athlete protection. These codes are often presented as part of National Coach Accreditation programmes inserted within programmes dealing with performance improvement of players. They just do not fit in these programmes.[9] Yet, as Brackenridge (2003: 10) suggests, coach accreditation bodies and sporting organizations both have a vested interest in dealing with these issues in order to safeguard 'the good name and integrity of sport [and] coaching'.

From an ethical position, the damage done to all female athletes by a single athlete accepting or tolerating harassment by coaches is marked. Dalmiya (1999) explains that the act of harassment is an attempt to annihilate the specific subjectivity of an individual, and tie his/her subjectivity to a powerless stereotype in society. Hence, the crime is against both the individual person and all other people in that class who must suffer the stereotype. She explains:

> [W]e may have an individual woman who is quite unaffected by the passes her boss makes or who even feels flattered by them. But in spite of this, an act of harassment remains morally reprehensible because by reinforcing stereotypes, it is detrimental to the class of women . . . Even when Rita thinks of *herself* as a foolish blonde, her boss in addressing her as a foolish blonde targets all blonde women and in so doing annihilates the particularity of each.
>
> *(ibid.: 59)*

This point provides the impetus for the next section of the chapter. While it may appear to be a dramatic shift to move from the sexual harassment and abuse of athletes (illegal behaviour) to a discussion of the consensual sexual relationships between coaches and athletes or former athletes, these sexual relationships may create stereotypes about women, even while the individual woman enjoys and benefits from the relationship. Hence, there is an ethical dimension to these relationships that goes beyond a discussion of individual choice.

Consensual sexual relationships between parties with different power

A graduate or undergraduate student is involved in an educational relationship with their supervisor or lecturer. This relationship, at its ideal, produces a good learning environment, where the person in power provides the student with knowledge, skills, counselling and professional orientations. The relationship necessarily involves a power difference; the supervisor is an expert in the field, may determine access to rewards for the student, and must evaluate the student (Blevins-Knabe 1992). Where this educational relationship coincides with some other form of relationship, sexual or otherwise, the ethicality of this other form of relationship is questionable, given the difference in power of the two parties (ibid.).

While sexual harassment, sexual abuse and 'consensual' sexual relationships with minors are all widely agreed to be exploitative, consensual romantic and/or sexual relationships between students and supervisors are more difficult to assess ethically, and produce less agreement about whether they should be banned (Blevins-Knabe 1992; Sullivan and Ogloff 1998). Research suggests that 15–20 per cent of female students have experienced some form of sexual relationship with educators[10] (Sullivan and Ogloff 1998). It is revealing that the most vulnerable female students (young women, single women who are just commencing graduate school, and women who have suffered from incest or assault) are over-represented in the figures (Blevins-Knabe 1992: Sullivan and Ogloff 1998).

While the psychological impact of such relationships has not been well studied in the educational setting, impacts within the therapy relationship have been documented that explain that clients eventually come to see such relationships as breaches of trust and professional responsibility, and that such breaches of trust may lead to impaired sexual relationships in the future, a distrust of therapists, psychotherapy, and members of the opposite sex generally, severe depression, hospitalization and suicide, and feelings of anger, rejection and abandonment (Shopland and VandeCreek 1991; Greenberg 1983, cited in Vasquez 1991). What is known regarding the student–supervisor relationship is that students often feel shame and blame themselves for the relationship and its effects as the relationship ends (Rutter 1989, cited in Blevins-Knabe 1992; Shopland and VandeCreek 1991), but that, over time, female students come to understand such relationships as coerced, even when they had perceived no coercion at the time of the relationship (Glaser and Thorpe 1986, cited in Skinner et al. 1995).

Survey results from current students reported by Keith-Spiegel, Tabachnick and Allen (1993, cited in Skinner et al. 1995: 132) suggested that the majority of students see direct sexual relationships between faculty and students as acceptable 'provided that grades had been submitted'. This was confirmed in Skinner et al.'s survey of over 800 students in the south-eastern United States. The ethicality of the sexual relationship for the current students was closely tied to the potential for ethical conflict with the existing educational relationship; that is, did the sexual relationship produce a dual relationship? Where no dual relationship was present, then current students were not particularly concerned. The current students also found it acceptable to terminate an educational relationship in order to pursue an intimate sexual relationship. The suggestion from this survey was that the major concern of current students was with the possibility for faculty engaged in dual relationships to act unfairly towards other students, and not with their own ability to give consent within the power-laden relationship (Skinner et al. 1995).[11]

In contrast, Glaser and Thorpe (1986, cited in Skinner et al. 1995) surveyed former students' perceptions on the ethicality of intimate supervisor–student relationships, and reported that 96 per cent of students considered such relationships as unethical when they occurred as part of an ongoing educational relationship, and 73 per cent still considered such relationships as unethical when occurring outside of any other educational relationship. This suggests that former students believe that the power differential between the two parties impacts on the capacity of the student to properly consent.

Blevins-Knabe (1992) suggests a series of questions that can be used to logically evaluate the ethical risk of forming any dual relationship with a supervisor. These questions are:

- Will the (broader) educational goals of the student be facilitated by the development of dependency on a special faculty member? Is the supervisor increasing the potential of the student, and other students, to be exploited?
- Will other students learn about justice and equitable treatment if one student is experiencing more favourable access to a supervisor?
- Does the student involved experience freedom of choice, or is the relationship exploiting the student's lack of alternatives?
- Is there actual or perceived loss of objectivity by the supervisor? Will male students believe that grades for females are unearned and related to physical attractiveness, and hence all members of the female group become tainted, and their abilities trivialized?
- Will future decisions regarding evaluation by the supervisor be compromised positively, or negatively, by either the ongoing relationship or termination of the relationship?
- Will students in the faculty consider all other members of staff with suspicion? Will the integrity and standing of the profession be compromised?

The questions are largely rhetorical, and suggest that the issues involved with dual relationships go beyond the idea of individual freedom, and must consider the effects that the relationship has on all others within the supervisor's world.

Research suggests that therapists who engage in sex with clients during the period of therapeutic treatment are often in distress themselves, and cannot objectively judge their own actions. Research also suggests that therapy and the goals of therapy are abandoned once the sexual relationship commences; that therapists in a sexual relationship are less likely to 'consult or refer the client even when the therapy process has clearly been compromised' (Bouhoutsos et al. 1983, cited in Shopland and VandeCreek 1991: 37). The American Psychological Association (APA) has recognized that any sexual intimacies between client and therapist not only will be harmful to clients, but will impact negatively on therapists, the therapeutic process and the profession as a whole (Shopland and VandeCreek 1991; Vasquez 1991).

It was the conflict between respect for an individual's rights and freedoms, and the professional concern for client welfare and the desire to do no harm that the ethics committee of the American Psychological Association debated when determining whether sexually intimate relationships between therapists and former clients should also be banned (Vasquez 1991). The APA decided that the professional duty to do no harm trumped any individual rights that the treated former client or the therapist might claim. Prior to this codification, the Ethics Committee of the APA often had to judge whether the termination of therapy was done 'fraudulently', in order to pursue a post-termination sexual relationship without contravening principles that prohibited sex with clients (Vasquez 1991; see also Steinberg *et al.* 2000). This codification makes unnecessary the need to judge reasons for termination of the therapy relationship.

Shopland and VandeCreek (1991) suggest that a number of theoretical perspectives, including the psychodynamic theory of transference, support a ban on post-termination sexually intimate relationships. These theoretical positions have been supported by state licensing boards, ethics committees, law courts and insurance organizations, such that all these bodies consider this type of relationship to be a breach of the ethical codes, and that any psychotherapist who engages in a sexual relationship with a former client is 'mishandling the transference phenomenon' (Cummings and Sobel 1985, cited in Shopland and VandeCreek 1991: 38). After termination of the therapy relationship, clients must still work out their feelings associated with transference, and may need to return to therapy at a later time. Commencing a sexual relationship with a former client at this time exploits these feelings of dependence and impacts on the possibility and success of returning to therapy (Shopland and VandeCreek 1991; see also Vasquez 1991). Even when this dependence has been worked out, the feminist perspective suggests that a power differential remains such that '[r]elationships established after termination may be friendly but they are not egalitarian' (Herman *et al.* 1987, cited in Shopland and VandeCreek 1991: 40).

Dual relationships in sport – ethical education for coaches

Kirby and Greaves' (1996) survey (cited in Brackenridge 2003) of 266 elite Canadian athletes revealed that 21.8 per cent of these athletes had engaged in sexual intercourse with a person in a position of power in their sport. This group of partners included coaches, administrators, doctors, physiotherapists and managers. Forced sexual intercourse, or rape, occurred in 8.6 per cent of cases. This leaves 13.2 per cent of cases involving apparently 'consensual' sexual intercourse between players and people in positions of power (Kirby and Greaves 1996, cited in Brackenridge 2003: 9).

Bringer *et al.*'s (2002) research on coaches' perceptions of the appropriateness of coach–athlete sexual relationships is the only research, empirical or logical, that I could find that deals with the ethicality of intimate sexual relationships between coaches and either current or former athletes, although much of what follows can be implied from the research on sexual abuse and sexual harassment by coaches of younger athletes, covered under the broader term of sexual exploitation. Their research, involving 19 male swimming coaches in four focus groups, responding to seven coach–athlete sexual intimacy stories, revealed that the perceptions of the coaches varied considerably regarding the appropriateness of intimate relationships with adult athletes. The responses ranged from complete opposition on the basis that such behaviour was both unprofessional and an exploitation of the athlete's lack of power, to viewing any restriction on such relationships as a restriction of civil liberties.[12]

Vasquez (1988) suggests a series of strategies for the prevention of counsellor–client sexual relationships that could be modified and applied to coach–athlete relationships. Although made over 20 years ago, her comments regarding the lack of training given to counsellors in ethical matters, including the ethics of forming sexual relationships with their clients, can be applied to the contemporary situation with coaches (see also Nickell *et al.* 1995). Most coaches receive no formal education about ethical analysis generally, or about the ethics of forming sexual relationships with their players or ex-players. At best, they receive some education about the coaching codes of behaviour, without the necessary skills to evaluate and decide ethical matters for themselves. In this situation, 'even the well-meaning counselor [or coach] can, and does, pose a threat to the client's [or athlete's] well-being' (Vasquez 1988: 238).

Vasquez goes on to explain that the mere exposure to professional codes of ethics will not be enough to produce a professional capable of ethical decision-making (1988; see also Leahy *et al.* 2002). What needs to be added in training programmes is the skills of improved sensitivity, ethical reasoning and decision-making. Counsellors and coaches should be given the opportunity to learn about ethical principles such as justice, beneficence and non-malfi·cence. As Nickell *et al.* (1995) remark, regarding the training of family and marriage counsellors in this area, it is unlikely that many therapists have the tools of an ethical education that would allow them to view their actions as exploitative and wrong, and guide their decision-making. This deficiency in education could produce 'maladaptive therapist responses' to any grey areas within the professional codes of ethical behaviour, where certain behaviours, such as hugging clients, may not be expressly prohibited by the code (ibid.: 323).[13] With these principles in hand, coaches could then reflect on the exploitative nature of dual relationships, the unfairness (actual or perceived) towards other athletes (Heywood 1999), the effects of certain types of behaviours like hugging or 'horseplay', and the loss of trust and esteem for the coaching profession as a whole, and embrace the restrictions placed on their freedom by the codes of behaviour.

Coaches need to develop sensitivity towards the ethical issues that impact on their professional relationships with their athletes. In order to prevent coaches unintentionally exploiting their positions of power over athletes, coaches could be made sensitive to the important factors that make the athlete vulnerable to the coach; factors such as the stage of imminent achievement, the excessive heterosexuality and homophobia of the female sports environment, the effects of low self-esteem and social isolation of athletes, the psychology of male–female relationships in the general society, the effects of transference in the coach–athlete relationship, and the various other factors that have been discussed in this chapter. To prevent later problems occurring, it is important that sporting organizations and coaches be able to recognize athletes who are vulnerable to exploitation, and these coaches act to help protect these athletes from victimization (Sullivan and Ogloff 1998).

Knowledge provided to coaches should also include the legal, judicial, psychological, social and medical effects that may emanate from the formation of a sexual relationship with a player. Toftegaard Nielsen's (2001: 165) questionnaire research with coaches from community to elite sport in Norway 'revealed a widespread ignorance of legal regulations governing this area and documented that coaches had lax attitudes towards being intimate with athletes'. Coach education programmes need to clearly emphasize to coaches the legal and club policy implications of decisions that they make regarding sexual relationships with players. While many organizations (unfortunately) do not make the formation of a sexual relationship with an ex-player grounds for dismissal from a position, many have in place bans on sexual relations with existing players.[14] Also, the law courts may view the deterioration of a previously believed 'consensual' relationship as an act of sexual harassment, given the relative power of the positions of coach and athlete in the relationship (Vasquez 1988). In terms of coach education and recruitment programmes, organizations must also be willing to provide continual training and feedback to coaches about these matters, and the programme must, at times, serve to 'prevent individuals who are unsuitable from entering the field' (ibid.: 241).

Coaches also need to develop self-awareness regarding their own sexuality, their ego and their power, and how these things can impact on their professional practices and their profession as a whole. Schoener suggests the following activity for counsellors, which could easily be modified for coaches:

> A counselor is asked to make a list of what one would do if one planned to seduce someone in one's work environment. How would you dress? . . . For what time of the day or night would you set the appointment? What tone of voice and body language and behaviors would you use? Through open dialogue [with peers], individuals participating in this exercise provide feedback to each other about behaviours that may be perceived or experienced as seductive or sexual in nature. Such outside peer observations help individual recognize their 'blind spots'.
>
> *(1987, cited in Vasquez 1988: 239)*

From these discussions, coaches may be able to develop preventative strategies regarding dress, environments and times of meeting with individual players, degrees and appropriateness of physical touch (Nickell *et al.* 1995), and methods of speech and body language that will preclude sexual attraction. The self-reflective coach will also reflect on boundaries in the relationship, as a safeguard against the formation of sexually based dual relationships (Shopland and VandeCreek 1991). The ethical coach will encourage parental monitoring of training sessions and games, and will discourage athletes from taking lifts from coaches to games and training or staying in rooms with coaches on trips.

Athletes need to be educated to recognize that any dual relationship is, by nature, exploitative and unacceptable (Sullivan and Ogloff 1998). That is, athletes need to develop the conceptual apparatus to describe sexual relations with their coaches as non-consensual, because of the differences in power (Bringer *et al.* 2002). Group meetings between students, or psychotherapy with a professional, may help the student to clarify 'contradictory emotions and perceptions of appropriate . . . behaviour' (Sullivan and Ogloff 1998: 243; see also Cense and Brackenridge 2001). Given the social and emotional isolation of some vulnerable athletes, both psychotherapy and group discussions may be useful tools to reduce vulnerability and perceptions of guilt and self-blame by the athlete who has entered into an intimate relationship with a coach or former coach.

From the athlete's perspective, it is also crucial that they are made aware of the legal and ethical responsibilities of the coach, and the grievance procedures that will assist them in claims against the coach. They must also feel supported by the organization in making such claims, a support that has often been neglected in the past. But reflection by the organization on the negative effects that such dual relationships have on future recruitment and success in the sporting programme should change this. Sporting organizations have a vested interest in dealing strongly and publicly with any breach of trust, professional codes or the law by their coaches (Brackenridge 1997).

Finally, sports organizations and society generally can provide momentum. Nickell *et al.*'s (1995) research on family and marriage therapists' responses to their own sexual attraction to their clients revealed that two factors were particularly important in preventing therapists from acting on their attraction. The first was that therapists sought out the support and counsel of supervisors. Sporting organizations should provide this form of mentoring to coaches, and provide coaching coordinators with training that allows them to provide support and guidance to their coaches. Coaching supervisors need to be 'proactive rather than reactive in their guidance' (ibid.: 324), by initiating discussions with coaches about the possibility of, and appropriate responses to, sexual attraction towards their players. Sporting organizations may also provide coaches with information about therapists who could help the coach to resolve countertransferent feelings towards athletes. Second, family and marriage therapists responded that State and Federal laws making intimate relationships with clients a felony, and professional codes of ethical behaviour that also prohibited such relationships, were both good-to-excellent influences on preventing the formation of sexual relationships. It may be time for all governments to enact laws regulating the relationships between coaches and athletes, and for coach accreditation bodies and sporting organizations to implement ethics education so that their coaches will embrace the underpinning foundations of these laws.

Conclusion

Brackenridge (2003) explains the importance of sporting organizations dealing with the sport-specific situational factors that they can control in order to prevent sexual harassment and abuse in sport perpetrated by (mostly) male coaches. She states:

> Most of us have no control over the intrapersonal and pathological factors that might cause someone to become sexually aroused to children or to unwilling adults. Sports administrators, leisure centre managers, park rangers, sports development officers, physical education teachers . . . do, however, have the capacity to influence risk analysis and prevention measures that might increase the efficacy of protection.
>
> *(2003: 7)*

The problem in dealing with some cases of sexual harassment and abuse in sports in the past is that sporting organizations have too often blamed the perpetrator as a deviant individual, and done little to educate the potential victims or monitor the recreation workplace. Recognizing and controlling the situational variables by educating athletes and installing external inhibitors to abusive coaching behaviour will help to prevent cases of sexual harassment and abuse (Brackenridge 1997).

In contrast, sporting organizations have not often recognized 'consensual' sexual relationships between coaches and athletes or former athletes as a problem at all. The professions of counselling and education are far advanced over the sporting profession in the recognition of the problems associated with dual relationships, and in dealing with these problems. It is time for sporting organizations to recognize that the power differential in athlete–coach relationships means that the possibility for consent to be 'voluntarily, knowingly, and intelligently' given by the athlete or former athlete is compromised by the prior coaching relationship. Further, regardless of the claims made by current athletes about their ability to give consent at the time of the dual relationship, research from the educational and therapeutic settings suggests that, in the future, many of these athletes will also suggest that their choices were coerced, and these athletes will also have to deal psychologically with breaches of trust and feelings of anger and rejection. Sporting organizations can help prevent these problems by introducing codes of behaviour that ban relationships between coaches and their current or former athletes, and implementing stringent punitive measures to encourage compliance with their codes of behaviour.

It is probably helpful to conclude the chapter with self-awareness and honesty. My wife of seventeen years is the mother of one of the junior basketballers that I coached. We began our relationship after I had commenced coaching her daughter. The dual relationship was particularly difficult to negotiate for both myself and my stepdaughter. I responded in what I now recognize to be a very inappropriate way. I made it more difficult for my stepdaughter to succeed by expecting more from her, punishing her more publicly for errors and denying her opportunities for elite-level coaching camps by giving invitations to other, less worthy team-mates. I feared charges of unfairness, and traded on my wife's and stepdaughter's love and affection. What I should have done was immediately terminate the coaching relationship, explain to my stepdaughter that this would prevent others from ascribing her successes to favouritism on my behalf, and enjoy a healthy parental relationship with my stepdaughter uncompromised by the coaching relationship. My awareness now does not make my guilt any less difficult to bear.

Notes

1 I agree with the feminist perspective that we should not suggest that sexual relationships between adult and adolescents are consensual.
2 Volkwein *et al.* (1997), Volkwein-Caplan and Sankaran (2002), and Fasting *et al.* (2007) all detail the physical, psychological, emotional and social impacts on the athletic victims of sexual harassment and abuse.

3 Dalmiya (1999) provides a fantastic ethical response to sexual harassment that demonstrates the reason that self-perception about the acts of harassment is normally a sufficient condition, but not a necessary condition. The harassment attempts to target and annihilate the individual woman at the same time as reinforcing negative and powerless stereotypes about the class of women. Even if the individual woman does not recognize her private harm, all women are affected negatively by the reinforcement of the stereotype.

4 Leahy *et al.* (2002) report similar figures with Australian elite and club-level athletes, but disturbingly also report that, for elite-level female athletes who have suffered sexual abuse, almost half of these athletes suffered the sexual abuse from someone associated with their sport.

5 This should not replace the various other mechanisms of control such as parental supervision, police checks, chaperoning, and openness with police investigations.

6 The courts will not differentiate between paid or unpaid employment when determining the vicarious liability of a sporting club (*Darren Kennedy v. Narooma Rugby League Football Club & Gary Pender (2001)* as cited on Play by the Rules (2009).

7 The Action Plan for Protection against Sexual Harassment and Abuse in Sport presented as Appendix A in the article by Fasting *et al.* (2003) should be compulsory reading for all sporting organizations, and could easily be modified to apply to 'consensual' adult relationships between coaches and players. The recommendations section in Wolohan and Mathes' (1996) article provides athletics directors and organizations with clear-cut policies that could help to prevent cases of sexual harassment from occurring and, hence, reduce the likelihood of successful litigation.

8 Sporting organizations become silent when confronted with issues of sexual abuse and harassment. On the website Silent Edge (Edgerton 1999), it was reported that

> [a]mid widespread allegations in the spring of 1998 that an ex-Wimbledon champion had been sexually abused by her coach from the age of 11, the Women's Tennis Association (U.K.) launched an investigation. Said the London Independent, 'Since then the WTA has refused to reveal anything about its findings and declines to explain why it hasn't turned the matter over to better equipped authorities – such as the police or therapists who have treated players traumatised by abuse on the tour. At the very least, it seems reasonable for the WTA to pass a code of conduct for coaches stipulating that unmarried girls shouldn't share hotel rooms with male coaches.' In early 1999, the WTA published a code of ethics which stipulates that coaches should not make any sexual advance to girls under 17.
>
> (London *Independent*, 27 July 1998; London *Guardian*, 31 January 1999, *cited by Edgerton 1999*).

9 Heywood (1999) adds that anti-harassment programmes in US college sports are often delivered by affirmative-action officers, and may not be taken seriously by coaches or athletes. The programmes do not originate from athletics departments, and may not be prioritized by coaches and directors.

10 For a review of the early research findings, see Skinner *et al.* (1995).

11 Gerard (1981, cited in Skinner *et al.* 1995: 139) reports that some upper undergraduate and postgraduate students in psychology in a university in California had objected to the APA prohibition on sexual relations between faculty and students in their ethical principles, on the basis that these students did not feel they needed 'the special attention afforded to psychotherapy patients'.

12 There was an excellent article in *Sports Illustrated* in 2001 that introduced the issue of the ethicality of sexual relationships between coaches and athletes. Although the early section of the article got bogged down on the performance effects of such relationships in a couple of case studies, the latter section of the article dealt directly with ethical issues (Wahl *et al.* 2001). The website Play by the Rules (2009) contains a section on intimate relationships between players and coaches that discourages such relationships, but does not call for a ban on relationships. The Women's Sports

Foundation (2009) website contains suggestions to sports administrators that they formulate clear rules that ban any intimate relationships between a coach and an athlete.

13 Nickell *et al.* (1995: 323) explain that, as in most professions, the ethical code of behaviour for the American Association of Family and Marriage Therapists is 'designed to be vague in order to leave room for interpretation'.

14 Bringer *et al.* (2002: 114–115) explain that the legal position in both Canada and the United Kingdom is that 'an adult athlete could bring charges of sexual assault against a coach, even if the relationship was "consenting"'. In addition, some sports organizations, such as the United States Olympic Committee, have produced a clear policy banning sexual contact between coaches and athletes or former athletes.

References

Blevins-Knabe, B. (1992) 'The ethics of dual relationships in higher education', *Ethics and Behavior*, 2(3): 151–163.

Brackenridge, C. (1994) 'Fair play or fair game? Child sexual abuse in sport organisations', *International Review for the Sociology of Sport*, 29(3): 287–297.

Brackenridge, C. (1997) ' "He owned me basically . . .": women's experience of sexual abuse in sport', *International Review for the Sociology of Sport*, 32(2): 115–130.

Brackenridge, C. (2003) 'Dangerous sports? Risk, responsibility and sex offending in sport', *Journal of Sexual Aggression*, 9(1): 3–12.

Brackenridge, C. and Kirby, S. (1997) 'Playing safe: assessing the risk of sexual abuse to elite child athletes', *International Review for the Sociology of Sport*, 32(4): 407–418.

Bringer, J., Brackenridge, C. and Johnston, L. (2002) 'Defining appropriateness in coach–athlete sexual relationships: the voices of coaches', in C. Brackenridge and K. Fasting (eds) *Sexual Harassment and Abuse in Sport: International Research and Policy Perspectives*, London: Whiting & Birch.

Burton-Nelson, M. (2002) 'Foreword', in K. Volkwein-Caplan and G. Sankaran *Sexual Harassment in Sport: Impact, Issues and Challenges*, Oxford: Meyer & Meyer Sport.

Cense, M. and Brackenridge, C. (2001) 'Temporal and developmental risk factors for sexual harassment and abuse in sport', *European Physical Education Review*, 7(1): 61–79.

Dalmiya, V. (1999) 'Why is sexual harassment wrong?' *Journal of Social Philosophy*, 30(1): 46–64.

Edgerton, E. (1999) 'Silent Edge', online. Available HTTP: http//www.silent-edge.org. (accessed 7 July 1999).

Fasting, K., Brackenridge, C. and Sundgot-Borgen, J. (2003) 'Experiences of sexual harassment and abuse among Norwegian elite female athletes and nonathletes', *Research Quarterly for Exercise and Sport*, 74(1): 88–97.

Fasting, K., Brackenridge, C. and Walseth, K. (2007) 'Women athletes' personal responses to sexual harassment in sport', *Journal of Applied Sport Psychology*, 19: 419–433.

Fejgin, N. and Hanegby, R. (2001) 'Gender and cultural bias in perceptions of sexual harassment in sport', *International Review for the Sociology of Sport*, 36(4): 459–478.

Heywood, L. (1999) 'Despite the positive rhetoric about women's sports, female athletes face a culture of sexual harassment', *Chronicle of Higher Education*, 45(18), online. Available HTTP: http://0-web.ebscohost.com.library.vu.edu.au/ehostt (accessed 24 March 2009).

Krauchek, V. and Ranson, G. (1999) 'Playing by the rules of the game: women's experiences and perceptions of sexual harassment in sport', *Canadian Review of Sociology and Anthropology*, 36(4): 585–600.

Lackey, D. (1990) 'Sexual harassment in sports', *Physical Educator*, 47(2), online. Available HTTP: http://0-web.ebscohost.com.library.vu.edu.au/ehostt (accessed 4 February 2004).

Leahy, T., Pretty, G. and Tenenbaum, G. (2002) 'Prevalence of sexual abuse in organised competitive sport in Australia', in C. Brackenridge and K. Fasting (eds) *Sexual Harassment and Abuse in Sport: International Research and Policy Perspectives*, London: Whiting & Birch.

Nickell, N.J., Hecker, L.L., Ray, R.E. and Bercik, J. (1995) 'Marriage and family therapists' sexual attraction to clients: an exploratory study', *American Journal of Family Therapy*, 23(4): 315–327.

Parker, C. (1999) 'Public rights in private government: corporate compliance with sexual harassment legislation', *Australasian Journal of Human Rights*, 5(1), online. Available HTTP: http:www.austlii.edu.au/cgi-bin/sinodisp/au/journals/AJHR/1999/ 6.html (accessed 16 March 2009).

Play by the Rules (2009), online. Available HTTP: http://www.playbytherules.net.au (accessed 19 February 2009).

Shopland, S.N. and VandeCreek, L. (1991) 'Sex with ex-clients: theoretical rationales for prohibition', *Ethics and Behavior*, 1(1): 35–44.

Skinner, L.J., Giles, M.K., Griffith, S.E., Sonntag, M.E., Berry, K.K. and Beck, R. (1995) 'Academic sexual intimacy violations: ethicality and occurrence reports from undergraduates', *Journal of Sex Research*, 32(2): 131–143.

Steinberg, B., Bloch, S., Riley, G. and Zelas, K. (2000) 'Revising the code of ethics of the Australian and New Zealand College of Psychiatrists: process and outcome', *Australian Psychiatry*, 8(2): 105–109.

Sullivan, L.E. and Ogloff, J.R.P. (1998) 'Appropriate supervisor–graduate student relationships', *Ethics and Behavior*, 8(3): 229–248.

Thornton, M. (2002) 'Sexual harassment losing sight of sex discrimination', *Melbourne University Law Review*, 22, online. Available HTTP: http://www.austlii.edu.au/cgi-bin/sinodisp/au/journals/MULR/2002/22.html (accessed 16 March 2009).

Toftegaard Nielsen, J. (2001) 'The forbidden zone: intimacy, sexual relations and misconduct in the relationship between coaches and athletes', *International Review for the Sociology of Sport*, 36(2): 165–182.

Tomlinson, A. and Yorganci, I. (1997) 'Male coach/female athlete relations: gender and power relations in competitive sport', *Journal of Sport and Social Issues*, 21(2): 134–155.

Tymowski, G. (1999) 'An ethical consideration of children's participation in high-performance sport', paper presented at the 7th International Postgraduate Seminar of Olympic Studies in 1999, online. Available HTTP: http://www.geocities.com/ olympic_seminar7/papers /tymowski.htm (accessed 16 September 2002).

Vasquez, M.J.T. (1988) 'Counselor–client sexual contact: implications for ethics training', *Journal of Counseling and Development*, 67: 238–241.

Vasquez, M.J.T. (1991) 'Sexual intimacies with clients after termination: should a prohibition be explicit?' *Ethics and Behavior*, 1(1): 45–61.

Volkwein, K.A.E., Schnell, F.I., Sherwood, D. and Livezey, A. (1997) 'Sexual harassment in sport: perceptions and experiences of American female student-athletes', *International Review for the Sociology of Sport*, 32(3): 283–295.

Volkwein-Caplan, K. and Sankaran, G. (2002) *Sexual Harassment in Sport: Impact, Issues and Challenges*, Oxford: Meyer & Meyer Sport.

Wahl, G., Werthein, L.J., Dohrmann, G. and Schechter, B.J. (2001) 'Passion plays', *Sports Illustrated*, 95(10): 58–70.

Walters, K. (2002) 'Vicarious liability – what does it mean in practice?' *Anti-Discrimination Commission, Queensland, Newsletter*, 3. Online. Available HTTP: http://www.adcq. qld.gov.au/newsletter/issue03/story6.html (accessed 4 February, 2004).

Wolohan, J.T. and Mathes, S. (1996) 'Title IX and sexual harassment of student athletes: a look back and to the future', *Journal of Sport Management*, 10: 65–75.

Women's Sports Foundation (2009) 'Sexual harassment – sexual harassment and sexual relationships between coaches, other athletic personnel and athletes: the foundation position', online. Available HTTP: http://www.womenssportsfoundation.org/Content/Articles/ Issues/Coaching/Sexual-Harassment–Sexual-Harassment-and-Sexual-Relationships-Between-Coaches-Other-Athletic-Personn.aspx (accessed 19 March 2009).

9

COACHING ETHICS AND PARALYMPIC SPORTS

Anne-Mette Bredahl

Introduction

Antoine (1996) argues that coaching Paralympic athletes has important and significant similarities with other forms of coaching, and, as such, a morally responsible Paralympic coach will require the standard catalogue of coaching excellences. According to DePauw (1990), the study of coaching in the context of Paralympic sports started in the late 1980s, and in comparison to coaching more generally, there is a paucity of research on the topic. Most of the extant research follows a dominant pattern focusing on technique development and performance enhancement. Unsurprisingly, much of this research concludes that most disabled athletes' performance can benefit from similar training regimes to those for able-bodied athletes, with some adaptations and modifications relating to the athlete's individual situation (Shephard 1990). Despite McNamee's (2008) observation that sports, as social practices, are inescapably ethically laden and that ethics should be at the heart of sport as a practical activity, ethical research and literature on the topic of Paralympic sport in general, and of coaching Paralympic athletes in particular, are scarce. The ways in which ethical issues influence a coach's role are explored at length in this book. Moreover, the desirable range of values, abilities and virtues a good coach requires to execute their role in a morally responsible way are tackled in various other chapters of this volume. These observations are equally relevant in the Paralympic context. Nevertheless, my aim in this chapter is to draw the reader's attention to a range of unique problems which a coach of Paralympic sports may encounter.

Above and beyond the standard scope of coach–athlete relations, Paralympic sports and athletes with disabilities give rise to additional important and ethically laden issues: these include the organization of Paralympic sport in terms of competitive categories; the increasingly commercial and professional nature of the Paralympic Games; and the type and severity of athletes' disability. The International Paralympic Committee (IPC) has a Code of Ethics in its handbook that outlines issues relevant for both coaches and athletes, for example in relation to fair play and rule-following: 'Coaches and team officials shall observe and follow the IPC Classification Code, the IPC Anti-doping Code, and all competition rules and regulations; and shall report any irregularity to the responsible officials' (IPC 2009a, *Handbook*, Section 2, Chapter 1.1, item 7.3). A code of ethics is welcome, but, as McNamee (2008) argues, it does not in itself immunize a practice from ethical problems. Before discussing the range of problems faced by Paralympic coaches, it is worth providing a brief sketch of the Paralympic Games and their history.

A short introduction to Paralympic sports and the Paralympic Games

Paralympic sports as a movement is relatively young compared to the Olympics (Steadward and Walsh 1986). The origins of the Paralympics lie in the rehabilitation of persons with congenital disabilities or with acquired injuries. An important milestone in sport for people with disabilities was the establishment of a spinal cord injury unit at Stoke Mandeville Hospital in England in the 1940s. The aim was to rehabilitate service personnel injured during the Second World War. Initiated by Sir Ludwig Guttmann, physical activity and sport became a central component of the rehabilitation, and was seen as an important and innovative tool to get a person back into an active and productive life after injury (Guttmann 1976; Scruton 1998; Anderson 2003).

As part of this process, Guttmann organized the first Stoke Mandeville Games in 1948 to coincide with the Olympic Games held in London that year. The participants were all people with spinal cord injuries, mainly from the United Kingdom. Howe (2008) suggests that it was Guttmann's vision, even then, that Games for people with disabilities should be held every four years in the same location as the Olympics. The first Games held outside the United Kingdom were organized in Rome in 1960. These Games are generally referred to as the first Paralympic Games (Howe and Jones 2006). They were the first full-scale event held in the same country and at the same time of year as the Olympic Games. The term 'Paralympic', however, was not used until 1964 in Tokyo. The first Winter Paralympics were held in 1976 in Örnsköldsvik, Sweden. After Seoul 1988, it was decided that the Paralympics would be held after each Olympic Games in the same venue. In 1989, the International Paralympic Committee (IPC) was established and marked the beginning of the Paralympic Movement (Howe 2008).

The term 'para' in relation to 'Paralympic' derives from Greek, meaning 'alongside' or 'beside'. As stated at the IPC webpage,[1] today the term 'para' is understood as combining the words 'parallel' and 'Olympic' as an illustration of how the two movements exist side by side. The Paralympic Games have evolved into elite international competition far removed from their roots in the values of *activity* and *participation* (DePauw and Gavron 2005; Howe 2008). The current organizational structure of the Paralympics, however, reflects the early participation-orientated

Games. Early on, a number of international organizations of sport for people with disabilities were formed to help facilitate participation and competition. In contrast to sport for non-disabled athletes, these organizations were not structured around individual sports *per se*, such as cycling, athletics and swimming, but related to particular types of impairment (such as spinal cord injuries, visual impairment, hearing impairment, cerebral palsy and amputations). The key function of these organizations was, and to some extent still is, to facilitate fair competition by grouping similarly disabled competitors together in order to minimize the effect of the disability on athletic performance. To this end, a classification system for each impairment group was developed.

The classification system and its challenges

In order to give athletes with very different physical and sensory abilities a fair chance to succeed in competition, all athletes are classified (medically) according to their disability. On this basis, they compete with others with similar disabilities on a 'level playing field'. For example, people with a certain level of cerebral palsy compete with others considered to experience the same level of impairment (caused by cerebral palsy or other disabilities). Early Paralympic contests were characterized by numerous classes which promoted inclusivity and maximized participation opportunities. Since then, the classification system has been under constant evaluation and modification in an attempt to make the classification reflect more accurately the range and scope of athletes' disabilities (Sherrill and Steadward 1993).

The IPC webpage states: 'Classification is simply a structure for competition. Not unlike wrestling, boxing and weightlifting, where athletes are categorized by weight classes.'[2] This is a little disingenuous, however, because classifying athletes with disabilities is far more complex than is suggested here. Classification in Paralympic sports relies on an invented system of categories that try to instantiate the type, degree and nature of certain disabilities, and their functional effects on athletes in relation to sporting challenges. Classifying disabilities is a controversial issue because, no matter how accurate the assessment is, there will always be a real or perceived functional difference (which may transfer into an athletic advantage) between the athlete with the most and least degree of disability within a class. From an ethical perspective, there are a number of areas of concern for coaches, athletes and administrators. These include the appropriateness of the categories to reflect the scope of disability, manipulating classification for dubious ends, and the marginalization effect of the categories themselves. It is important for the coach to be aware of these problems and recognize the implications for their athletes of engaging with the classification process.

Appropriateness of the categories

An issue for a coach to be aware of is that the present classification system is inflexible and can have a detrimental impact on an athlete. For example, the system does not easily accommodate athletes with more than one disability. A blind Paralympic skier who became paraplegic as a consequence of an injury during competition has to choose between competing as a blind skier or as a paraplegic skier. A sitting skier cannot manage the steep tracks that standing blind skiers can, and a blind sitting skier does not stand a chance when competing against sighted sitting skiers unless some form of 'compensation' is built into the rules. In this real example, the coach had to take the difficult decision to take this skilled and motivated skier off the team because there was no realistic chance of succeeding in either the available categories. Funding may not permit the coach to select athletes unless they have a realistic medal chance. If another category, *blind sitting skier*, had been available, this skier would have had a chance to excel, and the coach could have kept the athlete on the team.

Manipulating the classification system

Another dilemma for both coaches and athletes is that the outcome of the classification can profoundly affect the athletes' chance of succeeding. This might tempt some athletes to 'cheat' the classification process. A sitting skier[3] might cheat by deceiving assessors about their abdominal muscle function and balance. These are two key considerations that determine to which class the skier will be allocated. If the skier manages to mislead classifiers and competes against athletes with more severe disabilities, their chances of winning are significantly improved. Cheating the classification process is a viable option and can be a very real temptation for a coach. A corrupt coach could influence the process by encouraging their athlete to disguise or adjust their performance during the classification process. Although strategies have been implemented to increase the validity and reliability of the classification process, such as continued observation rather than a one-off test, some continue to try to manipulate the process.

One infamous example of cheating led to the suspension of the entire category of athletes with intellectual disabilities. It was discovered that the majority of the Spanish gold medal-winning basketball team for athletes with intellectual disabilities at the Paralympics in Sydney 2000 were ineligible to compete. One of the competitors was a journalist who later revealed the fraud (Davies 2000). It is clear that coaches were complicit in this fraud. The coaches and athletes in this case demonstrated a troubling lack of integrity which damaged the Paralympic Movement.[4] Manipulating the classification system, whether by deliberate fraud or by more subtle though still questionable means, can provide a potentially significant competitive advantage for the athlete. The coach and athlete, therefore, face difficult and important choices in light of the classification system. Do they seek to profit from the inherent difficulties in classifying, or do they behave with honesty and integrity, knowing that to do so might harm their chances?

In some categories, legislators have sought to eliminate the problem of deception. In the class for blind athletes, for instance, all competitors have to wear blinded goggles that, arguably, level the playing field. In other categories it is more difficult to control for the variability in functional disability. For example, competitors with extremely poor vision compete in the class for the partially sighted. Athletes with extremely poor vision therefore compete in a class with competitors whose sight, although not good, enables them to train and navigate without using a guide. The difference is illustrated by an example from the Paralympics in 2002. In these Games a skier with poor vision who competed in the class for partially sighted performed comparatively poorly. In the Paralympics in 2006, however, her sight had deteriorated completely and she was reclassified as a blind skier. She won both gold and silver medals. Favourable classification, therefore, has significant impact on medal chances in most sports.

Marginalization of certain athletes

Another issue a coach has to deal with is the potential marginalization effects classification has on individuals. Marginalization can happen in at least two ways. The first relates to membership of more severely disabled athletes in a team sport. Goal ball is a team sport developed for athletes with visual impairment, but individuals with the poorest sight have very little chance of selection.[5] Paradoxically, therefore, a game developed to give blind athletes a chance of competing in a team event is usually played by blindfolded partially sighted athletes. A coach who wants to win will not undermine the team's chances by selecting players of less ability, which is largely determined by the player's level of disability. In wheelchair rugby, on the other hand, every player is awarded a number of points according to their level of disability (with the most disabled athletes counting the *fewest* points). A coach can only field a maximum point value at any given time. The rule is designed to eliminate the exclusion from teams of the more severely disabled players. With the rule in place, good players with more severe disabilities become necessary for an eligible team. There is nothing to stop 'goal ball' developing a system similar to the one in wheelchair rugby.

The second issue of marginalization relates to the cause of an individual's disability. There is a general perception, echoed by coaches in particular, that the easiest way to get a medallist is to find an injured (formerly able-bodied) top athlete and introduce him or her to Paralympic sport. Working with a person with a congenital impairment is a far more difficult task. Ambitious coaches may choose to work with athletes whose disability is more favourable with regard to winning medals. These forms of marginalization are a consequence of the paradoxical effects of the classification system, which, although designed to maximize participation and inclusion, actually exacerbates a problematic value hierarchy of 'disability'.

The commercialization of the Paralympics; fewer classes and fewer medals

Since the Paralympics were aligned with the Olympics, they have been affected by the same market forces and commercialization pressures that characterize sport in the global market. According to Howe and Jones (2006: 33), 'The main concern of institutions such as the IPC is the efficient procurement and distribution of external rewards by making more money and packaging the most attractive and commercially viable product that will be sold to the highest bidder.' In order to make the Paralympics more commercial and to raise the value of medals, there has been significant rationalization of the number of competitive classes in the Games. Streamlining is considered necessary to make the Games more audience-friendly. Fewer classes mean fewer sets of medals awarded at each championship. A major problem with streamlining by combining classes is that athletes with different types and levels of disabilities end up competing against each other. Given the historical mission of the Paralympics – to organize sport according to similar disabilities to promote maximum participation – the proposed changes are potentially unfair and exclusionary. The IPC Code of Ethics (2009a, Chapter 1.1) states that '[a]thletic classification, which promotes sport participation of athletes with disabilities, is not discrimination but empowerment.'

Attempts have been made to compensate for differences among athletes with different levels of abilities within the combined classes;[6] however, Howe (2008) argues that the new system will exclude certain athletes, particularly those with the most severe disabilities. I have been a competitive Paralympic skier since 1992, and during those years the number of classes has been reduced to a third of the initial number. In the 1994 Paralympics, for instance, there were three classes for visually impaired women; today there is only one. The intention was to make one large competitive, but combined, class; however, the actual result has been a fall in the number of competitors from more than 30 participants in 1994 to around 10 female skiers competing in the Paralympic Games in 2006. It could be argued that, like the Olympics, the point of the Paralympics is to test the best athletes. In contrast to Olympic sports, however, athletes with disabilities have few alternative options to compete other than at the Paralympic Games. In other words, if a particular class is removed from the Paralympics, for all intents and purposes the competition in this event is all but obsolete. Such consequences appear at odds with the stated vision of the IPC (2009b): 'To Enable Paralympic Athletes to Achieve Sporting Excellence and Inspire and Excite the World',[7] and in the additional comments it states: 'the primary focus of IPC's activities, in the context of Paralympic athletes, is the development of all athletes from initiation to elite level'.

A positive result of the commercialization of the Paralympics is an improvement in the standard of performance. Some results at the Paralympics are getting closer to what is possible for elite athletes without disabilities (DePauw and Gavron 2005; Howe 2008). An athlete like Natalie Du Toit,[8] who won five gold medals at the Paralympics in 2008, also qualified for the Olympics a few weeks earlier, where she finished 16th in the marathon swimming competition. Brian McKeever,[9] who is a partially sighted multiple Paralympic champion, finished 21st (out of 125 skiers) in the 15 km event at the world championships for able-bodied in 2007[10] (without a guide). Athletes like Du Toit and McKeever can be seen as ambassadors who raise the profile of the Paralympics and its athletes. Despite some advantages, the commercialization of the Paralympics has exacerbated four ethical issues, namely, the exclusion of the most severely disabled, a change in coaching attitudes, problems with distributing scarce resources, and the temptation of dubious performance enhancement strategies.

The exclusion of the most severely disabled

Most nations' funding policies are tied to medal chances. If nations' funding criteria are based on medal chances, many athletes adversely affected by the change in classification will not be funded to go to the Paralympics. As mentioned, the excluded athletes are more likely to be those whose disability is severe. The added cost burden attached to athletes with severe disabilities further complicates the issue. An athlete with a more severe disability often has to depend on practical help to a greater extent in order to participate in sport in addition to support required in their daily lives. This requires more practical organization and also usually makes participation more expensive, due to the need for wheelchair-accessible hotels, adapted transportation and extra helpers. A coach may be tempted to (or forced to) focus on athletes whose requirements are less complex or athletes who are 'cheaper', for example athletes who do not need a guide or a person to help with personal care. One can take two athletes who have only one arm for the same cost as taking a blind athlete and a guide. This doubles the chances of winning medals for the same cost.

New types of coaches in Paralympic sports

The development in Paralympic sport from participation towards high performance has brought new challenges for coaches and coach education priorities (DePauw 1990; Sherrill 2003). The coaches who typically were involved with Paralympic sports in its earlier days often had their expertise in 'disabilities and their consequences', whereas the new types of coaches tend to have their expertise centred on the sport. Knowledge in one area does not exclude the other, but different types of coaches tend to have different strengths and weaknesses.

My experience is that the coaches who had been involved for a long time had a philosophy of participation and saw the possible broader rehabilitation benefits of participation in a person's daily life. Some of these coaches' sporting knowledge was limited and they had inflexible ideas about the potential of an athlete with disabilities. The new types of coaches, on the other hand, tend to approach participants as elite athletes with little consideration of the disability. For many elite Paralympic athletes, these new coaches have improved athletic standards (Bailey 2008; Howe 2008). The downside is that coaches new to Paralympic sports may find it difficult to appreciate the impact disabilities have on athletes. This lack of empathy might alter the sensibility of the coach–athlete relationship. This lack of understanding might be made worse by a general reluctance by athletes to share with the coach the particular difficulties they face as a consequence of their impairments. Talented athletes, particularly those with severe impairment, have quit the sport to avoid the awkward and uncomfortable feelings brought on by expressing to unsympathetic coaches the limits and problems they face when trying to develop their skills. Accidents have also occurred when athletes reluctant to show 'weakness' push themselves, or are pushed, beyond their abilities. It is important that coaches have a contextually sensitive understanding of performance enhancement in order to avoid such problems. To be a coach in Paralympic sports requires a greater level of empathy with one's athletes' unique circumstances and a sufficient level of knowledge of the challenges different disabilities present (DePauw 1990; Antoine 1996). This is not just a matter of optimizing performance, but more fundamentally a crucial moral responsibility to treat athletes with respect. The respectful coach is able to exercise good judgement in relation to the complex interaction between the objective challenges of the sport, the athlete's ability (including skill, technique, physique and courage), and the particular difficulties associated with the athlete's impairment and their individualized experience of it. The coach must decide how far to push the athlete while being aware of the nature and severity of the risks inherent, particularly in sports like biking or skiing. The standard catalogue of coaching attributes, knowledge, expertise, passion, virtue and good judgement (discussed elsewhere in this book) is perhaps even more essential in the context of Paralympic sports.

Economic support of athletes

Although there have always been differences between nations in the level of support given to Paralympic sports and to athletes, until fairly recently all the athletes were amateurs. Although many athletes continue to fund their own participation, others are professional. This picture varies between different nations. Some nations' financial backing is extensive, a fact reflected in the medal tallies at championships (Hodges 2008). In cross-country skiing, for instance, the mostly professional Russian and Ukrainian athletes completely dominated the 2009 IPC world championships, winning 72 per cent of the medals awarded.[11] Besides Russia and Ukraine, countries like the United Kingdom, the United States, Australia and South Africa also have professional athletes making their living from sport. Athletes from smaller nations like the Czech Republic and Denmark, however, have to fund their sports participation themselves. Good coaches will be cognizant of the implications for each athlete of their status as amateur or professional and tailor their training demands accordingly. Athletes' personal financial circumstances will determine the level of time and money an athlete can commit to the sport. Inequalities in financial support for athletes characterize most professional sports, with richer countries more able to support and finance participation at the Paralympic Games. Given the broader benefits of appearing at the Paralympics, namely the inspiration that athletes can provide for their nation's children and young people, it is important that raising finance is not an unduly prohibitive factor.

Coaches need to acknowledge the financial implications of their athletes' engagement. They need to be sensitive to the athletic/life balance, particularly of non-professional athletes. Some countries require their top athletes to have a part-time job or to study alongside their sports career. Coaches should help athletes get the balance right between pursuing victory today and planning for a life and career outside athletics in the future.

Rewards and the temptation of doping

Economic support and rewards have benefits, and can act as good and strong incentives for athletes to participate and do their best. They can, however, also have unintended consequences similar to those faced in the Olympics and other sporting arenas, namely an increased temptation to seek the benefits of performance-enhancing drugs (DePauw and Gavron 2005; Bailey 2008). When some Paralympic athletes are awarded 100,000 euros for a gold medal (Hodges 2008), they may well be tempted to take short cuts to victory, especially when the drug-testing regime in Paralympic sports is comparatively underdeveloped. In my 19 years as a Paralympic athlete, in total I was tested only three times (and always after medalling), and was never tested outside of competition. Even if I had been, I would not have been tested in a way that would reveal a type of doping that would be beneficial to use in an endurance sport like mine. The explanation given for the paucity of testing is economic, and the financial constraints are borne out by the fact that only the cheap urine test, and not the more expensive blood test, is used in Paralympic sport. The combination of increasing financial awards for medalling, and a minimal risk of being caught for drug use, certainly opens the door to doping. This temptation extends to coaches as well, because the financial reward often applies to both athlete and coach if medals are won. The extent to which coaches directly encourage athletes to use doping, or whether they simply 'turn a blind eye' to athletes who dope, may be difficult to quantify. Although positive doping tests are few and far between, it is possibly largely due to the poor testing process. It is likely that Paralympic sports are experiencing the same type of problems with doping as elite sports for able-bodied.

It is also known that some Paralympic athletes have used other dangerous practices classified as doping. One of these is called 'boosting', which is a process of raising the blood pressure dangerously by abnormal means (Bhambhani et al. 2009). This can, for instance, be done by an athlete with a spinal cord injury by inducing pain in an area without sensation, or blocking a urinary catheter[12] in order to 'shock the system'. The practice can help improve achievements considerably, but is a practice that can be life-threatening. Such practices as 'boosting' are types of 'doping' that require a different type of test to expose them.

An expanded doping test process in Paralympic sports could benefit the sport in many ways. First, it could serve as a protection for the athlete against being tempted or encouraged by others to dope. Second, it would enhance the chance of exposing athletes who do dope. Finally, it would give athletes with extraordinary results a chance to be acquitted of suspicion. For coaches to 'turn a blind eye', or even encourage athletes to use doping or dangerous practices, such as boosting, is unacceptable and violates the athletes' right to participate in a fair competition.

Endorsing or tolerating such practices neglects the well-being of athletes, and falls short of safeguarding their physical and mental health as outlined in the IPC Code of Ethics.[13]

Society's recognition of Paralympic sports

Overall, there has been a change in the way Paralympic sport is viewed by society. This is supported by increased media attention, and the fact that Paralympic Games attract more sponsors and spectators (Evaggelinou *et al.* 2005). But as DePauw and Gavron (2005) observe, there is a long way to go before Paralympic athletes (in general) get the same attention and support as Olympic athletes.

The historical background of Paralympic sport still influences the way many view it today. One example occurred when my guide/coach and I were selected for the Paralympics in 2006. The rule in our country is that one can apply for a week of extra leave from work if selected for major championships, so we did. Mine was granted, but my guide/coach's application was rejected on the grounds that 'the patient does not live in our country, so her participation in the Paralympic Games cannot be seen as a necessary part of her rehabilitation'. It would be unthinkable that somebody selected for the Olympics would have an application refused on those grounds. Participants at the Paralympics might have been patients at one point, and Paralympic sport motivated them to start training. Paralympic Games, however, are not (any longer) about the rehabilitation of patients, but about high–performance competition.

Recognition of Paralympic achievements varies from country to country, as illustrated by the economic support and rewards mentioned earlier. Also, the media attention and public recognition differ. In some countries, there are official welcomes and subsequent invitations from media and the head of state; in other countries, the Paralympics get little attention. All this affects the experiences of both the athletes and the coaches as credible practitioners. A lot of good work in promoting the Paralympic Games has been carried out over the years. If, however, Paralympic sport wants to be recognized more globally by society, then coaches, athletes and organizers need to continue to work on improving ethical matters, particularly a credible and effective anti-doping scheme.

Ethical codes and their relevance for coaches

For an organization like the IPC to have an ethical code of practice is necessary but not sufficient to ensure good practice. The fact that issues are mentioned in the ethical code unfortunately does not mean that people actually follow the code. The important issue is whether the values and principles embedded in the ethical code are actually manifested in the everyday practice of coach–athlete and coach–institution relations. There are a number of ways to improve ethical awareness and ethical conduct. One crucial requirement is to ascertain precisely what the level of engagement with ethical issues and with the ethical code is. An ongoing ethical audit would enable us to get a picture of what is actually going on at practitioner and coach level. Currently, I think ethical questions and concerns like those raised previously seem far away and largely irrelevant for coaches' everyday practice. The IPC does have an ethical committee, but the majority of coaches and athletes are largely ignorant of its existence and purpose.

The second important way of making ethics matter more to coaches in Paralympic sports is through better coach education. Coach education, as mentioned elsewhere in this book, requires more than familiarity with an ethical code. It would need to cultivate habits of reflection and good judgement in relation to ethical issues discussed above. Perhaps the central focus should be the classification system. Coach education would support coaches in tackling the complexity of the classification system and consider the potential ethical issues generated by its implementation. For example, coaches should reflect on whether the new system with fewer classes might disadvantage athletes with certain types of disabilities, and how to manage these issues. Coaches should be encouraged to contribute to a debate about how best to deal with the streamlining of categories in a morally sensitive way. For example, coaches could explore the expansion of 'the points system' in wheelchair rugby to other team sports and possibly relay teams. Reforming the current format in certain sports would both promote a more inclusive competitive structure and encourage national federations to nurture talented athletes with more severe disabilities. Coaches also need guidance on managing a limited budget without neglecting their moral obligations. In particular, the United Nations Convention on the Rights of People with Disabilities,[14] Article 5.2, states that 'States Parties shall prohibit all discrimination on the basis of disability and guarantee to persons with disabilities equal and effective legal protection against discrimination on all grounds.' It should be noted that this must include discrimination on 'economic grounds'.

Coach education is also needed to improve knowledge about different types of disabilities and their implications for athletes in sport and life in general. This would provide the coach with the requisite understanding to help treat athletes with dignity. Finally, coach education should cover doping and any associated risks. Coaches could, for example, take responsibility for their own athletes' clean status and safety by monitoring levels of erythropoietin (EPO).

Such education could potentially benefit from more involvement of former and present athletes, who could help present and debate relevant ethical issues, as they have personally experienced the consequences of the dilemmas. Athletes' experiences and practical knowledge could benefit the future of Paralympic sport even more if sports federations in the future could encourage more former Paralympic athletes to get involved in coaching and in developing Paralympics sports and the Paralympic Games.

Conclusion

In this chapter, I have described some of the ethical challenges to coaches in Paralympic sport. They arise in relation to a complex classification system, a commercially influenced streamlining agenda, funding priorities of national federations, and the unique problems faced by athletes with disabilities. Against this background, good coaches attempt to balance the needs of employers, the well-being and athletic ambitions of athletes, and the rules and regulations of the Paralympics, against their own goals and ambitions to succeed. It is important to help Paralympic coaches make the right decisions in this complex context. Whether they make decisions in a morally praiseworthy or blameworthy way depends on a whole host of factors discussed in detail throughout this book in general and in this chapter in particular. I believe that coach education tailored specifically to Paralympic coaches, which promotes understanding of the particular issues faced by Paralympic athletes, is fundamentally important. Education is required to cultivate and develop the appropriate range of abilities and dispositions so that coaches can adhere to and promote the values contained in the code of ethics of Paralympic sport.

Notes

1 See http://www.paralympic.org/release/Main_Sections_Menu/IPC/About_the_IPC/ (accessed 13 March 2009).
2 See http://www.paralympic.org/release/Main_Sections_Menu/Classification/ (accessed 30 April 2009).
3 A skier who uses a special kind of sledge fitted with a ski or skis in order to carry out the sport.
4 At the IPC General Assembly, on 23 November 2009, athletes with intellectual disabilities were reinstated and will compete again at the Paralympic Games 2012 in London. The issue of how to classify the athletes, however, remains unresolved.
5 People born blind have a bigger challenge in developing the same level of motor skills as (partially) sighted children (Bredahl 1997); also, learning new motor skills is more difficult without the assistance of *seeing* the movements.
6 In some cases, the more severely disabled get a percentage deducted from their finish time; in other cases, their performance is measured against the world record of the original class in which they competed.
7 See http://www.paralympic.org/IPC/Vision_Mission_Values.html (accessed 4 December 2009).
8 She has one leg amputated from the knee.
9 He is partially sighted.
10 See http://www.cccski.com/main.asp?cmd=doc&ID=1086&lan=0 (accessed 7 December 2009).
11 See http://www.ipcvuokatti2009.net/index_eng.asp?pid=153 (accessed 8 December).
12 The intention is to keep their bladders full and create a backflow to the kidneys, and thereby create stress on the body, which can produce a potentially performance-enhancing power surge in the body.
13 IPC (2009a) Code of Ethics, points 1.4 and 1.5s.
14 See http://www.un.org/disabilities/default.asp?navid=13&pid=150 (accessed 4 December 2009).

References

Anderson, J. (2003)' Turned into taxpayers: paraplegia, rehabilitation and sport at Stoke Mandeville, 1944–56', *Journal of Contemporary History*, 38(3): 461–475.

Antoine, K. (1996) 'The role of the coach in training the athlete with a disability', *British Journal of Therapy*, 3(8): 436–439.

Bailey, S. (2008) *Athlete First: A History of the Paralympic Movement*, Chichester, UK: John Wiley.

Bhambhani, Y., MacTavish, J., Warren, S., Thompson, W., Webborn, A., Bressan, E., Hedman, B., Van de Vliet, P., Pascual, J.A. and Vanlandewijck, Y. (2009) *Boosting in Athletes with High Level Spinal Cord Injury: Incidence, Knowledge and Attitudes of Athletes in Paralympic Sport*, World Anti-Doping Agency, Final Report, Montreal, Canada.

Bredahl, A.-M. (1997) *Kan man løbe fra problemerne?* Copenhagen: Hans Reitzels Forlang.

Davies, G.A. (2000) 'Disabled sport: Sydney cheats stripped of medals', *Telegraph*, 14 Dec.

DePauw, K.P. (1990) 'Teaching and coaching individuals with disabilities: research findings and implications', *Physical Education Review*, 13(1): 12–16.

DePauw, K.P. and Gavron, S.J. (2005) *Disability Sport*, Champaign, IL: Human Kinetics.

Evaggelinou, C., Giagazoglou, P. and Grammenou, A. (2005) 'Characteristics and attitudes of spectators attending the Athens 2004 Paralympic Games', Final Report, Bonn, Germany.

Guttmann, L. (1976) *Textbook of Sport for the Disabled*, Aylesbury, UK: HM & M.

Hodges, M. (2008) 'Ukraine punches above its weight', *China Daily*, Online. Available HTTP: http://www.chinadaily.com.cn/paralympics/2008-09/17/content_7034454.htm (accessed 5 May 2009).

Howe, P.D. (2008) *The Cultural Politics of the Paralympic Movement*, London: Routledge.

Howe, P.D. and Jones, C. (2006) 'Classification of disabled athletes: (dis)empowering the Paralympic practice community', *Sociology of Sport Journal*, 23: 29–46.

IPC (2009a) 'Code of Ethics', *IPC Handbook*, Online. Available HTTP: http://www.paralympic.org/export/sites/default/IPC/IPC_Handbook/Section_2/Sec_ii_Appendix_A_IPC_Regulations_on_Complaint.pdf (accessed 11 December 2009).

IPC (2009b) *Handbook: Paralympic Vision and Mission*. Online. Available HTTP: http://www.paralympic.org/IPC/IPC_Handbook/ (accessed 10 October 2009).

McNamee, M.J. (2008) *Sports, Virtues and Vices: Morality Plays*, London: Routledge.

Scruton, J. (1998) *Stoke Mandeville: Road to the Paralympics*, Aylesbury, UK: Peterhouse Press.

Shephard, R.J. (1990) *Fitness in Special Populations*, Champaign, IL: Human Kinetics.

Sherrill, C. (2003) *Adapted Physical Activity*, New York: McGraw-Hill Higher Education.

Sherrill, C. and Steadward, R.D. (1993) 'Paralympics 1992: excellence and challenge', *Palaestra*, 9: 25–42.

Steadward, R.D. and Walsh, C. (1986) 'Training and fitness programs for disabled athletes: past, present and future', in C. Sherrill (ed.) *Sport and Disabled Athletes*, Champaign, IL: Human Kinetics.

PART IV

Coaching in context

Contemporary ethical issues

10

COACHING AND THE ETHICS OF YOUTH TALENT IDENTIFICATION

Rethinking luck and justice

Richard Bailey and Martin Toms

The context: more money, more medals, more pressure

It is a truism that sport can be good for young people. There is now substantial evidence that participation in organized physical activities can result in a wide range of benefits, including positive contribution to their physical, social and emotional well-being (Siedentop 2002; Bailey 2006). Engagement in youth sport is perceived to be so worthwhile that governments around the world invest large sums of public money in its promotion. Successive UK governments, for example, have demonstrated great faith in the potential of sport for young people, and have probably invested more per capita than any other country; school sport alone has received more than £1 billion since 2003 (Green 2006). Other countries, too, have sought to reap the perceived benefits of sport for individuals and the wider society. Indeed, one international review found that the curriculum materials of each of the 52 countries surveyed made explicit reference to a range of pro-social outcomes putatively linked to participation in sport (Bailey and Dismore 2004). However, a succession of surveys have found considerable variation in the levels of human and financial resourcing allocated to such provision, with some educational systems (predominantly in the developing world) including very little formal sporting provision (Hardman 2008).

Investment in the development of the most able young people in sport has similarly been diverse in practice. Some countries, such as those from the so-called 'Eastern Bloc' (such as the former German Democratic Republic, Russia, and Bulgaria), established comprehensive systems which aimed to identify and scaffold talented young players towards elite success (Prescott 1999). While the 'Bloc' has fallen, aspects of its talent development practices (centralized finding and control, early selection, early specialization) can still be witnessed in regimes as diverse as China (Prescott 1999) and the United Kingdom (Bailey 2010).

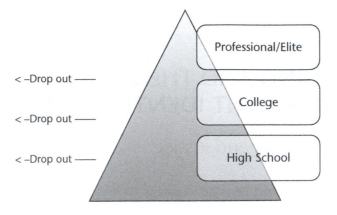

FIGURE 10.1   An example of *laissez-faire* talent development

Elsewhere, most clearly in the case of the United States (but mostly Western countries in general), talent development has taken a more *laissez-faire* approach, allowing individual interest, opportunity and capability to determine progression, at least during the early stages of the player's career (Bailey *et al.* 2010) (see Figure 10.1).

The rationale for such investment is, of course, somewhat controversial. In some centralized systems, such programmes are justified in terms of the wider benefit for society since, it is claimed, elite sporting success results in economic benefits, promotes grass-roots participation, and generates a 'feel-good factor' among the population and also a positive national 'image' abroad (DCMS /Strategy Unit 2002: 117). Elsewhere, talent development is considered an inherently worthwhile activity that helps young people realize their innate potentials (Winstanley 2003). And, of course, elite sports performance in many capitalist countries can be a source of enormous income generation and employment at both professional and collegiate levels (Lewis 2003).

Our main concern here is not so much with the scope of investment in sport, but with the utilization of such investment. The chapter starts, though, by exploring something far more complex and difficult to quantify financially – the concept of luck within the talent development process.

Policy documents tend to talk in generalities, and 'the case for sport' is often presented as if it refers to a relatively homogeneous group of activities. In fact, we might conceptualize sports participation in terms of three different goals: (1) public health goals; (2) educational goals; and (3) elite-development goals. Siedentop argued that there is an inevitable tension between these goals:

> One can legitimately question the degree to which elite-development goals of a junior sport system can be served as part of a comprehensive system and

still direct sufficient resources to achieve the educative and public health goals that are more fundamental to the system as a whole.

(2002: 396)

Underlying this statement is recognition of, perhaps, one of the most frequently overlooked issues of sports development: financial and logistical resources are finite, and increased investment in the support of one area necessarily requires relatively decreased investment in others. Also, substantial investment in the higher levels of sports performance is usually accompanied by pressure on all involved to deliver. For example, elite sport funding linked to Olympic sports in the United Kingdom is expected to reach £304.4 million for the Olympic funding cycle 2008–2012 (DCMS 2008: 4). This level of funding has been likened to a type of 'sporting arms race', as governments in pursuit of more medals invest further in elite sport because rival nations do, which in turn ratchets up further investment (Collins and Green 2007: 9). The consequences of a policy like this are clear: government officials and civil servants, national governing bodies, coaches, players and athletes will be placed under enormous pressure to achieve this ambitious goal. In fact, the nature of sporting competition means that a 'trickle-down' effect will take place whereby the greatest expectations will be forced on those who actual deliver success – the players and athletes. These people are, of course, already under enormous pressure from competing at the highest level, so their position is an unenviable one. Add to this the fact that the sheer quantity and duration of practice necessary to reach elite level mean that many of the potential players and athletes are still legally children (Bailey *et al.* 2010), and questions can be raised about the ethical nature of the enterprise. Yet while this is not a new observation within world youth sport, it is still commonplace within many nations and sports (David 2005). The pressure on young people to become 'early specializers' (i.e. to focus and train on a particular sport at a young age) is still evident, yet empirical analysis fails to find the evidence for this need (Bailey *et al.* 2010).

Questions about the ethical treatment of young people in high-performance sport are not new (e.g., Brackenridge and Kirby 1997). Paulo David (2005: 3) argues that '[h]uman rights and competitive sport are closely interwoven, despite the fact that they have ignored each other for decades . . . of all domains, sport is one of the few that has not yet been penetrated by children's rights.' With reference to the United Nations Convention on the Rights of the Child (1989), David sets out five possible sport situations that, in addition to the usual settings of discrimination based on sex, race, class and ability, can threaten the physical and mental well-being of children:

- involvement in intensive early training (violation of Article 19 – protection from child abuse and all forms of violence, and Article 32 – protection from economic exploitation);
- sexual exploitation (violation of Article 19 – protection from sexual abuse and violence);

- doping (violation of Articles 24 and 33 – right to health and protection from drugs);
- buying, selling and transfers (violation of Article 32 – economic exploitation, and Article 35 – protection from sale and trafficking);
- restrictions on education because of involvement in sport (violation of Article 28 – right to education).

Our intention in this chapter is not to revisit these themes; our sense is that they are starting to receive serious attention from scholars already. Our concern is a related matter, and one that has received almost no academic attention at all, namely that of luck within the talent development process. In fact, the locus of our concern is implicit in the Convention on the Rights of the Child (1989), itself. It states in Article 29(a) that 'States Parties agree that the education of the child shall be directed to: (a) the development of the child's personality, *talents and mental and physical abilities to their fullest potential*' (emphasis added). This statement has been interpreted by many to mean that it is possible to differentiate between appropriate and inappropriate talent development. Indeed, David himself writes:

> Competitive sports are not systematically harmful to health and they can be practiced safely by talented young athletes, as long as appropriate safeguards are in place. Many children are gifted in a particular field – whether sports, arts, music or another subject – that they can develop in a conducive environment, and if they are properly encouraged by adults. *Children with talent for sport have a right to expect support and guidance from their community.*
>
> *(2005: 34)*

We are inclined to agree with this position (who could argue with it?). However, we would draw the reader's attention to the final, italicized sentence of the quotation. The claim that talented players and athletes should receive appropriate support actually contains two parts: an explicit statement regarding the right to help; and an implicit presumption that such people are readily identifiable (because the concept of 'right' makes no sense without the associated notion that there is an evident population entitled to that right). Our contention in this chapter is that this presumption is unwarranted, at least in most developed countries:[1] the social and economic factors that mediate engagement, development and achievement in sport are such that it is simply not the case that children with talent necessarily receive support and guidance according to their needs. Consequently, these same factors also mean that some young people are given opportunities beyond their gifts due to the reinforcement of unearned privilege. Thus, aside from the more high-profile cases of unethical treatment of young players and athletes that were discussed above, talent development programmes, *per se*, are often unjust. Second, we frame this situation with reference to the philosophical concepts of 'luck' and 'responsibility', suggesting that it is both possible and necessary to distinguish different kinds of luck, in order to identify acceptable and unacceptable forms within the context of youth sport.

Talent development

Many people believe that talent in sport is innate, fixed, and affected only modestly by effort (Dweck 1999; Ommundsen 2003; Li *et al*. 2006). A version of this 'gene's-eye' account of performance is also held by many coaches (van Rossum and Gagné 1994) and academics (Bouchard *et al*. 1997; Hopkins 2001; Klissouras *et al*. 2007). Sigmund Loland offers a clear statement of this position when he writes:

> I have understood talent as genetic predispositions to develop performance
> . . . talent in sport . . . is an individual's genetic predisposition to develop phenotypes [an observable characteristic] of relevance to performance in the sport in question. The distribution of talent in the natural lottery is a random process. Moreover, we know that talent has significant and systematic influence on athletic performance, and that different sports require different talents.
>
> *(2002: 68–69)*

If the 'nature' stance is perceived as one end of a continuum, at the other end lies the 'nurture', or environmental position. According to this view, talent is primarily the result of practice and experience (Howe 2001). The most radical viewpoint representing the primacy of practice and environmental factors is the Theory of Deliberate Practice (Ericsson *et al*. 1993), which posits a direct relationship between the number of hours of high-quality practice and the performance level achieved.

In fact, it is very difficult to find a serious academic who holds extreme versions of either of these positions. If they existed, such fundamentalists would run the risk of ignoring one of the best-established findings of modern development science, namely that development is the result of an *interaction of genetic and environmental factors* (Bransford *et al*. 2000). Therefore, the bone of contention between the two camps is not whether genes or experience determine performance, but which is *most influential*.

For the purposes of this chapter, this conclusion is important because it undermines any simple equation of talent with natural dispositions: even the most genetically well-endowed player will fail to achieve if he or she is lazy, or unable to deal with success and failure. In fact, the research literature may have created an optical illusion through its findings in that, generally speaking, psychologists have been standard bearers for the environmentalist view while physiologists and geneticists have promoted the biological position. Therefore, the academic literature on talent has tended to pool towards either psychological or biological data. As we have argued elsewhere, however, participant development in sport cannot be understood fully without a sociological perspective as well (Bailey *et al*. 2010). There is very little discussion of the sociology of talent development, although talent is always socially situated and constructed. It is socially situated because talented individuals become so within catalysts such as milieu, persons, provisions and events (Gagné 2004), and it is socially constructed because the scope of the label 'talent' is defined by social and cultural values (despite the show's name, many of the acts presented on the various national versions of *Britain's Got Talent* – line-dancing dogs, using an axle grinder to create sparks against a metal thong, farting along to the Blue Danube – would not generally be considered suitable for talent development programmes).

What this means for our concern here is that there are likely to be a considerable number of mediating factors between any 'genetic predispositions' and actual sports performance. Many of the mediating factors are entirely beyond the control of the player or athlete, and to that extent could be said to be down to luck. From the perspective of a heavily funded activity like competitive sport, this raises important issues about social justice, because to abandon sporting opportunity to luck seems manifestly unfair. For the sports themselves, it raises serious concerns that the right people might not be identified and developed at the highest levels (or indeed at any level).

With these worries in mind, we turn to the concept of luck.

Talent and luck

Luck affects sporting performance in numerous ways. Loland (2002: 68) speaks about one aspect when he writes, 'The distribution of talent in the natural lottery is a random process.' Many of us had the misfortune to be born to the wrong parents, at the wrong time, and in the wrong place, and so were deprived of the chance of excellence in countless activities (in fact, we were all deprived in some respect or another). Innate giftedness is the paradigm case in the philosophical literature of luck, because it is a clear-cut example of an outcome over which we have absolutely no control. Susan Hurley, for example, distinguishes between 'thin' and 'thick' luck, with the former being the 'inverse correlate of responsibility' (2003: 107); in other words, it refers to those things for which an individual is not responsible. 'What is a matter of thin luck for an agent is what he is not responsible for, and what he is responsible for is not a matter of thin luck for him' (ibid.: 107). Thick luck, on the other hand, is *not* simply the inverse of responsibility. Rather, if something is a matter of thick luck, it is a somewhat open question whether an agent is responsible for it or not. An example of this might be a lottery. Loland's use of this term notwithstanding, generally speaking we have to choose to enter a lottery. However, we have little influence over its outcome.

There are other ways in which engagement in high-level sport might be affected by elements beyond our responsibility, and social and economic factors seem especially significant in this regard. Our aim here is not to review the literature (see, for example, Toms 2005; Bailey and Morley 2006; Bailey *et al.* 2010), but merely to highlight some findings that are indicative.

Social and economic aspects of talent development: a mini-review

1. Many children exhibiting signs of high ability during early childhood do not achieve high levels of performance in later life (Tannenbaum 1983). It seems

likely that a significant number of children never fulfil their early promise, due to developmental and maturational factors (Malina and Bouchard 1991; Abbott *et al.* 2002), and an inadequate or inappropriate social environment (Perleth *et al.* 2000). Of course, there is no way of calculating the number of potentially talented children who were born and brought up in non-supportive backgrounds and whose gifts were never realized, but we might presume that figure to be high.

2. One aspect of the talented young person's environment that has witnessed a considerable amount of research is the family (Côté 1999; Kay 2000, 2003). In his study of 120 musicians, artists, athletes, mathematicians and scientists, Bloom (1985: 3) found strong evidence that no matter what the initial characteristics (or gifts) of the individuals, unless there is a long and intensive process of encouragement, nurturance, education and training, the individuals will not attain extreme levels of capability in these particular fields. Patterns emerge from the literature to suggest there are some family characteristics that are facilitative of the development of high ability in a specific area (see Table 10.1). As Kay (2000: 151) summarizes, within the context of elite sport, 'Children are simply much more likely to achieve success if they come from a certain type of family.'

3. A considerable amount of academic research has examined the relationship between peer influence and participation in specific activities (Brustad 1993; Abernethy *et al.* 2002). Friendship seems to play a particularly significant role in decisions to invest time and effort in sports, compared with other domains. For example, Abernethy *et al.* (2002) reported that in the early stages of their careers, the Australian elite athletes in their sample all mentioned having a group of friends who were also involved in sport. Research in other areas presents the relationship between high ability and peer influence as problematic

TABLE 10.1 Social and economic influences on youth talent development in sport

Variable	*Source*
Parents achieved high standards in domain	Feldman and Goldsmith 1986; Rotella and Bunker 1987; Radford 1990
Relatively high socio-economic status	Rowley 1992; Duncan 1997; English Sports Council 1997
Ability and willingness to support and finance participation and specialist input	Rowley 1992; Kirk *et al.* 1997a; Kay 2000
Ability and willingness to invest significant time to support child's engagement in the activity	Yang *et al.* 1996; Kirk *et al.* 1997b; Kay 2000; Holt and Morley 2004
Parents as car owners	Rowley 1992
Relatively small family size	English Sports Council 1997
Two-parent family	Rowley 1992; Kay 2000
Attendance at independent school	Rowley 1992

Source: Based on Bailey and Morley (2006).

(Colangelo and Dettermann 1983; Winner 1996). There is some evidence that the possession of a gift or talent can endanger social acceptance, and this seems to be especially the case for girls (Luftig and Nichols 1991; Winner 1996).

4. It seems tautologous to claim that schools influence the development of talent in youth sport: in most countries, schools are the primary formal contexts for the introduction and development of sporting abilities in the young. Schooling certainly seems to be an important factor in children's cognitive and academic development (Ceci 1991), although individuals cited in Sloane and Sosniak (1985) attributed far greater influence to private teachers and professional artists. The limited autobiographical evidence available suggests that elite sports players are much more positive about their school experiences, with numerous high-level players and athletes crediting school physical education teachers with identifying and then nurturing their talents (e.g. Gunnell and Priest 1995; Redgrave 2000). However, while responsive and supportive physical education teachers constituted a necessary factor in the development of elite sports participation, they were rarely sufficient. Côté and his colleagues (2003) cite specialist coaches as one of the main sources of influence on children as they progress through their development in sport. In the early stages, the coach's role is generally supplementary to that of schoolteachers, offering structured practice activities and emphasizing basic skill development (Abernethy et al. 2002). Only later (at approximately 13 years of age, in the Abernethy et al. study) did the coach–athlete relationship become closer and more professional (Rowley 1992).

5. Finally, there is the role of geography: simply put, the area in which players grow up and facilities to which they have access will have a significant influence on their opportunities of sporting success. Common sense suggests that those from a large urban area, with all of the opportunities it offers, will have the most conducive environment for sporting success. Recent research, however, suggests this may not actually be the case. Côté et al. (2006) studied the birthplace of a multi-sport sample of elite North American players and concluded that children living in smaller cities have more opportunities for the development of sport expertise than their peers in larger cities or the countryside.

We trust that the relationship between luck and talent development in sport is sufficiently clear: if you are *lucky* enough to have a particular suite of genetic predispositions, that means you are able to move, react, and process information significantly better than your peers, and if you have wealthy, supportive parents who send you to a certain type of school, and if that school happens to have high-quality and committed teachers who excel in coaching your sport and high-quality facilities in which you can train, and if you live near an appropriate club or facility that can support you outside of school hours, and if you are fortunate enough to have a supportive group of siblings and friends, and if you are a boy, you are much more likely to achieve sporting success than if you lack, through no fault of your own, these social advantages.

To appreciate the inefficiency of this situation, think back for a moment to our account of the standard model of talent development in the West, which we introduced at the start of this chapter. The pyramid approach, in which fewer and fewer players train and compete at higher and higher levels, has been compared to a Darwinian process in which the relatively 'fit' survive at each level and the rest fall by the wayside (Kirk *et al.* 2005). Anecdotal evidence suggests that this metaphor has wide popular appeal among coaches and teachers: it might not be nice, but talent development requires selecting the best and rejecting the rest; it is the nature of the activity.

This is true in principle in the narrow context of elite sport, but our analysis reveals a flaw in the application of this approach. In order to understand this, it is necessary to appreciate that, according to evolutionary theory, selection is not indicative of an absolute superiority of organisms, but rather their relative, temporary superiority *within their niche*. In other words, the *best* do not survive, but rather the *best adapt* to specific environmental demands to survive (Daly and Wilson 1978). It may be possible, in theory, to utilize sufficient science and sense so that progression from one level of performance to another is based almost entirely on ability and/or predicted emergent ability (although this is certainly a very, very long way in the future), but this is not what happens now. On the contrary, as we have shown, young people are selected (in both the common and the Darwinian senses of that word) in terms of a range of elements that have nothing to do with their commitment or ability.

So luck matters, but so what? What follows from this discovery? We suggest a great deal follows. As we have implied earlier, it matters to us as taxpayers and members of the general public if a privileged few benefit and others are held back from sporting success for apparently arbitrary reasons. And it matters to sports national governing bodies if their pool of elite-level players have acquired their places due, to some extent, to fortuitous geography and maternity.

We concede that so far we have been using the term 'luck' in a number of different ways, and this may be unhelpful. Thomas Nagel (1979: 35) wrote that when we add up the different types of luck, the space that is left over that is free of luck seems to shrink 'to an extensionless point'. That may be the case, but we can at least put some sort of order to these types of luck.

Slicing up luck[2]

We need to be a little cautious in our use of the word 'luck' in this context. The word is used in a dazzling variety of ways in academic literature, and it seems wise to undertake some conceptual housekeeping at this stage. The best-known discussion of luck in philosophy is from a pair of articles, both called *Moral Luck*, by Thomas Nagel (1979) and Bernard Williams (1981), in which they comment on the notion that morality must be independent of luck in some sense. Nagel and Williams suggest that it is basic to our intuitive moral sense that what people are morally responsible for cannot depend on mere luck.

Another approach of slicing up luck is as follows (cf. Statman 1993; Lippert-Rasmussen 2005):

1. Resultant luck – the outcomes of our actions are affected by luck, e.g. training to be a philosopher of sport just prior to the sudden creation of a number of appointments in that area.
2. Circumstantial luck – the circumstances in which one acts introduce luck. For example, by chance, a young athlete finds himself attending a club run by an expert coach for a certain sport, and his career benefits as a result of this.
3. Constitutive luck – luck affects the kind of person you are. For example, some long-distance runners and cyclists have freakishly low resting heart rates, and because of this, it makes sense to say that they were genetically lucky, within the context of cycling or running.
4. Antecedent causal luck – there is luck in the way one's actions are determined by antecedent circumstances. For example, children born into 'sporty' and supportive families are more likely to be motivated and better prepared to engage with sport than those who are not so fortunate.

These analyses are interesting in their way, but are of limited value to us if we are seeking to distinguish different forms of luck with a mind to informing policy or practice. Another way of thinking about luck highlights what we think is closer to the central issue at stake. Dworkin (1981) and Cohen (1989) distinguish between 'brute' and 'option' luck. Option luck refers to that for which we are responsible, by taking risks, for example. But we are not responsible for brute luck. There is a significant body of literature within egalitarian and social justice theorizing that suggests that their most fundamental aim is to neutralize luck (Arneson 1989; Roemer 1998). And this has predominantly been taken to mean brute luck (Cohen 1989). In other words, these egalitarians aim to neutralize the influences on distribution for which we are not responsible.

John Rawls (1971: 104) maintained that, '[n]o one deserves his place on the distribution of native endowments any more than one deserves one's initial starting place in society'. To this we could retort that sporting success is attributable to more than innate talent, and that dedication, determination, a strong mental attitude and extremely long hours of practice are also important. Rawls, however, was ready for this counter, arguing that these qualities, too, can be seen as products of luck:

> The assertion that a man deserves the superior character that enables him to make the effort to cultivate his abilities is equally problematic; for his character depends in large part upon his fortunate family and social circumstances for which he can claim no credit.
>
> *(1971: 104)*

So, does it follow that talented players ought to be handicapped in some way to counterbalance their natural gifts? It would certainly change the nature of sport:

Two identical people playing tennis . . . but neither could ever win. The game would never get beyond 40–40, or perhaps, since neither was the least bit better than the other, the first rally of the match would be interminable, or at least last until both players dropped from exhaustion, presumably at the same time.

(Wilson 1966: 73–74)

Rawls' solution to this problem is that talents represent common assets that benefit all, and they are just because principles of justice are the result of

an agreement to regard the distribution of natural talents as a common asset and to share in the benefits of this distribution whatever it turns out to be. Those who have been favored by nature, whoever they are, may gain from their good fortune only on terms that improve the situation of those who have lost out.

(1971: 101)

In other words, Rawls is arguing that unequal distribution of a resource like talent can be justified if the practices that generate such inequalities operate in the long-term interests of the disadvantaged; the talented athlete has effectively been nationalized (Simon 1991).

This solution does not seem adequate either as it seems to overlook a number of key features of high-level sports performance, for example that inequality is due to the interaction of the expression of the talent and the responses of those witnessing to it. Thus, rewarding achievement reflects societal evaluations and celebrations of what some 'lucky' individuals do with their gifts, gifts to which they are not merely contingently attached but which may reflect their nature too (ibid.). Moreover, in suggesting that talents are in some way owned by the community, Rawls contravenes the intuitive view that we do, in fact, own our own minds and bodies (Nozick 1974), and therefore ought to have some say, at least, about the services to which they are put. Finally, Rawls seems to be implying that their realization ought to be fair. Any benefit that might accrue to a minority of exceptional sport performers is fatally undermined if those performers earned their exulted position through undeserved advantage due to, for example, parental income or school quality. In other words, while the possession of talents may not be equitable, opportunities for their development must be. Luck neutralization need not, therefore, be anti-talent, but rather anti-privilege.

Hard luck and soft luck

From the considerations outlined above, it seems that luck, *per se*, is not of greatest concern, but rather a particular form of luck. To be clear, our concern here is the sporting context. We are equivocal about the scope of luck that ought be curtailed in the wider society, but it does seem reasonable to suppose that individual differences, which generate much of the challenge and excitement of sport, ought not be neutralized as a matter of course (stepladders for short basketball players, handicapping of the fastest sprinters, and telescopic lenses for short-sighted golfers could all be classified as luck-neutralizing strategies, but seem to betray something of the spirit of sport).

While we do not wish to further complicate the earlier discussion of luck, our suggestion is that there are two types of luck that are of particular relevance to this discussion: luck that is modifiable and luck that is not. Examples of the former are numerous, but include the quality of physical education, the quality of coaching and parental income. An example of the latter might be genetic inheritance. The second form of luck seems necessarily more difficult to address. The former can be called 'soft luck', the latter 'hard luck'. Soft luck is avoidable and can be directly addressed; hard luck is unavoidable, and cannot be 'corrected' directly.

This distinction is important because it is cognizant of the nature of sport and the importance of some types of individual differences in it. At the same time, it honours the spirit of the luck neutralization position, but only when that luck is soft (i.e. is modifiable). Therefore, this perspective does not abandon social responsibility; on the contrary, it makes an explicit case that those who benefit from privilege are not further privileged, and those who are relatively disadvantaged are supported. This seems warranted because, on the one hand, youth talent development is predominantly supported from the public purse, and the public has a right to expect that expenditure will be distributed fairly. On the other hand, even if youth sport was an entirely private affair, society would still be justified in intervening in defence of the welfare of some of its most vulnerable members.

Conclusion

Elite sport is costly, for society and for the players/athletes who engage in it. Unlike most other contexts of sport, those performing at the highest levels are working in a necessarily selective environment. Selection is acceptable if it is the result of an individual making the most of the innate gifts available (of hard luck). It is not acceptable if opportunities are presented to persons heavily mediated by social and environmental happenstance. In other words, we are arguing that elitism is a reasonable (perhaps attractive) element of competitive sport; exclusivity is not acceptable, if that term is understood to mean that groups are selected and not appropriately supported into or out of talent development programmes based on little more than an accident of geography or upbringing.

We are not suggesting that socially fortunate players achieve sporting success entirely due to their social backgrounds. Obviously, practice and dedication are vitally important to their success. However, we do maintain that success is generally much easier for groups from fairly clearly defined social backgrounds (in the United Kingdom, these backgrounds include those of wealthy, white boys). We also suggest that selection onto talent development programmes for a minority (and consequently de-selection off for a much larger group) is mediated to such an extent that it is not possible to say with any confidence that the 'winners' are the most talented because the whole process is infused by soft luck at every point. This is unnecessary, wasteful and unfair.

What does this mean for coaches? To begin with, it is important to abandon the naïve notion that ability is the only factor that determines success in talent development systems. However talented the members of a selected cohort might be, we can say with some confidence that they do not represent all, or even most, of the most able young people available. Rather, they are the lucky ones whose abilities and commitments have survived the social and financial obstacles that are almost inevitable features of sport in the Western world. This awareness alone ought to generate a sense of dissatisfaction, whether for moral reasons (it is not fair that so many potentially able young people are expelled through no fault of their own) or for more pragmatic ones (success is much more difficult without access to the best players). We have a bolder proposal, too. Rather than simply acknowledging the structural unfairnesses within talent development systems, coaches (as well as their administrators) can challenge them. If luck is as influential in the process as we have indicated here, then it will be worthwhile exploring opportunities to *neutralize luck*. In other words, a strategic use of the resources available to coaches (which includes their time and expertise) ought to be dedicated to breaking down barriers to participation and progression. To do this might reveal numerous talented young people who are otherwise hidden or expelled from the system; it also has the happy moral coincidence of being the right thing to do.

Notes

1 It is highly likely that this contention holds in all non–Communist states (and probably also those); however, we will be citing literature from the developed world in this instance, so our claim is suitably restricted.
2 This discussion relies on Bailey (2007).

References

Abbott, A., Collins, D., Martindale, R. and Sowerby, K. (2002) *Talent Identification and Development: An Academic Review: A Report for sportscotland by the University of Edinburgh*, Edinburgh: sportscotland.

Abernethy, B., Côté, J. and Baker, J. (2002) *Expert Decision-Making in Team Sport*, Canberra, ACT: Australian Institute of Sport.

Arneson, R. (1989) 'Equality and equal opportunity for welfare', *Philosophical Studies*, 56: 77–93.

Bailey, R.P. (2006) 'Physical education and sport in schools: a review of benefits and outcomes', *Journal of School Health*, 76(8): 397–401.

Bailey, R.P. (2007) 'Talent development and the luck problem', *Sport, Ethics and Philosophy*, 1(3): 367–377.

Bailey, R.P. (2010) *Gifted and Talented Physical Education and Sport: A Review of Principles and Practice*, Loughborough: Youth Sport Trust.

Bailey, R.P. and Dismore, H. (2004) *Sport in Education: The Worldwide Review*, Berlin: ICSSPE.

Bailey, R.P. and Morley, D. (2006) 'Towards a model of talent development in physical education', *Sport, Education and Society*, 11: 211–230.

Bailey, R.P., Collins, D., Ford, P., MacNamara, A., Toms, M. and Pearce, G. (2010) *Participant Development in Sport: An Academic Review*, Leeds: sports coach UK.

Bloom, B.S. (ed.) (1985) *Developing Talent in Young People*, New York: Ballantine Books.

Bouchard, C., Malina, R.M. and Pérusse, L. (1997) *Genetics of Fitness and Physical Performance*, Champaign, IL: Human Kinetics.

Brackenridge, C.H. and Kirby, S. (1997) 'Playing safe? Assessing the risk of sexual abuse to young elite athletes', *International Review for the Sociology of Sport*, 32(4): 407–418.

Bransford, J.D., Brown, A.L. and Cocking, R. (eds) (2000) *How People Learn: Brain, Mind, Experience and School*, Washington, DC: National Academy Press.

Brustad, R.J. (1993) 'Youth in sport: psychological considerations', in R.N. Singer, M. Murphey and L.K. Tennant (eds) *Handbook of Research on Sport Psychology*, New York: Macmillan.

Ceci, S.J. (1991) 'How much does schooling influence general intelligence and its cognitive components? A reassessment of the evidence', *Developmental Psychology*, 27: 394–402.

Cohen, G. (1989) 'The currency of egalitarian justice', *Ethics*, 99: 906–944.

Colangelo, N. and Dettermann, D.F. (1983) 'A review of research on parents and families of gifted children', *Exceptional Children*, 50(1): 20–27.

Collins, S. and Green, M. (2007) 'The Australian Institute of Sport', *Journal of the Academy of Social Sciences in Australia*, 26(2): 4–14.

Côté, J. (1999) 'The influence of the family in the development of talent in sport', *The Sport Psychologist*, 13: 395–417.

Côté, J., Baker, J. and Abernethy, B. (2003) 'From play to practice: a developmental framework for the acquisition of expertise in team sports', in J.L. Starkes and K.A. Ericsson (eds) *Expert Performance in Sport: Advances in Research on Sport Expertise*, Champaign, IL: Human Kinetics.

Côté, J., MacDonald, D., Baker, J. and Abernethy, B. (2006) 'When "where" is more important than "when": birthplace and birthdate effects on the achievement of sporting expertise', *Journal of Sports Sciences*, 24: 1065–1073.

Daly, M. and Wilson, M. (1978) *Sex, Evolution and Behavior*, North Scituate, MA: Duxbury Press.

David, P. (2005) *Human Rights in Youth Sport: A Critical Review of Children's Rights in Competitive Sport*, London: Routledge.

DCMS (2008) *Playing to Win: A New Era for Sport*, London: DCMS.

DCMS/Strategy Unit (2002) *Game Plan: A Strategy for Delivering Government's Sport and Physical Activity Objectives*, London: Cabinet Office.

Duncan, J. (1997) 'Focus group interviews with elite young athletes, coaches and parents', in J. Kremer, K. Trew and S. Ogle (eds) *Young People's Involvement in Sport*, London: Routledge.

Dweck, C. (1999) *Self-Theories: Their Role in Motivation, Personality, and Development*, Philadelphia, PA: Psychology Press.

Dworkin, R. (1981) 'What is equality? Part Two: equality of resources', *Philosophy and Public Affairs*, 10: 283–345.

English Sports Council (1997) *The Development of Sporting Talent 1997*, London: Sports Council.

Ericsson, K.A., Krampe, R.T. and Tesch-Römer, C. (1993) 'The role of deliberate practice in the acquisition of expert performance', *Psychological Review*, 100: 363–406.

Feldman, D.H. and Goldsmith, L. (1986) *Nature's Gambit: Child Prodigies and the Development of Human Potential*, New York: Teachers College Press.

Gagné, F. (2004) 'Transforming gifts into talents: the DMGT as a developmental theory', *High Ability Studies*, 15(2): 119–147.

Green, M. (2006) 'From "Sport for All" to not about "sport" at all? Interrogating sport policy interventions in the United Kingdom', *European Sport Management Quarterly*, 6: 217–238.

Gunnell, S. and Priest, C. (1995) *Running Tall*, London: Bloomsbury.

Hardman, K. (2008) 'Physical education in schools: a global perspective', *Kinesiology*, 40: 5–28.

Holt, N.L. and Morley, D. (2004) 'Gender differences in psychosocial factors associated with athletic success during childhood', *The Sport Psychologist*, 18: 138–153.

Hopkins, W.G. (2001) 'Genes and training for athletic performance', *Sportscience*, Online. 5 (1), Online. Available HTTP: http://www.sportsci.org/jour/0101/wghgene.htm (accessed 20 February 2001).

Howe, M.J.A. (2001) *Genius Explained*, Cambridge: Cambridge University Press.

Hurley, S. (2003) *Justice, Luck, and Knowledge*, Cambridge, MA: Harvard University Press.

Kay, T. (2000) 'Sporting excellence: a family affair?' *European Physical Education Review*, 6: 151–169.

Kay, T. (2003) *The Family Factor in Sport: A Review of Family Factors Affecting Sports Participation: Report Commissioned by Sport England*, Loughborough: Institute for Youth Sport.

Kirk, D., Carlson, T., O'Connor, T., Burke, P., Davis, K. and Glover, S. (1997a) 'The economic impact on families on children's participation in junior sport', *Australian Journal of Science and Medicine in Sport*, 29(2): 27–33.

Kirk, D., O'Connor, T., Carlson, T., Burke, P., Davis, K. and Glover, S. (1997b) 'Time commitments of junior sport: social consequences for participants and their families', *Journal of Sport Behavior*, 20(1): 51–73.

Kirk, D., Brettschneider, W.-D. and Auld, C. (2005) 'Junior sport models representing best practice nationally and internationally', *Junior Sport Briefing Papers*, Canberra: Australian Sports Commission.

Klissouras, V., Geladas, N. and Koskolou, M. (2007) 'Nature prevails over nurture', *International Journal of Sport Psychology*, 38(1): 35–67.

Lewis, M. (2003) *Moneyball*, New York: Norton.

Li, W., Lee, A. and Solmon, M. (2006) 'Gender differences in beliefs about the influence of ability and effort in sports and physical activity', *Sex Roles*, 54: 147–156.

Lippert-Rasmussen, K. (2005) 'Justice and bad luck', in E.N. Zalta (ed.) *The Stanford Encyclopedia of Philosophy*, online. Available HTTP: http://plato.stanford.edu/entries/justice-bad-luck/ (accessed 20 November 2006).

Loland, S. (2002) *Fair Play in Sport: A Moral Norm System*, London: Routledge.

Luftig, R.L. and Nichols, M.L. (1991) 'An assessment of the social status and perceived personality and school traits of gifted students by non-gifted peers', *Roeper Review*, 13: 148–153.

Malina, R.M. and Bouchard, C. (1991) *Growth, Maturation and Physical Activity*, Champaign, IL: Human Kinetics.

Nagel, T. (1979) 'Moral luck', in *Mortal Questions*, New York: Cambridge University Press.

Nozick, R. (1974) *Anarchy, State, and Utopia*, New York: Basic Books.

Ommundsen, Y. (2003) 'Implicit theories of ability and self-regulation strategies in physical education classes', *Educational Psychology*, 23(2): 141–157.

Perleth, C., Schatz, T. and Mönks, F.J. (2000) 'Early identification of high ability', in K.A. Heller, F.J. Mönks, R.J. Sternberg and R.F. Subotnik (eds) *International Handbook of Giftedness and Talent*, 2nd edn, Oxford: Elsevier.

Prescott, J. (1999) 'Identification and development of talent in young female gymnasts', unpublished PhD thesis, Loughborough University.

Radford, J. (1990) *Child Prodigies and Exceptional Early Achievers*. New York: Free Press.

Rawls, J. (1971) *A Theory of Justice*, Cambridge, MA: Harvard University Press.

Redgrave, S. (2000) *Steve Redgrave: A Golden Age*, London: BBC Books.

Roemer, J. (1998) *Equality of Opportunity*, Cambridge, MA: Harvard University Press.

Rotella, R.J. and Bunker, L.K. (1987) *Parenting Your Superstar*, Champaign, IL: Leisure Press.

Rowley, S. (1992) *TOYA and the Identification of Talent*, London: Sports Council.

Siedentop, D. (2002) 'Junior sport and the evolution of sport cultures', *Journal of Teaching in Physical Education*, 21: 392–401.

Simon, R.L. (1991) *Fair Play: Sport, Values and Society*, Boulder, CO: Westview Press.

Sloane, K. and Sosniak, L. (1985) 'The development of accomplished sculptors', in B.S. Bloom (ed.) *Developing Talent in Young People*, New York: Ballantine Books.

Statman, D. (ed.) (1993) *Moral Luck*, Albany, New York: State University of New York Press.

Tannenbaum, A.J. (1983) *Gifted Children: Psychological and Educational Perspectives*, New York: Macmillan.

Toms, M. (2005) 'The developmental socialisation of young people in club sport: an ethnographic account', unpublished PhD thesis, Loughborough University.

van Rossum, J.H.A. and Gagné, F. (1994) 'Rankings of predictors of athletic performance by top level coaches', *European Journal of High Ability Studies*, 5: 68–78.

Williams, B. (1981) *Moral Luck*, Cambridge: Cambridge University Press.

Wilson, J. (1966) *Equality*, New York: Harcourt, Brace and World.

Winner, E. (1996) *Gifted Children: Myths and Realities*, New York: Basic Books.

Winstanley, C. (2003) *Too Clever by Half: A Fair Deal for Gifted Children*, Stoke-on-Trent: Trentham Books.

Yang, X., Telema, R. and Laakso, L. (1996) 'Parents' physical activity, socioeconomic status and education as predictors of physical activity and sport among children and youths: a 12-year follow-up study', *International Review of the Sociology of Sport*, 31(3): 273–287.

11

COACHING AND THE ETHICS OF PERFORMANCE ENHANCEMENT

Irena Martínková and Jim Parry

Introduction

When we think of performance enhancement in sport, our minds turn automatically to the issue of *illicit* performance enhancement – for example, by means of doping – and of course we shall give full consideration to such matters. However, we should never lose sight of the fact that the primary purpose of the coach is to help the athlete to improve and enhance their performance. Regardless of whatever aims, methods, values and virtues the coach might espouse, this is their defining aim *qua* coach: to contribute to the enhancement of the athlete's (or the team's) performance. The aim of this chapter is to examine ethical issues that arise within this context.

There are many ways in which performance enhancement can be achieved, including rigorous and systematic training, a proper diet, management of injuries and injury risks, and improvements in motivation and other psychological factors. A wealth of scientific information is now available to coaches and other specialists in order to achieve enhancements, and to fine-tune the various processes. Much of this is often considered ethically unproblematic.

However, there are also other avenues available for the coach that seem to (or are believed to) provide improvement, but which raise concerns because of their legal or ethical status. This chapter will explore the key ethical issues involved in performance enhancement generally, including harm, exploitation, paternalistic decision-making (both for adults and children), individual freedom and informed consent. It will do so with special reference to three concerns: (1) the use of illicit performance-enhancing drugs; (2) the use of permissible supplements; and (3) the morality of certain approaches to training.

Doping

As we have already noted, the first thing that comes to our minds when we think about performance enhancement in sport is doping. And when we think about doping, we usually think about drug-taking. The 'official' definition of doping is, however, wider than this.

What is doping?

Article 1 (on the Definition of Doping) of the World Anti-Doping Code (WADA 2009a) defines doping as the occurrence of one or more of the anti-doping rule violations set forth in Article 2 of the Code. Article 2 basically cites the use or attempted use by an athlete of a prohibited substance or method (as described in Article 4), and includes rules relating to athlete whereabouts, the refusal or evasion of test procedures, and to the possession, trafficking or administration of a prohibited substance or method.

Why do athletes use doping?

As well as direct physical performance enhancement via drug-taking, there are many other reasons given for doping, which refer to the supposed additional or accompanying benefits, for example:

- decreased recovery period, allowing more intensive training;
- masking the presence of other drugs;
- making the weight;
- staying the course (simple endurance – e.g. long-distance cycling);
- psychological edge (promoting the athlete's confidence);
- keeping up with the competition (coercion – pressure to follow suit).

Why do we think that doping is wrong? – the main arguments

Pre-competition agreements

The primary wrong lies in simple rule-breaking. The rules function as a kind of pre-competition agreement which specifies an athlete's eligibility to compete and his or her rights, duties and responsibilities under the agreed rules. What is wrong with doping is the secretive attempt to evade or subvert such a 'contract to contest', an explicit example of which is the Olympic Oath, by which athletes swear that they have prepared themselves ethically, and will keep to the rules. To subvert the contract to contest threatens the ethical basis of sport, jeopardizes the integrity of the sporting community and erodes public support and trust.

However, the rules themselves require a basis of justification, since the anti-doping rules must appeal to some issue of principle in addition to rule adherence. Considerations advanced include the following:

Unfair advantage

Arguments against performance enhancement through doping are not simply arguments against performance enhancement, since that is what athletes constantly seek to achieve by training, coaching, nutrition, the application of sports science, etc. Neither are the arguments simply against performance enhancement by means which confer an unfair advantage, since many legal means might be seen as 'unfair', being beyond the resources of most countries. Rather, a relevant argument should be made specifically against *unfair advantage conferred by illegal means*.

Harm

Many argue that doping may be harmful to the individual athlete, either because the substances are inherently harmful, or because they have been administered without medical supervision, or because they have been inadequately tested. Further, it is argued that harm to other individual athletes is caused by the coercion they feel to follow suit in order to maintain competitiveness.

Social harm

Recently, though, commentators have also observed a social harm. With the huge expansion in the market for drugs in gyms and fitness clubs, there is now an emerging claim for a further wrong: that, by modelling doping as a lifestyle, athletes contribute to the social problem of thousands of sport, fitness and bodybuilding fans consuming substances whose long-term effects are unknown. Athletes, it is said, should be more aware of their social responsibility.

Why do we ban doping?

It is one thing to say that doping is wrong, and quite another to ban it, which requires the apparatus of testing, judicial procedure and enforcement. So alongside such principles as those given above, we also see various rationales for testing and enforcement, including:

- fairness preservation (against unfair advantage);
- athlete protection (against harm to health and reputation);
- deterrence via detection, with the threat of punishment (which might, on the one hand, serve both of the above seemingly legitimate rationales, but might, on the other, serve more questionable purposes, such as lifestyle prescription or 'role model' requirements).

However, there are also two kinds of arguments against a ban. The first is 'empirical', suggesting that we cannot test effectively and fairly, because:

- there is inadequate coverage (not enough resources for testing and testers, or not enough support from civil authorities);
- the tests are not good enough (one test for EPO had only 92 per cent accuracy, and the cycling federations were afraid to have their decisions tested in court, since they could have been ruined by one court action);
- athletes with the best knowledge and resources know how to avoid detection, which is why the testing procedures catch so few (there is a suspicion that, out of the relatively few cases of detection, there are a relatively large proportion of cases where the athlete was convicted of some very minor infraction, or on a technicality, or for a non-performance-enhancing substance, or where there is a reasonable doubt that the athlete did anything wrong at all);
- there are many cases which seem to be simple mistakes.

The second kind of argument is 'moral', suggesting that we should not ban on grounds of infringement of liberty and should not test on grounds of invasion of privacy. This kind of argument would also point to the many cases of injustice in the history of testing and enforcement, and to the tyranny of value and lifestyle prescription.

Why isn't it just down to individual choice?

Some argue that a ban is simply parentalist – that we cannot justify interference in the individual athlete's decision-making processes. Tamburrini (2000: 215), for example, says, '[T]he ban on performance-enhancing methods constrains the professional activities of athletes, and . . . the reasons often advanced to support that constraint do not stand criticism.' However, Schneider (2005: 40) argues that the 'individualistic' view fails to give adequate recognition to the private/public distinction. It seems to suppose that any individual's 'private' views and decisions (such as to engage in doping, or to seek performance-enhancing genetic technology) are privileged, and should be taken into account by any existing institutions (such as sports practices). Schneider objects that such private views should not be allowed to 'trump' the values expressed in and through the practice – that there is a 'public' view here that should take precedence. Sports are communal practices, and encapsulate certain shared views, adherence to which is a prerequisite of entry and participation. Of course, rules change – sometimes as a result of pressure from within the practice, and sometimes from without – but only (in some sense) *with the consent of* the practice. Why should people who want 'clean' sport have to accept dopers?

Some have suggested that the way forward for dopers is that they should announce themselves as dopers, and set up their own versions of various sports. But this will not solve our problem, because there is no guarantee that some dopers will not refuse to identify themselves as such, since they presently only succeed in their plans if they are secretive – just as at present there is no guarantee that any individual would deny himself the advantage of pretending to be clean while secretly doping.

If he does not respect the anti-doping rules now, why should he respect the clean/doped distinction later?

The ethical basis of the idea of sport

Let us comment upon a positive feature of the debate about performance-enhancing drugs. The drugs debate has forced everyone to think in ethical terms, and to appeal to ethical principles. But if we take these appeals seriously, and follow them through, there are some interesting consequences. Assume that drug-taking in sport is wrong, and ask the question: '*Why* is it wrong?' The answers we have given above were all stated in terms of some ethical principle that is claimed to be central to our idea of sport, which drug-taking allegedly violates. Let us revisit two of those arguments and see where the underlying principles lead us:

Unfair advantage or inequality of opportunity

Some say that what is wrong with drug-taking is that it confers an unfair advantage. Notice that no one can (sincerely) make this objection to drug-taking unless he is sincere in his commitment to sport as embodying fairness, and as disallowing unfair advantages as being against the idea of sport.

However, many of those who hold this objection against drug-taking seem perfectly prepared to allow various kinds of very obviously unfair advantages. For example, only certain countries are able to generate and enjoy the fruits of developments in sports science; and only certain countries are able to take advantage of the knowledge and technology required for the production of specialized technical equipment. Is this fair? The company that produced the so-called 'moon-bikes' for the US cycling team in the 1984 Olympic Games later shamelessly marketed them under the slogan: 'The Unfair Advantage'.

Let us widen the issue: it seems to us a fact that international competition is grossly unfair, because some countries have the resources to enhance the performance of their athletes, and some do not. Those nurtured within advanced systems might take time to consider the extent to which their performances are a function not just of their abilities as individual sportspeople but also of the social context within which they have been nurtured. Have not their performances been enhanced? Are not their advantages unfair?

Consistency requires that we revisit the whole idea of disadvantage, and also inequality. While there are many kinds of inequality that we could not (or should not) eliminate, there are also many *unfair* inequalities that could be addressed by simple changes in current practice, or in current rule formulations. For example, why not include more 'ethnic' sports in the Olympic programme, rather than continuing the present Western hegemonic domination? Kabbadi, a sport popular on the Indian sub-continent, is a sport based on the game form of 'tag', which is known in most societies in the world. It requires minimal facilities and no equipment. Why should we Westerners not have to learn such sports and compete on those terms, rather than collude in the disappearance of indigenous sport forms in favour of our own curriculum?

Anyone who has a genuine concern about (and relies on arguments against) unfair advantage in the case of doping should also be prepared to revisit and reconsider unfair advantage arguments in other contexts.

Rule-breaking, or cheating

Others say that drug-taking is wrong simply because it is against the rules of competition – and, of course, if we wish to participate, we should all obey the rules of the present competition, whatever they are. However, not everyone actually does obey the rules of competition – sometimes not even the rule-makers themselves. For example, pace-making is against the rules of the IAAF, although it is allowed so as to facilitate record-breaking attempts in the commercial promotion of media spectacle, and no one is disqualified. In fact, runners can earn large fees for performing this 'service'. If officials so readily flout their own rules, they are poorly placed when athletes do the same, or when critics demand better justification for the rules that presently exist.

In a world where the values of sport are sometimes forgotten under the pressures of medal-winning and the marketplace, it ill behoves those responsible to turn a moralistic eye on athletes. Why should athletes take any notice of the moral exhortation of those who have profited from the commercialization of sport, when they see the true values lived and expressed by those around them?

The drugs debate has made everyone stand on ethical principle. But think how sport might develop (what it might become) if those principles were not merely used opportunistically over the drugs issue, but rather were acted upon consistently in the interests of truly fair competition and equality of opportunity. We think that there is an opportunity here to open up debate again about the ethical basis of sport, so that our sports practice (and the sports science and training theory that support it) become rooted in firm principles that encapsulate what we think sport *should be*. If we think that what is wrong with doping is that it denies an equal opportunity to others, then just this thought should cause us to revisit other examples of unequal opportunity, and to re-examine our attitudes towards those examples. In the same way, if we think that what is wrong with doping is that it presents an avoidable harm to athletes, then just this thought should cause us to revisit other examples of sport practices that result in avoidable harms (short-term and long-term) to athletes, and to re-examine our attitudes towards those examples. Unfortunately, this kind of consistency in the application of our principles seems to be a rare commodity – we often seem unwilling to extend our ethical thinking beyond examples which already seem obviously wrong to us. We need to think more extensively about the values of the thing we value – sport.

Some might see the above as wishful thinking, but we do not think so. Every coach has countless opportunities in their daily work and practice to display their values to athletes – to explain and express what the internal values and the internal logic of sport must mean for anyone who wants to participate in an appropriate manner. But even if such an approach were to be rejected, we still have to say now what we think about the specific issue: why we think it is wrong to take dope.

Our main answer is that it would be wrong to take enhancers if they are banned, because it is simple rule-breaking. If anyone seeks to evade any rule for advantage, especially when they do it knowingly and secretively, then that is the clearest possible case of cheating. True, there may well be arguments outstanding regarding the justice, relevance or importance of the rule itself, but so long as the rule is the rule we ought all to obey it, on pain of sanction. To get into the Ritz, a man must wear a tie. Whether or not this is a stupid or trivial requirement is irrelevant to whether he gets into the Ritz. There are plenty of places to eat, but if he wants to eat at the Ritz, he had better wear a tie.

Sports competitors prepare and compete on certain more or less precise understandings described by the rules. Any attempt to evade these rules for advantage is cheating. It is an attempt to subvert the very basis upon which the activity alone is possible; it is to pervert the logical and ethical basis of the whole social practice of sport. *This* is the greatest harm perpetrated by doping cheats and those coaches, managers and medics who assist them: not the alleged medical harm to self or the coercion of others, but the harm to self and others caused by behaviour which threatens the social practice of sport itself.

After all, athletes are subject to an extra and special set of logical and ethical considerations *just because* they seek to enter the cooperative enterprise of competing with and against others in sporting contests. As 'contractors to contest', they must accept certain constraints in order to count as acceptable opponents. And one such putative constraint is that against doping in sport. Dopers disqualify themselves.

Supplements

In the case of doping, there is at least a certain amount of clarity – we have the 'WADA list' as a (fairly) clear guide as to what is banned (WADA 2009b). Since the main and most generally accepted argument against doping is quasi-legal (it is against the rules), it might be thought that anything *within* the rules, such as 'supplements' of various kinds, would be ethically unproblematic. After all, what athletes need to 'supplement' is their normal food intake, and a food is something taken simply in order to maintain life, health or growth. But there are difficulties even with this: to maintain life or health at what level? A 'normal' level? – how are we to specify that? To assist growth to what degree? And what are my 'needs', anyway? When diseased or deficient in some way, are we not treated with drugs or supplements? (We might see this as 'medical supplementation'.)

Imagine that some young athletes in power or combat sports begin to supplement their food intake in order to 'bulk up'. They simply eat more and different foods. Then they might discover a supplement like whey protein, after which they might go on to take creatine (which many see as a borderline case), and some of them might further consider using anabolic steroids. So how are we to see the two intermediate steps between the food and the dope (whey protein and creatine): as a harmless extension of food, or as the slippery slope to doping?

Sometimes supplements are used instead of doping. Some seek to gain the supposed benefits of doping while evading the anti-doping rules by using substances that are not actually banned. Richard Quick, a swimming coach who sees himself as someone 'on the cutting edge of what can be done nutritionally and with supplements', seeks to maximize supplement efficacy. He is quoted as claiming that his athletes can do 'steroid-like performances' while trying to 'keep up with the people who are cheating without cheating' (Sokolove 2004: 53). Notice that the meaning of cheating here is given solely in terms of what the rules currently say or do not say. However, if there are indeed legal substances that can enhance as well as steroids, it is unclear why more athletes are not using them. It is also unclear why they are not on the WADA banned list.

For example, creatine is a legal substance that has been taken by professional athletes in Europe and the United States for many years. It seems to help muscles work harder for longer and improve recovery time. The athletes Linford Christie and Sally Gunnell, and the footballer Ian Wright, admit to having used it, and the footballer Glenn Hoddle both used it as a player and condoned it as a coach (Warshaw 1998). These athletes used creatine to obtain the enhancements and advantages supposedly conferred by steroid usage, and they chose creatine because it was not on the banned list, as did many Italian footballers over the past 30 years.

However, the fact that it was not banned did not safeguard the Italian footballers from serious harms. Recent epidemiological studies have shown a high risk for ALS (amyotrophic lateral sclerosis – a rare and devastating neurodegenerative disease of unknown aetiology) among Italian footballers (Belli and Vanacore 2005; Vanacore *et al.* 2006), and creatine usage is identified as a possible cause. There is also evidence that it can cause kidney and liver damage (Warshaw 1998). Even if there were no harmful effects, however, there is no certainty that the substance will produce the desired effects. The most common adverse effects reported to be associated with creatine include fluid retention and weight gain, and these effects may actually be detrimental in some sporting events (Ambrose 2004). So any coach advocating or supplying creatine takes risks with regard to the athlete's health and with regard to performance detriment.

Plans for nutrition, supplementation, enhancement and doping can be so comprehensive and elaborate that, from the point of view of the athlete, it can be difficult to see where one begins and the other ends. There has also been some official confusion over the relative seriousness of a particular drug, for example in cases involving modafinil. When Kelli White, who was a training partner of Dwain Chambers, tested positive at the World Championships, the International Association of Athletics Federations (IAAF) classified modafinil as a mild stimulant. 'The classification meant White faced disqualification and losing her 100 and 200m gold medals – but no ban. The new WADA list of prohibited substances, published on Jan. 1, however, includes modafinil as a major stimulant' (Knight 2004).

So was she taking a mild or a major stimulant? Did she take it or was she given it to take? Did she really appreciate what she was doing and what the consequences might be? 'Kelli White . . . lost her medals and prize money after a drug test showed that she had taken the stimulant modafinil. "After a competition," she said, "it's hard to remember everything that you take during the day" ' (Sokolove 2004: 52). How revealing – this suggests a regime designed by a team of support staff, to which the athlete submits. Even some 'clean' athletes take a cocktail of pills that they hope will compensate for the supposed advantages of the banned substances taken by the cheats who risk detection. The British tennis player Greg Rusedski took such a cocktail every day (Hart 2004), with a detailed and systematic diary – and we should assume that this is the rule rather than the exception among elite athletes, many of whom tread a fine line between the legal and the illegal. This imposes a tremendous responsibility on all who might be involved in these matters – especially those charged with duties towards athlete care.

So, again, how are we to see athletic supplementation – as innocent as food, or as questionable as dope? Our short answer will be: if it is for maintenance or health purposes (sustaining/compensatory/restorative), it is more like food, therapy or medicine; but if it is strictly for performance purposes (enhancement), it is more like dope.

We should first of all note, though, that the term 'enhancement' actually covers both of the above cases, and is ambiguous here. It could mean 'compensatory/ restorative' – that is, supplements that compensate for a temporary incapacity (like iron for anaemia) or restore my powers (like smelling salts to revive me) or guard against a possible dysfunction (like salt for cramps). These are supplements that allow the best 'me' to attend and compete at present – they enable my best performance on the day. Or it could mean 'baseline performance-enhancing' – that is, supplements that aim to enhance my capacity to produce better performances in general and in future. These are supplements that aim to produce a new and better 'me'.

Now we can apply these observations as follows:

1. In the sense of food supplements, athletes *must* take supplements. They need to supplement a 'normal' food intake in order to support their extra activity, which is greater than that of the average non-athletic citizen. In the case of elite athletes, it can be enormously greater. Long-distance runners and cyclists, tennis players, and footballers take on extra water because of the dangers of dehydration, and extra calories because of the large quantities their bodies use and lose. So such supplementation is inevitable and unproblematic.

2. In the case of compensatory/restorative supplements, there does not seem to be any objection. It is the duty of athletes to be at their best, and to be as well prepared as possible for competition. If that means taking a prescribed medicine to maintain the capacity to train or perform, this does not seem unfair. If that means taking a vitamin E pill (an anti-oxidant) to combat atmospheric pollution during a marathon race, then, in the absence of further objections, this would

on the face of it seem unproblematic. And, in the case of legitimate medical need, WADA recognizes rule-governed Therapeutic Use Exemption.

3. In the case of baseline performance-enhancing supplements, however, athletes take them for much the same reasons as some athletes take drugs, and they may be similarly willing to risk their safety and their health, and to inadvertently test positive for doping. In addition, despite the fact that supplements are not illegal, and even if they were shown to be safe and not harmful, there is the suspicion in some minds that taking them alters the conditions of the contest in favour of those who can afford them, who are prepared to take them, and who are able to gain benefit from them, and that this constitutes an extra element of unfairness in the contest – an unfair advantage that the supplement-taking athlete is quite prepared to accept for him or herself. In reply, it might be said that supplements are at least available widely and legally, and that any unfairness is no worse than already existing unfairnesses.

However, it is not simply a matter of deciding what kind of supplement/enhancer to take or not to take. We have to consider the practical problem of the efficacy of those supplements available to the athlete, which also raises ethical issues of safety and possible harms, deception, and informed consent.

Supplement efficacy

Guarantee of quality of substance – fraud

The first practical problem for athletes and their advisers is that because supplements are not drugs, they are not subject to the same rigorous testing and monitoring of production procedures, and so we cannot be confident of either their composition or their effects.

Maughan offers a caveat and a conclusion:

> Some supplements contain excessive doses of potentially toxic ingredients, while others do not contain significant amounts of the ingredients listed on the label . . . Many of these supplements confer no performance or health benefit, and some may actually be detrimental to both performance and health when taken in high doses for prolonged periods.
>
> *(2005: 883)*

So our first problem lies in ensuring that the advertised substance is present in the advertised quantity.

Guarantee of quality of substance – contamination

As noted above, and despite recent initiatives by the European Union to tighten up procedures, there are still no binding regulations for supplement manufacture and supply. Our second problem, then, and one that has produced a huge number of positive dope tests, lies in inadequate production procedures resulting in possible contamination with a banned substance. For example, Greg Rusedski tested positive for nandrolone, a performance-enhancing substance on the WADA banned list, but it turned out that it had been present in a contaminated supplement supplied by his professional association, the ATP (the Association of Tennis Professionals) (Bose 2004). In order to be safeguarded, we need to know that the substance is pure, and we need to guarantee non-contamination. This is not a simple matter. After studies suggested that 15–20 per cent of supplements were contaminated, the British Olympic Association issued the following position statement on its website: 'UK athletes are strongly advised to be extremely cautious about the use of supplements . . . strongly advised not to take supplements' (BOA 2009). This warning is backed by the research evidence: 'There is also new evidence that some of the apparently legitimate dietary supplements on sale contain ingredients that do not appear on the label but that are prohibited by the doping regulations' (Maughan 2005: 883). 'A significant proportion of nutritional supplements manufactured worldwide contain non-listed contaminations with anabolic-androgenic steroids, whose ingestion may lead to positive doping test results' (Striegel *et al.* 2005: 723).

We should mention here examples of both accidental and deliberate contamination. In the former, the problem may rest with the raw materials used, or with the manufacturing process, or with inadequate testing, or with unreliable suppliers. The classic example is of a supplement made with the same equipment previously used to make a steroid. The athlete takes what he or she thinks is the supplement, and tests positive for the steroid. In the latter, the motivation of the manufacturer might be to bring about an actual ergogenic effect (so that the product really is seen to 'work'), or to bring about another effect so as to make the athlete think that the substance is actually working (for example, a little added amphetamine to give an immediate buzz).

Efficacy of the substance

However, assuming that we do have the actual 'pure' substance, and not some fraudulent or contaminated version of it, this does not get us out of the woods. One big question still remains: how do we know that a particular supplement is ergogenic (i.e. improves performance), inert, or ergolytic (i.e. reduces performance, or is detrimental to health)? The problem here is our ignorance: there is very limited research evidence one way or another.

For example, take a very commonly used supplement – anti-oxidants. We do not even know much about the many different individual anti-oxidants to be found in various foods, and how they function within their food context. But athletes consume them in tablet form, in isolation from their food context. We do not know whether this might alter their effect, whether to render them inactive, or to produce detrimental side-effects, or to increase their benefits – we just do not know.

Furthermore, typically, neither do we have any account of the possible inter-actions between various supplements being consumed, or, in very many cases, any account at all of the possible interactions between them and any nutrients or drugs also being consumed. For example, many people trying to reduce their cholesterol levels are also dieting to lose weight, and might eat grapefruit. However, it has recently been discovered that grapefruit should not be eaten when taking cholesterol-reducing drugs, because it interferes with a liver enzyme.

Our levels of ignorance ensure that many decisions about what to eat or use for the best are taken on very inadequate empirical grounds – partly because our knowledge is limited at the macro-biochemical level; and partly because we know so little about *ourselves* and our individual, particular microbiological responses. We are each different, and our bodies respond differentially, as anyone will know who has had to diet seriously – often it is a matter of finding what will work for *oneself*. This means that many of us are conducting physiological experiments on a population of one: ourselves.

So sometimes recommendations regarding supplements are made without adequate knowledge or evidence of efficacy, sometimes in response to advertisements or anecdotal recommendations, sometimes because a particular substance is currently fashionable, and sometimes in the spirit of 'if it does them no good, at least it will do them no harm'.

From the above discussion, we can distil some recommendations that we think will be useful for the coach's deliberations and decision-making.

Issues for the coach

Empirical issues that a coach should consider in relation to supplements include the following:

*   What is the scientific or clinical evidence?
*   What are the specific and non-specific effects?
*   What is the evidence on *this* population? (Some experiments on dope and supplements have been conducted on non-athletes, or on non-elite athletes, which compromises the validity of the results for the population relevant to the coach.)
*   What is the effect on *this individual* athlete?
*   Do we know enough about levels? (Can one overdose on them?)
*   Do we know enough about combinations?
*   Is there a placebo effect? (And does this raise issues of deception?)
*   Is anyone looking at the nocebo effect? (i.e. when one feels worse having taken it).

Ethical issues that coaches should consider include the following: exploitation, fraud, consent, health, safety and athlete protection, for example:

- awareness of exploiting and fuelling an athlete's insecurity, desire to win, dependency on the coach, etc.;
- ensuring they are knowledgeable and well-informed in matters upon which they offer advice;
- supporting governing bodies in devising systems for safe supplements;
- ensuring that athletes are able to give their fully informed consent;
- taking responsibility for advising athletes on risk avoidance.

Butcher (2004) notes the duties of all involved to reduce or minimize the risks faced by athletes, and the 'tangled responsibility' that results in ethical requirements of all stakeholders, as follows:

- *The supplement industry* bears responsibility for consistently good manufacturing processes and quality control. It should also ensure honesty in description, giving reliable information (accurate labelling), and making claims to efficacy only when supported by evidence.
- *Sport scientists* should avoid prejudicial relations with the industry in order to preserve their objective status. Collusion with sponsors and apparent endorsement of products bring risks of bias.
- *Governments* must consider the dangers of an unregulated supplement industry, but also the needs of athletes subject to government-mandated doping controls.
- *Sports authorities* should be looking for a coordinated system for safe supplements.
- *Athletes* should ensure that they are knowledgeable and aware of the issues, and that they obtain products from reliable sources. Elite athletes (or those with adequate resources) might even test their own supplements.

Training methods

While doping is widely seen an ethically problematic form of performance enhancement, and certain forms of supplementation also attract a certain suspicion, training is usually seen as something unproblematic – simply as a necessary part of preparation. We see it as normal that the athlete must submit him or herself to a training regime, which is something to be undertaken by (even endured by) the athlete for his or her own good. However, training is also a form of performance enhancement.

If training were something decided upon and designed by the athlete for his or her own purposes, there could be little ethical complaint. The main problem here lies in the prescription of a training programme by one person for another, which raises issues of parentalism, especially when there are dangers and risks of the harms of over-training, or failure to treat the athlete as autonomous (of which more in a moment), or otherwise to respect the athlete's humanity.

Issues to do with training methods perhaps arise most starkly in the treatment of children, but of course they are also present with older athletes. The dangers of over-training and inappropriate methods have long been recognized, as have the duties of the coach to be knowledgeable and well informed, to take care over the appropriate design of training sessions and schedules, and to monitor athletes for signs of weariness and distress.

The possible adverse effects of intensive training include:

- 'external force' injuries (rugby tackle; falling from apparatus, etc.);
- overuse injuries (recurring stress to joints);
- impaired growth (skeletal; delayed menarche);
- psychological issues (prolonged stress or anxiety; influence of over-zealous or intrusive coach or parents; effect of over-training on educational attainment or social development; increase in aggressive behaviour outside of sport, etc.);
- burn-out, drop-out, retirement (cf. Rowley 1992: 4).

However, the coach's responsibilities extend beyond harm avoidance, and include responsibilities to the athlete for his or her development, both in the sporting sense and in the wider sense of leading the person towards maturity – if we are thinking at all in an 'athlete-centred' way (e.g. Kidman 2005).

This section will look at issues to do with the control of the coach over training and over other, wider aspects of the coach–athlete relationship, illustrating the ethical dangers of dominance in general by focusing on the clear example of the child athlete. It tries to show how our interest in developing an ethical understanding of sport and coaching coheres with an account of the child (or the athlete) as a developing moral agent. It further tries to show what is wrong with parentalism in the coaching relationship more generally, and how it may lead to abuse.

Parentalism

Schrag's (1977) account of parentalism, centred on the notion of the child, begins with the political notion of freedom. If we see human freedom as an inviolable right, how do we justify parentalism, which is defined as the coercion of people in their own interest? In a just society, parentalism would be virtually absent – but in our society we accept parentalism over children, while rejecting it for adults. So on what criterion do we make the adult/child distinction? Schrag rejects linguistic develop-ment, reproductive capacity, rational decision-making and maturity as candidates, and argues that there is no clear distinction to be made.

Instead of insisting on such a distinction, we might adopt a utilitarian stance, as follows. If left to their own devices, children are unlikely to find their own happiness. So they must submit to the parentalistic rule of others who are more likely to choose wisely. However, if we are identifying individuals who are unlikely to choose wisely, this group will include some adults, too. So the utilitarian procedure does not permit a sharp distinction between child and adult. Rather, development from one to the other is gradual, and varies across individuals. So the problem here is that it is very difficult to identify a precise point – say, the age of 16 – across the population (or even within the career of an individual) where more wise than unwise choices are likely to be made.

So, the danger of such a utilitarian stance is that it would undermine the cultural pattern that protects the freedom of adults against parentalistic encroachment – and this pattern requires the support of some view that insists on the idea of a firm boundary between the two stages, even if it is difficult to specify its basis.

One conclusion we may take from the above speculations is that parentalism is not always wrong. Sometimes it is necessary for some people (and we assume especially and mostly for young children) to be helped, advised, and led towards what will be in their best interests. But with maturation, people need such influence less and less, so that parentalism becomes gradually redundant.

Another possible conclusion is that children should be treated as different, and as requiring special support and consideration. However, since there is no clear division between childhood and adulthood, a special responsibility is imposed upon us not to assume that all children share (or lack) common capacities; but to monitor for (and to treat individuals according to) their emerging capacities.

Among these capacities is an emerging autonomy – the capacity gradually to assume full responsibility for one's choices and actions. Such a capacity is central to the development of the individual as a moral agent, and is acknowledged in Article 5 of the UN Convention on the Rights of the Child 1989 (see David 2005, Chapter 3) as the basis for the recognition of children as fully fledged subjects of rights, and as important for the overarching aim of 'progressive empowerment'.

Among our other responsibilities towards children, then, is a special responsibility to be child-centred, in these two senses: first, to notice, respond to and nurture their emerging capacities; and second, to do so in ways that maximize their future capacities for autonomous and open-ended development. If this is 'child-centredness', then we would also argue for 'athlete-centredness' in the coaching relationship, for both children and adults.

That is to say, coaches have a special responsibility to notice, respond to and nurture their athletes' emerging capacities; and to do so in ways that maximize their future capacities for autonomous and open-ended development.

Similarly, in arguing that some children participating in the world of high-performance sport are being harmed, and that their futures are being foreclosed, Tymowski (2002: 6) proposes that

> [E]lite sport children require a form of paternalism [*sic*] that protects their interests while at the same time is autonomy-respectful. This is actualized by a bifurcated rights system, which works towards securing non-harmful sports practices and preventing the premature foreclosure of life opportunities for elite child athletes post-sport.

The same applies to adult athletes. While the responsibilities of the coach to promote development, to avoid harm and to provide benefits are starkly revealed in the case of children, the arguments alerting us to both the dangers and the opportunities of parentalism apply with even greater force in the case of adult athletes.

Coach domination and athletes' rights

All sport (including children's sport) is organized and controlled by adults in powerful positions vis-à-vis the athletes, which creates conditions under which domination and exploitation may thrive. This is especially true given the level of trust accorded to adults by children (see McNamee 1998). There are obvious moral dangers here, since adult power over children is expressed in many ways, via two assumptions that are in tension:

- the assumption that children are mini-adults – since some child athletes compete at very high levels, expectations may be held that children should be able to handle certain situations and emotions in the ways that adults do;
- the assumption that children are unable to take decisions for themselves – as soon as adults get involved, they tend to exert undue influence or to take over completely.

So, even where the coach has good intentions towards the athlete's improvement, it is easy for a parentalist concern for the athlete to develop in ways that undermine his or her level of maturation, or fail to respect his or her emerging autonomy. We may sometimes observe some of the following aspects of domination and exploitation in relationships between coaches and both children and adult athletes:

- the 'achievement by proxy' syndrome, in which athletes become the vehicles of the coach's ambition (Tymowski 2002, 3.5.2.3, quoting Tofler *et al.* 1998);
- domination over training, using pain and training as punishment;
- domination over the body (food, nutrition regime enforcement, weight, shape, etc.);
- domination over lifestyle (dress code, parties, hairstyle, friendships, etc.);
- invasion of privacy (control of sleep, sex life, relationships, etc.).

The language of rights

Given these concerns, it is important that athletes' rights are established and implemented. Our previous analysis of the concept of 'child' generates a set of rights, some of which are shared with adults, but some of which are specific to children. One of the earliest statements is the Bill of Rights for Young Athletes proposed by Martens and Seefeldt (1979), which suggests the following rights:

- right to participate in sports;
- right to participate at a level commensurate with each child's maturity and ability;

- right to have qualified adult leadership;
- right to play as a child and not as an adult;
- right of children to share in the leadership and decision-making of their sport participation;
- right to participate in safe and healthy environments;
- right to proper preparation for participation in sports;
- right to an equal opportunity to strive for success;
- right to be treated with dignity;
- right to have fun in sports.

In the case of adult athletes, it is over twenty years since Bruce Kidd (1979) was suggesting athletes' unions to fight for athletes' rights. His arguments, very similar to the ones employed above in the case of children, spring from the belief that the opportunity for self-development in high-performance sport is a basic human right.

Some have criticized such statements, which utilize the language of athletes' rights, because they are often presented without justification as a set of claims or demands. However, it is also possible to express our concerns through the language of welfare, emphasizing the duties and responsibilities of coaches. Two primary duties owed to others are those of non-maleficence ('do no harm') and benevolence ('do what benefits'), and we can apply those to coaching as follows.

The athlete's welfare – non-maleficence

The dangers of sport – things we should seek to avoid?

- physiological stress or damage;
- overtraining as a risk to health, well-being and the development of sporting potential;
- nutritional problems, food supplements, drug misuse;
- psychological impact – pressure, stress, burn-out;
- over-specialization on sport to the detriment of other aspects of life;
- over-specialization on one sport;
- lifestyle requirements – the denial of childhood and the oppression of the adult.

The athlete's welfare – benevolence

The benefits of sport – things we should seek to provide?

- satisfaction in participation and achievement;
- self-esteem from being and being seen as good at sport;
- confidence in facing challenges and in risk-taking;
- peer acceptance and peer relationships;
- bodily well-being;
- personal identity and role definition.

Obviously, we are now squarely in territory which can be described as political, as well as ethical, and this requires that coaches examine their own motivations, engagements and commitments.

Conclusion

The astute reader will have noticed that, in the foregoing, it has been impossible to discuss issues of performance enhancement without presupposing (or taking an overt stance upon) wider considerations. But, in this, we are not alone – every coach is in the same position. There is no escape from ethical and political thinking – no escape from devising a coaching 'philosophy'.

For our part, we should confess to a central commitment to a 'humanistic' stance on these matters, which means at least an 'athlete-centred' approach to the coach–athlete relationship and a non-instrumental approach to the values of sport.

An *athlete-centred approach* springs from a belief (with Kidd 1979) that the opportunity for self-development in high-performance sport is a basic human right (see also David 2005; Kidman 2005). Over many years, Bruce Kidd has developed a view of the role of the sports coach as one that promotes the humanizing of sport and de-emphasizes the one-dimensional and instrumental aim of producing winners. This involves seeing the athlete in his or her fullness and complexity as a human being, first and foremost.

The coach is not a value-neutral agent who simply organizes athletes' sporting activities. He or she is, just like the rest of us, 'situated' – inhabiting their own social context and following their own objectives, one of which is to help the athlete to improve and enhance his or her performance.

Obviously, self-reflection is necessary to identify the values underlying the coaching process (see Lyle 2002). For this, coaches have to clarify their personal objectives as well as objectives for their athletes' participation. Coaches may seek to earn a living, to gain public recognition, to have social contact, to have fun, to travel or simply to be in charge. It is not a problem that coaches should have their own objectives, as this is what usually keeps them in the work, but they should make clear what these objectives are. Only then can coaches distinguish between their own interest and the interests of the athlete, so as to be able to ensure that they do not impose their interests on the athlete.

Second, the self-reflection of the coach is also necessary so that athletes might also clarify what they seek for themselves, so that both parties can situate themselves within the relationship. For any particular objective held by one of them might be complementary to, or inapplicable to, or contrary to an objective held by the other. Clarification, and the resolution of conflicting objectives, would seem essential to a healthy coach–athlete relationship – one that promotes mutual objective-seeking and minimizes exploitation, domination and excessive control, and that seeks a coherent, productive and mutually satisfying way of coaching.

Making the coach's and athletes' objectives clear is a prerequisite for developing any coaching 'philosophy' (Kretchmar 2005), which is to *coherently* and *consistently* guide future activities. 'A philosophy provides boundaries within which the coach–athlete relationship can be located' (Cassidy *et al.* 2008: 55). It is one way of setting the limits of coaching, so that no one feels oppressed or abused during the training and coaching process, and so that it actually assists the athlete. This is necessary especially when coaching has the potential to dominate and harm (Kidman and Hanrahan 2004).

A *non-instrumental approach to the values of sport* emphasizes the intrinsic values that are at the heart and soul of each sport. We describe the benefits of sport in both intrinsic and extrinsic ways. We emphasize the internal satisfactions and intrinsic values of the activity as well as the many benefits that participation and success may bring. However, there are many ways in which athletes' participation in sport may be used instrumentally in the interests of others. We have already noticed the phenomenon of achievement by proxy, but there are other instrumental motivations that may lead to a contradiction between the athlete's participation and the supposed benefits.

Insofar as coaches owe duties to athletes in respect of their development, coaching should be guided first and foremost by intrinsic values: towards those values that make each particular sport uniquely what it is, not towards extrinsic values that may be achieved in many alternative ways; towards education, not just training (Jones 2006); aiming at development, not exploitation; empowerment, rather than control. Insofar as coaches are educators (and surely they must be, at least in part) they must first of all have in mind the benefits of participation to the athlete, not to others.

References

Ambrose, P.J. (2004) 'Dietary supplements used in sports', *Journal of the American Pharmacological Association*, 44(4): 501–516.

Belli, S. and Vanacore, N. (2005) 'Proportionate mortality of Italian soccer players: is amyotrophic lateral sclerosis an occupational disease?', *European Journal of Epidemiology*, January, 20, 3: 237–242.

Bose, M (2004) 'Don't blame me, says Rusedski', *Daily Telegraph*, 10 Jan. 2004. Available HTTP: http://www.telegraph.co.uk/sport/tennis/atptour/2371000/Dont-blame-me-says-Rusedski.html (accessed 20 April 2010).

British Olympic Association (2009) 'Advice to UK athletes on the use of supplements', Online. Available HTTP: http://www.deafukathletics.org.uk/supps.pdf (accessed 20 April 2010).

Butcher, R. (2004) *Ethical Challenges and Responsibilities in the Production, Regulation, Prohibition and Use of Supplements,* CCES Discussion paper, online. Available HTTP: http://performancetrainingsystems.net/Resources/CCES-EthicalChallengestoSupplements.pdf (accessed 20 April 2010).

Cassidy, T.G., Jones, R.L. and Potrac, P. (2008) *Understanding Sports Coaching*, London: Routledge.

David, P. (2005) *Human Rights in Youth Sport*, London: Routledge.

Hart, S. (2004) 'Rusedski seeks compensation', *Sunday Telegraph*, 11 Jan. web-published at http://www.encyclopedia.com/doc/1P2-8915036.html (accessed 20 April 2010).

Jones, R.L. (2006) *The Sports Coach as Educator*, London: Routledge.

Kidd, B. (1979) 'Athlete's rights, the coach, and the sport psychologist', in P. Klavora and J.V. Daniel (eds) *Coach, Athlete and the Sport Psychologist*, Champaign, IL: Human Kinetics, pp. 25–39.

Kidman, L. (2005) *Athlete-Centred Coaching: Developing Inspired and Inspiring People*, Christchurch, NZ: Innovative Print Communications.

Kidman, L. and Hanrahan, S. (2004) *The Coaching Process: A Practical Guide to Improving Your Effectiveness*, 2nd edn, Palmerston North, NZ: Dunmore Press.

Knight, T. (2004) 'Athletics: WADA warn of long-term THG danger', *Daily Telegraph*, 30 Jan. 2004. Available HTTP: http://www.telegraph.co.uk/sport/othersports/athletics/2372121/Athletics-WADA-warn-of-long-term-THG-danger.html (accessed 20 April 2010).

Kretchmar, R.S. (2005) *Practical Philosophy of Sport and Physical Activity*, Champaign, IL: Human Kinetics.

Lyle, J. (2002) *Sports Coaching Concepts: A Framework for Coaches' Behaviour*, London: Routledge.

Martens, R. and Seefeldt, V. (1979) *Bill of Rights for Young Athletes*. Available HTTP: http://www.educ.msu.edu/ysi/parents/billofrights.htm.

Maughan, R.J. (2005) 'Contamination of dietary supplements and positive drug tests in sport', *Journal of Sports Sciences*, 23(9): 883–889.

McNamee, M. (1998) 'Celebrating trust – virtues and rules in the ethical conduct of sports coaches', in M. McNamee and S.J. Parry (eds) *Ethics and Sport*, London: Routledge.

Rowley, S. (1992) *TOYA – Project Description*, London: The Sports Council.

Schneider, A. (2005) 'Genetic enhancement of athletic performance', in C. Tamburrini and T. Tännsjö (eds) *Genetic Technology and Sport*, London: Routledge.

Schrag, F. (1977) 'The child in the moral order', *Philosophy*, 52(200): 167–177.

Sokolove, M. (2004) 'The shape to come', *Observer Sports Magazine*, 8 Feb.: 50–57.

Striegel, H., Vollkommer, G., Horstmann, T. and Niess, A.M. (2005) 'Contaminated nutritional supplements – legal protection for elite athletes who tested positive', *Journal of Sports Sciences*, 23(7): 723–726.

Tamburrini, T. (2000) 'What's wrong with doping?' in C. Tamburrini and T. Tännsjö (eds) *Values in Sport*, London: Routledge.

Tofler, I.R., Knapp, P.K. and Drell, M.J. (1998) 'The achievement by proxy spectrum in youth sports: historical perspective and clinical approach to pressured and high-achieving children and adolescents', *Child and Adolescent Psychiatric Clinics of North America*, 7(4): 803–820.

Tymowski, G. (2002) 'Rights and wrongs: a philosophical consideration of children's participation in elite sport', unpublished PhD thesis, University of Gloucestershire.

Vanacore, N., Binazzi, A., Bottazzi, M. and Belli, S. (2006) 'Amyotrophic lateral sclerosis in an Italian professional soccer player', *Parkinsonism and Related Disorders*, 12(5): 327–329 (Jun Epub 2006 Feb. 3). Available HTTP: http://www.ncbi.nlm.nih.gov/pubmed/16459125 (accessed 19 November 2009).

WADA (2009a) *World Anti-Doping Code*, online. Available HTTP: http://www.wada-ama.org/en/World-Anti-Doping-Program/Sports-and-Anti-Doping-Organizations/The-Code/ (accessed 19 November 2009).

WADA (2009b) *Prohibited List*, online. Available HTTP: http://www.wada-ama.org/en/World-Anti-Doping-Program/Sports-and-Anti-Doping-Organizations/International-Standards/Prohibited-List/ (accessed 19 November 2009).

Warshaw, A. (1998) 'Football: drugs in Serie A – Italy sinking deeper into scandal', *Independent*, online. Available HTTP: http://www.independent.co.uk/sport/football-drugs-in-serie-a---italy-sinking-deeper-into-scandal-1178042.html (accessed 13 October 1998).

12

ETHICAL ISSUES IN COACHING DANGEROUS SPORTS

Emily Ryall and Steve Olivier

The crew was leery; Carlos and I argued about the change in plans. Yes, Audrey was making a substantial leap in a sport where progress was typically measured in one- to five-meter increments, and her previous personal best, which set a female record a year earlier in Fort Lauderdale, was 130 meters. And, yes, I was asking her to descend another forty-five meters, a full ten meters beyond the maximum depth recommended even for recreational scuba divers. But she was in a groove, in the zone, and both Audrey and I felt we should capitalize on it. Neither of us thought we were being reckless.

(Ferreras 2004: 7)

In his biography, Pipín Ferreras recounts the world record free diving attempt made by his student and wife, Audrey Mestre, that ends tragically with her death – a death that Ferreras admits he was, in some part, responsible for. Ferreras was Mestre's coach and mentor, and while she freely chose to participate in such a dangerous sport, it was, as he acknowledges, his own relentless competitive spirit that encouraged Audrey time and again to push the limits of human capability.

Introduction

This chapter will deal with the ethical questions surrounding the responsibilities of coaches towards those they coach. In particular, we will attempt to evaluate two competing positions: one that insists that coaches have a fundamental moral duty to protect those in their care from harm, and the other that maintains that a coach's role is simply to best facilitate the desires, no matter how risky or dangerous, of those who have chosen to utilize the coach's expertise.

While we hold that a libertarian[1] position ought to be taken with regard to individual participation in dangerous sports and leisure activities (cf. Olivier 2006), our view depends on the assumption that it is generally a single person that is involved in these activities,[2] that coercion is absent, and that the person is mature and rational. However, when participants are coached and when others are involved (e.g. in team sports), we adopt a slightly more paternalistic stance. In these instances, the presence and participation of others, with the attendant complications regarding consequences, inform our view. Furthermore, we provide a conceptual analysis of the term 'coach' which suggests there is a tacit agreement by the athlete to relinquish aspects of his or her autonomy to the coach.[3]

Before continuing, it is necessary to construct a broad typology that informs our position. It may be that some delineation is required between those activities that have historically been labelled as 'free' or 'extreme' sports (such as surfing, skateboarding, mountain biking, climbing and BASE jumping) where participants generally set their own agendas and challenges and are not subject to formal instruction or coaching, and those potentially dangerous sports that rest on a long-established structure and organization (such as rugby, boxing, martial arts and ice hockey).[4] While we would take a libertarian stance with regard to the former category, including situations where others (e.g. family, and rescue teams) might be affected, such discussion is beyond the scope of this chapter, and has been dealt with elsewhere (Olivier 2006). And even though we acknowledge that the former pursuits are becoming increasingly embedded in 'mainstream' and commercial culture, and that they bear witness to rising organization and commodification, including formal instruction and coaching,[5] we confine ourselves to the latter category, considering the obligations that a coach has towards participants in a slightly more formal setting.

A primary question of this chapter is 'to what extent should coaches allow their athletes to be exposed to risk in sport?' In attempting an answer, we will focus on what 'coaching' means, reflect upon the value of participating in dangerous sports, and consider the duty and obligations that coaches have towards those under their instruction. Subsequently, we will attempt to reach a satisfactory conclusion that allows us to defend a libertarian position despite ceding some ground to paternalists. Prior to doing so, we will attempt to clarify what we mean by risk, and by dangerous sports. Russell (2005) provides an apposite definition of what constitutes a 'dangerous' sport as opposed to 'nondangerous' sport. The former has, at its heart, 'a significant risk of loss of, or serious impairment to, some basic capacity for human functioning' (ibid.: 4). In the latter, risk is peripheral (e.g., pulling a muscle in attempting a tennis shot). What the so-called dangerous sports have in common is that while serious attempts are made to manage the risks (e.g. training, safety equipment), the real possibility of death exists (see Olivier 2006). The distinction between the types of activities is useful when defending the value of participation in dangerous sports, as we later do, but the concept of risk should also be accepted to hold a degree of fluidity and not solely applied as a predetermined label to particular activities. If it is accepted that risk is also dependent on the competence and judgement of an individual, as we will argue, then risk in sport can also be applied to some situations in those sports that Russell labels as 'nondangerous'.

Distinguishing between coaches and instructors

It would seem non-contentious to say that not all sports have 'coaches', for the term is generally applied only to sports that require ongoing management and skill development (although more common than it used to be, it is still relatively rare to hear the term 'climbing coach', though 'climbing instructor' is commonly used). As such, it might be that a distinction ought to be made between the terms 'coach' and 'instructor'. However, most definitions of the terms are synonymous. For instance, the standard definition is to categorize a coach as 'an instructor, or trainer' (*The Collins Pocket English Dictionary* 1981; *The Concise Oxford English Dictionary*, Soanes and Stevenson 2008). In turn, an 'instructor' is generally defined as a 'teacher', and a 'teacher' as someone who 'gives knowledge and insight'. As such, all three, 'coach', 'instructor' and 'teacher', are used interchangeably. To further complicate matters, some terms are culture-specific, and there are even variations within countries. Nevertheless, a subtle distinction can and ought to be made, for our normal usage suggests that a coach is much more involved in the continued performance development of the athlete, whereas an instructor provides the athlete with the fundamental skills and knowledge which the athlete can later perform, hone and improve without the instructor's presence. To illustrate, consider the difference between a swimming coach and a swimming instructor. The latter imparts elementary skills and knowledge which, once acquired, allows an individual to enter the water without risk of drowning, whereas the former holds a more sustained presence in the lives of those they are coaching in order to provide assistance in reaching particular goals (e.g. to improve stroke technique, times, positions in races, or distance covered). Such a distinction would support the direction promoted by organizations such as the National Coaching Foundation, which now emphasize a holistic approach to coaching rather than the traditional and narrow focus upon improvement of psycho-motor skills; the latter emphasis we reserve for the role of 'instructor'.

A distinction may also be found in the style in which information and knowledge are imparted, for while an instructor is generally regarded as using an autocratic approach, coaching encompasses a wider range of methods. The contemporary coach often attempts to manipulate the environment, including an athlete's psychological state, in order to elicit a certain reaction or response, particularly as preparation in facing novel or problem situations. This is in contrast to an instructor, who equips the athlete with the foundational skills and knowledge in order to be able to participate in that activity *qua* that activity. To reiterate, one might say that an instructor provides the elementary skills in order to ensure that that individual is not simply able to participate in that activity, but also to do so safely. Hence, the aim of a swimming instructor is to enable an individual to keep afloat and swim to safety; that of a driving instructor to keep road accidents to a minimum; that of a sky-diving instructor to ensure people can jump from planes and not to their death; and so on. A coach, on the other hand, often works with already competent individuals in that particular sport to improve performance further, for example performing complex skydiving manoeuvres and formations in team contexts. Whether such a conceptual distinction leads to a difference in ethical responsibilities between the two is a question that emerges from such discussion, and one which will be dealt with throughout this chapter.

The value of dangerous sport

Prior to any consideration of the role that a coach or instructor plays in enabling participation in dangerous sports, it is necessary to reiterate the value of such activities, for any defence will give weight to the position that we are advocating. Russell (2005: 14) maintains that its value is found in its capacity for self-affirmation in that '[i]t can incorporate a challenge to capacities for judgment and choice that involves all of ourselves – our body, will, emotions, and ingenuity – under conditions of physical duress and danger at the limits of our being'.

In contrast, non-dangerous activities suffer a degree of anaemia. Arguably, participating in dangerous activities is the difference between watching the shadows in Plato's allegory of the cave, and doing the 'real' thing. Admittedly, such a position may be exaggerated, for there is a lot to be said for achievements of a non-dangerous nature, such as writing a novel or bringing up children to be decent and well-rounded citizens, but the raw phenomenological sense one gets from pushing one's body to the limits is valuable in a much more abrupt and immediate way. Nowhere is this more so than in activities which bring one's mortality to the fore; for whereas one's failure to write a great (or even published) novel may lead to loss of esteem, and one's awareness of the chance that one's children may turn into criminals or thugs leads to sadness and frustration, participation in dangerous sports opens more immediate and seemingly serious possibilities. That is not to say that discovering one's children are corrupt or violent is less serious than suffering a broken leg skiing, but rather the boundary between success and failure in the latter is one that appears suddenly and with little opportunity for correction, whereas the former is a much more gradual process of realization. Ultimately, and as Howe (2008: 9) notes in her consideration of value in remote sport, the value in these activities is found in their potential to 'affirm one's existence, and den[y] one's transience and insignificance'. In this, we create a paradox whereby one is both confronting and, at the same time, avoiding one's mortality and fragility. Ultimately, risk in sport is valuable because it amplifies

> the imperative that operates in all sport to concentrate on the moment [and] to effect the crucial connection between awareness and embodiment. Risk sharpens the attention to detail and to one's priorities and values . . . Risk contributes to the clarification of who we are, what we value, and what we are willing to do about it. It is a valuable element in developing a knowledge of one's self.
>
> *(ibid.: 13)*

Yet this is not to say such risk and danger to one's body is the primary motivation for participation, for this would suggest a particular masochism and self-loathing that do not fit into our picture of an athlete. Rather, the point of the activity is its constitutive goal(s): to finish the race, to score a knock-out, to touch the ball over the try line, and so on. The value of such sports is achieving such goals despite the risk to one's body.[6]

Opponents of such a view may concede that dangerous sport provides some opportunity for self-understanding and personal growth, though they may disagree that this outweighs the responsibility one holds towards others and society in general. They even may rightly argue that individuals who choose to put themselves in dangerous situations because they believe it increases their authentic being have made a poor or misguided judgement when they have dependants to care for, or place others (such as rescue teams[7]) in danger as an unintended consequence. And it is here that we are confronted with the question as to the role that the coach plays in all of this; for a coach has a direct effect upon and engagement with the individual who is making such decisions.

The duty of care and other paternalistic responsibilities

The issue here is whether a coach has a duty of care that extends to a paternalistic intervention to prevent an individual's participation in an activity if that coach believes that there is a strong possibility that the athlete may suffer injury or death in the process. If we accept that a coach's role is to 'help [athletes] improve their performance and reach their full potential' (Kent 1997), and that participation in dangerous activities provides an avenue for *self-affirmation*, how are they to balance this against other paternalistic responsibilities which such a role holds? For, in returning to our conceptual discussion, it would not be unusual for those under the supervision of a coach or instructor to be called protégés, a term which is synonymous with 'dependant', 'charge' or 'responsibility', and deriving from the Latin 'to protect'. If we are content to apply the term 'protégé' equally to both those being coached and those under instruction, then it would suggest that, *by definition*, despite any conceptual distinction, both coaches and instructors have a responsibility for those under their guidance.[8] On the other hand, it could be argued that a good coach will recognize the value of the affirming properties of an activity, note the athlete's rational will to engage in the activity, and provide the best risk-managed environment possible. This holds for the so-called 'extreme' and for the more traditional dangerous sports. Such a view would fulfil the paternalistic responsibilities, and thereby properly advance the welfare of the protégé.

Let us hold in mind a variety of hypothetical situations that we will consider throughout this discussion. The first sees an established rugby team severely depleted in numbers for a forthcoming match. To fulfil the fixture they will need to play an adult beginner who has barely been to more than a couple of training sessions and has not been taught all the required elementary skills of the game, particularly those required in contact and collision situations, such as where to place one's head and neck when tackling. However, this novice is willing and enthusiastic to start for the team. The second example sees a young, but adult, cricket player fielding at short leg without a helmet. There is no requirement for a fielder in this position to wear a helmet but most usually choose to do so. The third example sees a fairly inexperienced but gung-ho skier consistently deviate from the line taken by her instructor down the slope, in order to take advantage of the powder and attempt some complex manoeuvres. Let us say that in each of these examples, the coach or instructor holds the belief that the athlete involved does not have the skills and knowledge to deal effectively with situations that are likely to occur, i.e. the rugby player does not have the ability to tackle or be tackled safely, the cricketer does not have the reactions to avoid being hit by a full-blooded hook shot, and the skier does not have the capacity to judge the terrain and complete the necessary turns. The pertinent questions here are: are the examples ethically equivalent, and are the coaches or instructors under any obligation to act in a particular way?

Creed v. Drago: should Rocky have intervened?

However, prior to a detailed discussion of these particular examples and in order to gain a richer understanding of the context surrounding such questions, we will turn to a storyline from *Rocky IV* which sees Apollo Creed come out of retirement to fight the far superior Russian Ivan Drago. Before the fight, Rocky, who is managing/coaching Creed, expresses his unease about Creed's ability and suggests that the fight should be postponed. Creed vehemently disagrees and replies that the fight should go ahead as planned. However, by the end of the first round it is obvious that Creed is completely outclassed and is brutally battered from Drago's power and superior fitness. Assessing the situation, Rocky remonstrates that he wants the fight to end but Creed insists that Rocky is not to throw in the towel. The second round begins and while Rocky is deliberating between Creed's wish to remain in the ring and his own judgement that the situation is becoming unacceptably dangerous, Drago delivers the knock-out blow that proves to be fatal.

This fictional example provides a valuable illustration of the difficulties that a coach faces in balancing an individual's desires with his or her own judgement. Arguably, it was Creed's pride and patriotism (for Creed remonstrates with Rocky that there is a greater anti-Soviet purpose to the fight) that led to his downfall. While Rocky could see that Creed was no match for Drago, he chose to support[9] Creed into the ring and abide by his wishes until the end. The question is whether Rocky had a duty to intervene before it was too late. Should Rocky have insisted the fight be postponed or cancelled? Should he have thrown in the towel as soon as he saw that the fight was lost? For ultimately, Rocky's decision, or lack of one, contributed to Creed's death.

Anderson (2007), in her consideration of the role of physicians in sport, argues that paternalistic intervention *is* required when a situation is deemed (by the medical staff in this case) to be likely to result in significant harm to the individual involved. Anderson's example is also from the boxing ring. This time, the tale is of a boxer who has recently suffered a head injury from a motorcycle accident but still wishes to fight despite the likelihood of death were he to receive another blow to the head. The justification for such intervention is found in a doctor's duty to balance an athlete's wishes against the aims of medicine and the Hippocratic Oath. Anderson does admit, however, that other than withholding treatment, medical staff have little power to intervene in a paternalistic way. This is not the case for a coach, who wields far greater power in allowing or limiting an individual's participation in an event. Anderson would undoubtedly argue that a coach has an equivalent, or even greater, duty to prevent the boxer from fighting (until he has fully recovered, at least); and in Rocky's case, he had an obligation to intervene in Creed's participation.

Mill's libertarianism and dangerous sports

The scenario illustrated by the *Rocky* movie is not uncommon in sport (although the outcome might not often be as serious). Creed's attitude replicates what Coakley (2007) defines as the 'sport ethic', whereby the values found within a sporting culture expect individuals to sacrifice themselves (though only up to a point; of which death is not a part) for the greater good. In Creed's case, he felt the responsibility of the American (and Western) ideology weighing upon him. In other cases, individuals are prepared to suffer from fear of being ostracized or admonished by their group, even if such a fear is a false perception. In the 2009 Six Nations rugby match between Scotland and Wales, the Scottish winger Simon Webster was knocked out in a tackle but after coming to, he continued to play. It was only when the referee spotted him vomiting on the pitch minutes later and ordered that he be substituted, that he left the pitch. The Scottish coaching staff were probably, to a greater or lesser extent, aware of Webster's injury but allowed Webster to continue. Although Webster made a full recovery, a similar case had far more tragic consequences. Australian player Ian Tucker died from head injuries following a match in 1996 after he continued playing despite receiving treatment for concussion earlier in the game. In all these three cases, the injured athlete continued playing despite the coaching and medical teams being aware that they had sustained an injury. Let us assume (although it is not known in Webster's and Tucker's case) that the individuals involved were adamant that they be allowed to continue despite their injuries and suffering. We could therefore say that all three coaches emulated Mill's (1962) libertarian stance. As Mill states:

> [T]he only purpose for which power can be rightfully exercised over any member of a civilized community, against his will, is to prevent harm to others. His own good, either physical or moral is not a sufficient warrant. He cannot be rightfully compelled to do or forbear because it will be better for him to do so, because it will make him happier, because in the opinion of others, to do so would be wise, or even right. These are good reasons for remonstrating with him, or reasoning with him, or persuading him, or entreating him, but not for compelling him or visiting him with any evil in

case he do otherwise . . . Over himself, over his own body and mind, the individual is sovereign.

(1962: 73)

Rocky certainly attempted to remonstrate, reason, persuade and entreat with Creed, but eventually left Creed to make the final decision. It may well be that the coaching teams in both rugby examples did the same to a limited extent, although perhaps they ultimately relied on the advice of their medical team, who would have made an assessment as to the nature of the injuries. Mill would argue that there was nothing more that Rocky *ought to* have done; that Rocky had an obligation *to allow* Creed to continue to participate. We are right to voice our opinions but, according to Mill, the choice must be left for the individual. Yet there are two problems with such a stance. The first is that such a position assumes that one is able to be fully autonomous and free in one's decision-making. The second is that such a position does not allow for a situation whereby individuals (either tacitly or explicitly) transfer their right to autonomy to a coach, on the grounds that those in such positions are able to provide an objective assessment of the situation when that individual may be clouded with the 'red mist' of emotion.

The problem with a libertarian stance is that even taking out of the equation the usual philosophical problems associated with the concept of 'free will', to insist that an individual has absolute autonomy over her decisions is to oversimplify things. It is rarely the case that an individual is able to make a decision without the influence of others, and this is particularly so in the case of team sports, where one's actions directly and materially affect others. Indeed, on this Mill does not disagree; for he says that it is perfectly legitimate to verbalize and persuade others of our own judgements. Yet the distinction between entreating someone to act in a particular way (which Mill accepts) and compelling them (which Mill rejects) is difficult to clearly establish. Let us return to one of our initial examples to illustrate: although the novice rugby player wants to play rugby, she may well not yet feel confident in actually doing so. Yet she is also aware that the team is short of players and her team-mates will appreciate having her on the pitch even if she is unable to play to their standards. Other people with an interest in the sport tell her that being thrown in at the deep end is one of the best ways of learning about the game. Furthermore, likely social acceptance from an already-bonded sub-cultural group might act as a powerful motivating factor in persuading her to play. Despite all of these influences, a libertarian would argue that the player is able to make an autonomous decision. Yet this clearly is not the same type of autonomous decision a lone individual makes about whether they watch the tennis or the football on television that evening. In the case of the novice player, it could be argued that a degree of coercion or sanction (e.g. not being selected again) might be present, which is not present in deciding which television programme to watch. This is the case even if the coercion to play is not explicit but merely perceived. The problem for Mill is that such a conception of autonomy requires both that an individual is strong-willed and confident enough to make rational decisions despite the rhetoric of others, and that others who attempt to remonstrate, cajole and persuade do so in a reasonable and decent way.

The second problem is the one that is more pertinent for this chapter. Vallentyne (2009) states that ownership rights, that is, the right one has to do as one wishes with something (of which an individual is a *self-owner*), consist of five aspects: (1) sole control over its use; (2) compensation if it is used by another without permission; (3) rights to enforcement or restraint if the latter are violated; (4) capacity to transfer ownership to others; and (5) immunity to non-consensual loss of ownership.

Transferring autonomy to the coach

It is the transference of ownership that seems most interesting in considering the role of the coach. Could it be argued that when an individual agrees to be coached or instructed, she is acquiescing to the transfer of ownership of her 'self'? When an individual presents herself to a coach, she does so with the understanding that the coach has something to offer, i.e. knowledge and expertise. Presumably this knowledge and expertise extends to advice about whether to participate or not, or whether certain aspects of a sport are beyond the potential participant's current safe limits. In return, does the athlete agree to relinquish her autonomy? Such agreement might be seen to be made with the recognition that in allowing the coach to make decisions on her behalf, she will be more likely to achieve what she desires, namely *self-affirmation*.

One area where this transference of autonomy could perhaps be most useful is in the assessment of risk. An accurate assessment allows for a judgement to be made as to whether one is able to deal with that risk. Could we argue that in recognizing the position of an individual as being one's coach, the athlete is voluntarily transferring the assessment of her capabilities to that coach? Yet this appears to take Mill's position too far, for he again reiterates:

> [N]either one person, nor any number of persons, is warranted in saying to another human creature of ripe years, that he shall not do with his life for his own benefit what he chooses to do . . . Considerations to aid his judgment, exhortations to strengthen his will, may be offered to him, even obtruded on him, by others: but he himself is the final judge.
>
> *(Mill 1962: 133)*

So when we ask, 'What is the role of a coach in situations whereby a player has over-assessed his ability to deal with risk?', a libertarian would assent to that player's wish regardless of the consequences. If we consider the second of our cases, which sees a confident but novice cricketer volunteer to field at short leg without a helmet, the most a coach would be able to do (according to Mill) is to remonstrate, persuade or cajole the player to make an alternative choice (to wear a helmet). It may be that there are alternative measures the coach could take in overcoming this problem. The coach may argue on the grounds of a tactical decision that the individual would be better positioned elsewhere, or that someone else is more skilled to take a catch and thus positively affect the outcome of the game. But this only works in a competitive situation whereby a coach can make strategic decisions to optimize a team's end (i.e. to win the game). In non-game-related or non-competitive situations, a coach or instructor cannot fall back on this strategy. In the case of the wayward skier, if an instructor is uneasy with her athlete's assessment of ability and perception of risk, the choices are more limited. Either the instructor continues with the lesson, doing her best to equip the individual with the skills required to carry out the moves she attempts but also allowing the athlete to put herself at what the coach believes to be 'unnecessary' risk,[10] or the instructor refuses to continue with the instruction unless the individual agrees to yield to her will.

Nevertheless, it is important to highlight Mill's reasoning for his conclusion. In this, he argues that '[a]ll errors which he is likely to commit against advice and warning are far outweighed by the evil of allowing others to constrain him to what they deem his good' (ibid.: 133). This suggests that it is better, for the greater good, to allow individuals to take risks. It is this acceptance of risk that leads us to a position of self-affirmation. In a similar vein, Breivik (2007) maintains that developing a culture of risk acceptance, as opposed to risk avoidance, achieves the balance desired between a safe society and a good life. He states: 'One should not only accept, but even seek, risks when the odds are good enough, mastery is possible and the total expected outcome is positive' (Breivik 2007: 12).

It is Breivik's caveats that one should note here: *when the odds are good enough, mastery is possible, and the outcome is positive.* Who is better placed to enable such outcomes than a coach, instructor or teacher? If an individual seeks out a person who they believe is able to impart expertise and allow them to master skills, then upon agreement of such a role, the coach takes on the responsibility to equip these protégés with the tools to be able to negotiate dangerous or risky situations safely. Few people who participate in dangerous sports do so with a desire for death; rather, it is the taste of outwitting injury and death that is savoured.

Again, it needs to be reiterated that there is a difference between risky/dangerous sports and sports that contain risks, as Russell (2005) makes clear in his discussion on the issue, and this may have an important effect on our analysis of a coach's role. If we are to take a libertarian stance, then we need to take into account that it is much more likely that those individuals who participate in dangerous sports are aware of, and require, the inherent risks involved in that activity than those who take part in non-dangerous sports. A reasonable and competent adult *knows* that sailing in open water in a force eight wind is hazardous but that is what makes it exciting and exhilarating, whereas the dangers of impalement for an individual practising the javelin are those to be avoided and not pursued. As such, to say that the latter willingly participated in a risky situation when she trips and impales herself is to misrepresent a libertarian stance. As the possibility of such an event is unlikely, and certainly not part of the value of participation, it would be reasonable to say that a javelin coach has a responsibility to ensure that those she is teaching are taught the correct techniques of carrying the javelin as well as to ensure that the practice area is free from any hazards. It is not the will of the individual practising the javelin to covet the risks of participation, and the coach should take this into account. In contrast, the instructor of the sailor who looks at the stormy seas with an eager anticipation has a different role to fulfil.

Dangerous sports, self-affirmation and the sublime

As Ilundain-Agurruza (2007) notes in his exegesis between extreme sports and the Kantian conception of the sublime, the sublime is experienced through precariously balancing on the edge of a (real or metaphorical) precipice in the full knowledge that a slight slip would lead to certain death. It is even more relevant to our consideration of the role the coach plays in all this, when Ilundain-Agurruza goes on to say:

> The goal is to be neither far behind the edge of the precipice nor over it, but right at it. The extreme demands that we get as close to danger as possible while staying right on the edge of safety, barely holding the temptation to take one more step. The antinomy, as an aesthetic principle of artistic appreciation, is not easy to develop. It requires a discriminating sense of taste – different arts placing particular demands – developed through attentive exposure to, and critical reflection on, art works. Likewise, mastering the paradox of danger of the extreme involves abilities that need to be developed to a high degree by means of practice and experience of the requisite skills for the given sport or activity.
>
> *(ibid.: 157)*

Like Breivik, Ilundain-Agurruza also maintains that mastering dangerous situations requires the mastery of skills and abilities. If we are to accept that coaches, by definition, exist in order to improve the skill level of their protégés, and that mastery of dangerous situations requires a greater level of skill and ability, then it appears that the role of the coach is to enable one to confront and prevail over dangerous situations. In this, a coach has a responsibility to equip his or her athletes with the tools to be able to cope effectively with risk and danger in sport, including the skill of recognizing when to back off and when not to initiate the activity.

Here, one might retort that rather than creating a safer environment for the athlete, athletes will desire to push the boundaries of their activity further, hence making it more dangerous. There is evidence that 'risk' athletes do exactly that: go higher, harder and faster, and it has been suggested that there may be an association between the experience of dimensions of flow (the optimal psychological state underpinning peak performance) and the compulsion to engage in an activity (Partington *et al.* 2009). If such an experience occurs at the metaphorical precipice between life and death, then whatever the level of skill and ability with which that individual is equipped, they will forever be positioning themselves on the edge. Yet this edge in real terms becomes more and more precarious; for there is a difference in consequence between making a mistake and falling 2 metres, and slipping and falling 200 metres. Opponents may argue that for this type of athlete at least, an instructor would inadvertently increase the risk involved. In response, we would maintain that these types of athletes do not generally have coaches or instructors. They are individuals who are self-taught and self-sufficient. They have surpassed the level of expertise that any coach can offer. Also, any training that they might receive, and their experience in their sport, actively encourage risk recognition, assessment and mitigation. To argue that a coach inherently increases the risk to an athlete is to misrepresent the reality of the situation involved.

Rather, we ought to consider the usual position of coaches or instructors, in that they provide an individual with the tools to be able to recognize and deal effectively with potentially dangerous situations. So in the case of our novice rugby player who does not have the skills to tackle properly, she is putting herself in a more dangerous situation on the pitch than a player who does have those skills. One might say that it is the role and duty of the coach to provide that player with the appropriate skills. Yet the relevant question must be whether that duty is solely dependent on the consent or request from that individual. If we are to take a libertarian standpoint, then the answer, of course, must be in the affirmative: an individual who does not wish to learn important skills from the coach but who still wishes to participate should be allowed to do so.

Conclusion

In conclusion, then, it appears that a coach does have a role to play but it is one that must be directed by the individual under instruction. The coach ought not to coerce the athlete into participating in risky situations when she does not wish to, but should allow an individual to takes risks even if the coach feels apprehensive as to her ability to cope with such risks. But a coach has a further responsibility in providing her athletes with the best tools, skills and knowledge available to be able to accurately assess risk and to be able to deal with dangerous situations, thus providing opportunities for *self-affirmation*. This may not be the conception of the coach with which we are most familiar, but it is the one to which all coaches should aspire if they are to take seriously the autonomy of others and the value of participating in dangerous sport.

As an epilogue, let us return to our cases and examples to provide some moral direction. Despite the tragic consequences, Rocky ought to be commended for allowing his friend and athlete, Apollo Creed, to enter the ring despite his reservations as he recognized the autonomy of Creed's decision and the possibility for self-affirmation. In the case of the novice rugby player, the coach has a primary obligation to ensure that the player is provided with the foundational skills to experience a game of rugby as a valuable and self-affirming experience; and arguably such an experience would require the possession of contact skills since they are a constitutive aspect of the game. However, if these skills were not apparent and the novice genuinely (and this is something that the coach must judge) desired to participate in a game, the coach ought to acquiesce. This is also the case for the enthusiastic but reckless cricket player and the wayward skier. The coach may wish to remonstrate, cajole, entreat and persuade those under instruction to make an alternative choice, but if the individual holds to the original decision, the coach ought to work in a way that allows for the best possible realization of the individual's desired outcome. With regard to the example given at the outset in the account of Audrey Mestre's attempt to break the world free diving record, arguably Ferreras, her coach and husband, embodied Mill's conception of the libertarian. It may be conceded that, with hindsight, Ferreras was reckless in persuading Audrey to dive to that depth, but he did so from the belief that she had the capability of achieving it. Audrey, too, wanted to push herself to the limits, not because she particularly desired to break records but simply because she found it such an incredibly self-affirming experience.[11] Though Audrey paid the ultimate price for her choice, Ferreras was right in allowing her to do so. The autonomy of the athlete and the value she sees in her participation in dangerous sports ought to be respected and remain paramount.

Notes

1 In this we ascribe to Mill's (1962) conception of the term, in that an individual's autonomy is the primary value and that regardless of the judgement of others as to the appropriateness or sagacity of an individual's decision, they have no moral authority to prevent it.
2 To keep the issues to the minimum, the remit of this chapter is the consideration of adult athletes and not those under 18 years of age. In all examples given, it is assumed that the individuals involved are rational adults.
3 It is this conceptual analysis of the term 'coach', rather than any other individual involved who would not be labelled as a 'coach', that leads us to acknowledge some degree of paternalism. This would therefore rule out the adoption of a paternalistic stance by those who, for example, provide the financial and practical support that enables an individual to engage in dangerous sporting and leisure activity.
4 These lists are indicative rather than exhaustive.
5 See later for a distinction between coaching and instruction.
6 One also needs to be careful not to over-glamorize the concept of *self-affirmation* in the way in which Russell arguably does with a consideration of the term from the perspective of romantic militarism. Such a 'gung-ho' and non-self-reflective conception is not one to be particularly admired or valued. In contrast, the type of *self-affirmation* that perhaps holds real worth is the existential kind, even if this is only pre-consciously acknowledged by the individual involved.
7 See earlier point about the scope of this chapter.
8 There may be differences in the degree to which they are responsible (which *is* dependent upon the conceptual distinction) but these will come to light in our subsequent discussion.
9 Or at least chose not to paternalistically intervene.
10 As commented upon later in the text, there is inherent risk in all activity; when walking along a street there is the risk of being mown down by a speeding car that has mounted the pavement, but this risk is beyond the control and bounds of what one would wish to call a reasonably lived life. In contrast, running blindly across a busy eight-lane motorway when there is a pedestrian walkway above is not a necessary part of living a reasonable life. There will undoubtedly be some disagreement where the distinction lies between a valuable (self-affirming) experience that minimizes unnecessary risk and a reckless and non-valuable experience where unnecessary risk is taken, but the point being made is to

acknowledge the coach's or instructor's judgement in determining where inherent risk
ends and unnecessary risk begins.
11 If, of course, we are to accept Ferreras's portrayal of Audrey Mestre and his account of
the events involved, since it is in his biography that these events are recalled.

References

Anderson, L. (2007) 'Doctoring risk: responding to risk taking in athletes', *Sport, Ethics and Philosophy*, 1(2): 119–134.
Breivik, G. (2007) 'The quest for excitement and the safe society', in M. McNamee (ed.) *Philosophy, Risk and Adventure Sports*, London: Routledge.
Coakley, J. (2007) *Sport in Society*, 9th edn, London: McGraw-Hill.
Collins Pocket English Dictionary (1981) Glasgow: William Collins.
Ferreras, P. (2004) *The Dive: A Story of Love and Obsession*, London: HarperCollins.
Howe, L. (2008) 'Remote sport: risk and self-knowledge in wilder places', *Journal of the Philosophy of Sport*, 35(1):1–16.
Ilundain-Agurruza, J. (2007) 'Kant goes skydiving: understanding the extreme by way of the sublime', in M. McNamee (ed.) *Philosophy, Risk and Adventure Sports*, London: Routledge.
Kent, M. (1997) *Food and Fitness: A Dictionary of Diet and Exercise*, Oxford University Press. Oxford Reference Online. Available HTTP: http://www.oxfordreference.com/views/ENTRY.html?subview=Main&entry=t38.e389 (accessed 15 October 2009).
Mill, J. S. (1962) *Utilitarianism, Liberty, Representative Government*, London: J.M. Dent.
Olivier, S. (2006) 'Moral dilemmas of participation in dangerous leisure activities', *Leisure Studies*, 25(1): 95–109.
Partington, S., Partington, E. and Olivier, S. (2009) 'The dark side of flow: a qualitative study of dependence in big wave surfing', *The Sport Psychologist*, 23: 170–185.
Russell, J. (2005) 'The value of dangerous sport', *Journal of the Philosophy of Sport*, 32(1): 1–19.
Soanes, C. and Stevenson, A. (eds) (2008) *The Concise Oxford English Dictionary*, 12th edn, Oxford University Press. Oxford Reference Online. Available. HTTP: <http://www.oxfordreference.com/views/ENTRY.html?subview=Main&entry=t23.e10754> (accessed 15 October 2009).
Vallentyne, P. (2009) 'Libertarianism', in *Stanford Encyclopaedia of Philosophy*, online. Available HTTP: http://plato.stanford.edu/entries/libertarianism/ (accessed 15 October 2009).

13

A DEFENSE OF EXPATRIATE COACHING IN SPORT

Cesar R. Torres

Introduction

The latest wave of sport globalization has increased and accelerated all sorts of transnational exchanges between institutions and peoples. Coaching is one area in which the transnational character of sport has become evident. This is the case not only at national competition but at the international level as well. Whereas national teams have traditionally been led by coaches of the same nationality, globalized national sport officials have recently been keen on hiring foreign coaches to lead their teams. For example, New Zealander Robbie Deans coaches the Australian men's rugby union team and Italian Fabio Capello coaches England's men's football side. In the 2008 Olympics, Argentine Raúl Lozano, Japanese Masayo Imura, and Frenchmen José Ruiz managed Poland's men's volleyball, China's women's synchronized swimming, and Mali's women's basketball teams, respectively.

The appointment of foreign coaches to lead national teams has generated a great deal of controversy. These coaches have frequently been criticized in both their home and their adopted countries. In the former, coaches are accused of disloyalty, defection and even treason. In the latter, coaches are portrayed as non-representative of national sporting cultures, which makes it difficult for the public to identify with them. Many believe that hiring foreign coaches violates the unwritten principle of international sport which mandates that national teams be led by compatriots. At the center of the controversy is the belief that putting foreign coaches in charge of national teams flies in the face of patriotic duty. For the critics, hiring a foreign coach to train a national team is simply unpatriotic.

In this chapter, I will examine the ethics of coaching a foreign national team.[1] I will argue that it does not constitute a breach of patriotic duty. In doing so, I will critique the extreme patriotism which regards expatriate coaching as unpatriotic. Moreover, I will argue that expatriate coaching promotes a set of desirable values that is likely to enhance international sport competition, foster intercultural interaction, and foster national solidarity. My analysis will be inspired by the writings of Nicholas Dixon, Stephen Nathanson and Martha C. Nussbaum, who argue for an alternative position to extreme patriotism, namely, moderate or sensitive patriotism. The limits and conditions of this kind of patriotism imply moral regard for people from other countries. In a nutshell, moderate or sensitive patriotism will allow me to argue that expatriate coaching is not antipatriotic and has, potentially, many beneficial effects for the coach's home country as well as the adopted one.

Extreme and moderate patriotism in sport

Amor patriae is at the very heart of patriotism. That is, patriotism is characterized by love of *patria* or country, which involves 'identification with it and a special concern for its well-being and that of compatriots' (Primoratz 2008: 206). As such, patriotism is displayed in different realms, including the sporting world. Coaches and players of national teams typically regard themselves as the embodiment of their country's sporting cultures while officials, supporters, and journalists embrace and encourage that sentiment. The former believe they have to defend a characteristic national playing style and the latter demand them to be loyal to it. Coaches, players, officials, supporters, and journalists alike identify with their country and are concerned about the national team's fortune on the playing field. Since these patriots love their country, they all wish their national team to win, and suffer with its sways. In an important sense, national teams are perceived as potent means to both express national identity and become associated with compatriots in the national community.

Despite its seeming innocuousness, patriotism has troubled many morally conscientious people and, therefore, has been seriously scrutinized. This is so because of a widespread interpretation of what patriotism entails. This view was forcefully summarized, and ridiculed, by Bertrand Russell, who considers that patriotism is 'a willingness to kill and be killed for trivial reasons' (1928: 184). Russell's dictum echoes the ideas of Leo Tolstoy, for whom patriotism invariably leads to war.[2] Regardless of whether Russell and Tolstoy overstate the warring tendencies of patriotism, they pointedly underscore the dangers implicit in having a special concern for one's fellow countrymen and women. Stephen Nathanson explains the rationale behind these dangers:

> If one cares only for one's own nation and if – as seems plausible – one's nation could profit from things of value possessed by other nations, then if possible, one's nation should engage in any activities necessary to obtain the desired goods. Since we can suppose that other nations will not voluntarily give up their valued possessions, then warfare becomes the inevitable policy choice for those who can expect victory.
>
> *(1989: 537)*

Even if patriotism does not necessarily result in war, the required commitment to one's country and the special concern owed to one's people may easily develop into an exclusive concern for one's country and its people, enmity toward other countries, and the acceptance of morally questionable practices in the name of one's country's and its people's well-being. This is what lies behind the use of the common phrase 'My country, right or wrong.' For these extreme versions of patriotism, wars included or not, whatever policies hold the country together and advance its interests are worthy of support. To think and act otherwise is simply to be disloyal.

Although it seems generally true, as Nicholas Dixon argues, that 'patriotism in sport will rarely result in wars or any kind of general mistreatment of citizens of the rival nations' (2000a: 74–75), examples of bellicose activities occasioned by sport are not difficult to find. One of the most notable is the so-called 'football war' of 1969 between El Salvador and Honduras. The qualifying games for the 1970 World Cup between the two countries that gave the war its name led to much disorder and violence but did not cause it. They served, though, as catalyst for hostilities related to existing profound disagreements, tensions, and instability, both inside each of the two countries and between them. The war was not over football but extreme patriotism did show its ugly face in those games.[3] This case seems to reflect George Orwell's position that '[a]t the international level, sport is frankly mimic warfare' (1950: 152). Orwell did not think that sport was the cause of international animosity. Yet his belief that its confrontational character facilitates the emergence of undesirable behavior toward one's rivals and their supporters made him fret about extreme patriotism in sport.

While indeed extreme patriotism in sport rarely leads to war or severe conflicts in which, paraphrasing Orwell, only the shooting is lacking, it can generate reprehensible attitudes and behaviors. Sometimes the excesses of patriotic ardor are confined to the playing field, such as when physical violence or verbal abuse occurs between coaches and players of rival countries. Occasionally, those excesses spill over to the crowds which confront either in the stands or in the stadium's immediacies. At other times, by making inappropriate patriotic remarks in the form of chants or slurs against rival countries, the crowds attempt to negatively influence their performance. Yet it is not too uncommon for coaches and officials to encourage and coerce their athletes to engage in morally dubious practices in the name of national prestige and superiority. Consider, for example, the cheating, abusive training techniques, or perilous tactics rationalized in the name of victory for one's country. In many instances, these practices jeopardize the well-being not only of the rival country's athletes but also of one's own, who become instruments of extreme patriotism's mission to ratify national superiority and dominance. The media are oftentimes willing to advance this instrumentality as patriotic while portraying rival countries in a negative light and their athletes as heartless competitors.

What characterizes all these forms of extreme patriotism in sport is either 'a simple lack of moral regard for athletes, coaches and other people from rival countries' or 'a callous disregard of the welfare of our own athletes', and in some cases both at the same time (Dixon 2000a: 75). Critics of patriotism argue that this lack of moral regard for other country's people and even one's own is incompatible with, and in fact renounces, 'such basic moral notions as universal justice and common human solidarity' (Primoratz 2008: 211). It is precisely for this reason that Russell and Tolstoy reject patriotism and call for egalitarian cosmopolitanism, which proposes that duties to humanity take precedence over particular obligations imposed by the love of one's country. For them, much of the antagonism and misunderstanding among countries originates in patriotism. Because many critics, including Orwell, consider that patriotism in sport has similar flaws and damaging consequences, they reject international sport competitions such as the Olympic Games and even advocate their dismantling. Indeed, it was not infrequent during the first seven decades of Olympic competition to read adverse comments on the enterprise and even predictions of its imminent collapse due to the undesirable displays and effects of patriotism.[4] Perhaps ironically, and in spite of Pierre de Coubertin's insistence on its cosmopolitan character, the Olympic Games has been constructed as an arena for the manifestation of patriotic loyalty and superiority.[5]

Some philosophers, uneasy with the choice of an egalitarian cosmopolitanism that excludes love of country and particular obligations to one's compatriots or a patriotism that denies universal moral considerations such as impartiality, equality, justice, and common humanity, have searched for a middle position. For instance, Nathanson (1989, 1993) defends a version of patriotism that allows for love of country and a special concern for one's compatriots while respecting universal moral rules, making it neither exclusive nor uncritical. In doing so, he acknowledges the moral worth of foreigners and recognizes moral constraints to the pursuit of one's country's interests and goals. This moderate patriotism does not imply hostility toward other countries, respects their negative rights, and permits having some concern for their interests, needs, and goals. As Nathanson (1993: 38–39) explains, 'Moderate patriotism, then, is morally superior to extreme patriotism because it is consistent with a recognition of human equality and the universality of basic rights that belong to people simply by virtue of their humanity.'

Martha C. Nussbaum has recently defended a brand of patriotism that also combines patriotism with universal human values. Her sensitive patriotism highlights the crucial role that one's country plays in a meaningful life. As she explains, 'currently, and for the foreseeable future, nations are critical for the promotion of people's well-being and life opportunities' (2008: 82). Nussbaum sees the risk of emptiness of meaning in denying particular attachments that are so dear to people. Nevertheless, she understands love of country within 'the constraints of some strong duties to humanity' and proposes that we 'then ask ourselves how far we are entitled to devote ourselves to the particular people and places whom we love' (ibid.: 80). Her appeal to sensitive patriotism is one that departs from one's particular emotional attachments and 'accepts the constraints of global justice' (ibid.: 80). Nussbaum's sensitive patriotism is, much like Nathanson's, critical, inclusive, respectful of other nations' negative rights, and constrained by universal moral principles. In other words, it is not 'My country, right or wrong' but rather, approval when right and moral criticism and fighting to mend its ways when wrong. That is, the former is morally unacceptable because it does not withdraw support from immoral practices.

Moderate patriotism appears to be morally unobjectionable and as such, as Nathanson notes, it 'is a morally permissible ideal' (1993: 48). In this sense, Nathanson clarifies that his 'defense of patriotism does not imply that anyone ought to be a patriot. That only follows if we assume that one's country is worthy of patriotic duty' (ibid.: 48). Although Nussbaum is not explicit about it, one can speculate, considering her emphasis on the role of nations as collective expressions of human autonomy and the sentiments that bind citizens together, that she may tend to see this kind of patriotism as required. Although interesting in itself, the issue of whether moderate patriotism is obligatory surpasses the purposes of this chapter. What is relevant here is that this kind of patriotism, which by respecting the negative rights of the people of all countries prevents *prima facie* harming them, is morally permissible.

Even if only permissible, it is not difficult to find examples of moderate patriotism in sport. Many sportspeople all over the world support their national teams and want to see them win without exhibiting hostility or obnoxiousness toward rival competitors or supporters. Others actively denounce and oppose any kind of cheating or perilous tactics that their own national team may use in order to get an undeserved competitive advantage. What is more, some practices actually protect the welfare of players from rival countries. For instance, the prevalent practice of kicking the ball out of bounds in international football games when a player is presumed injured is much celebrated as an instance of sportspersonship. In fact, abstaining from enacting it, even when one's side could benefit from such abstention, is typically decried around the football community. Some other practices in international football such as pre- and post-game handshakes, as well as the exchange of jerseys at the conclusion of games, symbolize moderate patriotism. All these examples show concern for rivals and a willingness to recognize, and treat, them as equals.

Dixon (2000a: 85) provides a summary of what moderate patriotism can accomplish in sport by way of an example: 'Even partisan fans of their national team are able to recognise and applaud skilful play by foreign opponents, and this too helps even potentially jingoistic supporters to recognise foreign opponents as people who deserve respect and admiration.' If extreme patriotism is regrettable in sport and elsewhere in society, moderate patriotism seems to be not just permissible but also admirable and desirable. Clearly, for many, playing for, identifying with, and favoring their national teams in international sport does involve respecting rivals and, on occasion, assisting them and celebrating their outstanding performances. For them, fair and decent competition trumps the idea of winning at all costs. Moderate patriots in sport see rivals as human beings rather than as anonymous enemies to be conquered. As moderate patriotism indicates, patriotism does not inevitably entail moral disregard for people of other countries. On the contrary, it 'distinguishes between harming outsiders (which it forbids) and, on the other hand, bestowing benefits on our compatriots that we do not extend to outsiders (which it allows)' (Dixon 2000a: 81).

Moderate patriotism has been criticized from two opposing viewpoints: universalism or cosmopolitanism and extreme patriotism. For the former, it is incompatible with universal and impartial justice; for the latter, it is an emasculated or empty version of patriotism. Although space does not allow for a complete discussion of the debate, it is worth noting that proponents of moderate patriotism base their defense against the 'incompatibility argument' on the notion that special or particular duties and allegiances can be aligned with the demands of impartial and universal justice. In this sense, Nathanson argues that 'a morality that is both impartial and universal can recognize legitimate forms of partiality towards people with whom we share special ties' (1993: 76). This is so because he takes universality to mean standards that apply to everyone rather than identical treatment to everyone.[6] In turn, moderate patriots respond to the charge of 'emptiness', emphasizing that while critical and inclusive, they are not neutral in every conflict. If a conflict is legitimate and unavoidable, moderate patriots support their country but such support is not unconditional or automatic and carries a deep sense of regret.[7] As Nussbaum proposes, inspired by the writings of Johann Gottfried Herder, sensitive patriotism 'would breed contempt for aggression against other nations and, equally, for internal hatreds and group animosities' (2008: 84). Proponents of moderate patriotism have convincingly defended their thesis and shown its permissibility and desirability.

Extreme patriotism and expatriate coaching in sport

Most condemnations of expatriate coaching in sport come from advocates of extreme patriotism. In their home countries, some expatriate coaches have had their sense of patriotism questioned. Consider the case of American Mike Bastian, who coached China's women's softball team in the 2008 Olympics. His acceptance of the Chinese offer did not sit well with the American softball community. For instance, using undeniably extreme patriotic jargon, Ronnie Isham, Director of National Teams for USA Softball, contended in reference to Bastian that:

> It's a lot lower-level than going to war. . . . But when you're trying to develop a program and a team and an individual to be an elite athlete and contend for a gold medal, and you have somebody who's your neighbor working with a foreign country to do the same thing, then yes, it is somewhat of a betrayal.
> *(Heller 2008)*

Although Bastian claims that he was just 'helping softball grow and develop in China' and that he is 'a proud American, I love America, I love USA Softball' (ibid.), he acknowledges being blacklisted, and being called a traitor and an enemy by his compatriots. Similar to Bastian's experience is that of Japanese Masayo Imura, who coached China's women's synchronized swimming team to a bronze medal in the 2008 Olympics, the country's first medal in the sport in Olympic competition. Imura, a pioneer of her sport, 'was labeled a traitor by many Japanese colleagues and fans when she took the China job' (ibid.). This type of accusation is not unfamiliar to American Joe Soares, who, after an illustrious playing career with his country's wheelchair rugby team, moved on to coach Canada's and Great Britain's national squads. Mark Zupan, a current star of the American team, has asked of Soares' coaching career, 'How's it feel to betray your country?' (*Murderball* 2005).

Extreme patriots consider coaches who cross borders treasonous. Arguably this is so because, for these critics, expatriate coaches not only fail to stand by their countries but actually assist rival countries. This is exemplified by Bastian's recollection of an American softball player's forthright reaction to having him in the opposite dugout. She explained, 'You gotta understand that you're the enemy now, and the way I play the game is that I hate my enemy' (Heller 2008). The construction of rivals as enemies and the concomitant feeling of hate toward them represented in this comment demonstrate moral insensitivity and go well beyond patriotic feelings of love of country and goodwill toward fellow compatriots. It is important, nevertheless, to address the extreme patriots' charge that expatriate coaching constitutes treason and is, thus, unpatriotic.

By claiming that expatriate coaches betray their country and become traitors, extreme patriots imply, at least, that these coaches have negative feelings toward their native countries and, at worst, that they are willingly trying to see their native countries harmed. These are quite the sentiments of a country's enemies. In political and judicial circles, treason is typically associated with the attempt to subvert the established order in one's state or impair its well-being. That is, it involves the intention to endanger one's own country's national security. For example, *Black's Law Dictionary* defines treason as the 'offense of attempting by overt acts to overthrow the government of the state to which the offenders owes allegiance; or of betraying the state into the hands of a foreign power (1979: 1345; see also Wild 2006: 259). Unsurprisingly, in ancient times, Cicero commented that 'No wise man ever felt that a traitor ought to be trusted' (1966a: 163) and that if a state and its body politics were to be preserved and prosper, it is 'against evils from within, against plots devised at home [that we must be on our guard]' (1966b: 487).

In light of what treason involves, it is difficult to see how expatriate coaching typifies it. Expatriate coaches train foreign national teams to succeed on the playing field in international competitions and presumably to represent the best of and advance the country's sporting culture. As such, their job does not require negative attitudes toward, or the harming of, their homelands, much less collusion with people from the adopted country to overthrow the governments of their home countries, cause upheaval in them, or wage war against them. Of course, some expatriate coaches might, in theory, be so motivated. However, such potential motivation does not demonstrate that expatriate coaching is inherently treasonous any more than all coaching methods are thought to be impermissible because some are abusive, and conducive to injuries and, in extreme cases, to athletic incapacitation. Agreeing to coach a foreign national team does not automatically convert the expatriate coach into a traitor to his or her originating country, one whose goal is to undermine its body politic. Defending himself against accusations of treason, Deans, the New Zealander who coaches the Australian men's rugby union team, supports this view, arguing that 'treason is when you're putting your nation at threat. This isn't war, it's a game. Lives are not at risk' (Anon. 2008b).

Critics of expatriate coaching may accept that it does not involve treason in the political and judicial senses described above but still contend that it demonstrates disloyalty to the coach's own national sporting culture, its practices, traditions, and history. Following Alasdair MacIntyre's communitarian conception of patriotism (1995), critics may assert that as a member of that culture, one's identity is bound up with it and, as a result, should respect it.

There are at least three responses to this argument. First, coaching a foreign national team and remaining loyal to one's own national sporting culture seem to be compatible. In fact, expatriate coaches typically honor that culture by advancing its best practices and traditions in their adopted countries. Expatriate coaches do not renounce their identities at the airport and are not expected to do so. It is because of who they are and where they come from that they are, in fact, esteemed and hired. Coaching a foreign national team does not necessarily involve this sense of disloyalty. Second, the fact that a coach owes her sporting identity to her country's sporting culture does not attach her to that culture for life. She may decide to part ways with it and allow her sporting identity to evolve in a different direction. Human identities are not rigid. Third, critics of expatriate coaching are at risk of demanding loyalty to the coach's native sporting culture simply because it is hers. This would be uncritical and exclusive, traits of extreme patriotism found unbefitting above. Even MacIntyre advocates this kind of partiality only for situations in which one's country's survival and 'large interests' are at stake (1995). Applied to the issue at hand, how could expatriate coaching jeopardize the survival and 'large interests' of a coach's native sporting culture? The question is especially valid because lending countries' sporting cultures tend to be more vibrant and successful than receiving ones. An expatriate coach's contribution to the latter does not amount to an equivalent subtraction from the former. Expatriate coaching is not a zero-sum situation; indeed, lending countries do not give up having coaches for their national teams when one of their own agrees to coach a foreign national team. Furthermore, not only do they continue having coaches, but most of the time they appoint the ones thought to be best qualified for the job.

Yet critics of expatriate coaching may agree to all this but still contend that expatriate coaching is disloyal in that it fails to give preference not just to an abstract notion of a coach's national sporting culture, but to the actual athletes and supporters of one's own country. This would be the case only if a coach refused an offer to work for her own national team and chose to coach a rival nation. I am afraid that this is not too often the case; normally, coaches who have been offered a position to coach their national teams are more than willing to do so. If a coach is not extended an offer by her own country but accepts one from a rival country, there is no favoritism and, therefore, no disloyalty involved. Logically, there must be at least two coaching offers, one from one's country and a second from another country, in order to favor one over the other. However, it is appropriate to highlight that not all cases in which a coach rejects an offer to coach her home national team are morally problematic, whether an offer by a rival nation is tendered at the same time or not. That evaluation would depend on such factors as whether her home's government is a democracy or a dictatorship, whether it is involved in a war or obstructs political adversaries' activities, or whether the national sport governing body treats its affiliates and athletes with decency and demonstrates progressive and inclusive policies. Finally, it should be pointed out that patriotism is permissible and desirable but not mandatory. In that sense, refusing to coach one's own national team or accepting an offer to coach that of another country does not inevitably fail the athletes and supporters from the coach's home country.

Another objection raised by critics of expatriate coaching relates to the welfare of the coach's own sporting community. The objection is that an eventual victory by the national team led by the expatriate coach over her home country's national team would be harmful to the latter. This objection has no force. Dixon argues that 'athletes' attempts to win and fans' preferences for their own country's athletes in international sporting contests inflict no significant harm on people in other countries' (2000a: 82). It does not seem to matter whether the coach of a national team is an expatriate or a compatriot. A loss, in itself, does not inflict significant harm on the losing side and its supporters. While, as Dixon asserts, athletic losses result mainly in disappointment, they do not result in harm to the body politic and basic human capacities (2000b). In a Lockean sense, athletic losses bring no injury to 'the material reality of the body and where the object is freedom' (Scarry 1996: 100). To assume that a national team's loss at the hand of a foreign national team coached by an expatriate inflicts harm to a nation's welfare misguidedly implies that international competitive sport tests the worth of one's country *qua* country and constitutes a battle between clashing political or ideological worldviews. On the contrary, the central purpose of a sporting contest is to demonstrate and determine athletic superiority. For this reason, 'disappointment and the possibility of losing self-esteem are the inevitable and unobjectionable accompaniment of any actions in a competitive context' (Dixon 2000b: 95). That is, because of the structure of competitive sport, disappointment will take place whatever the nationality of the rival coach. Such contingency is not the making of rival coaches, whether foreigners or compatriots, but inherent in competitive sport.

There are two other critiques of expatriate coaching advanced by extreme patriots. These critiques originate mainly, although not exclusively, in expatriate coaches' adopted nations. First, oftentimes these coaches are accused of not representing the national sporting cultures of their adopted countries, which makes it difficult for the public to identify with them. Bastian admits to this, recognizing that on one occasion 'The Chinese leaders were embarrassed because I wasn't "acting Chinese" ' (Heller 2008). This accusation, though, is valid for both foreign and native coaches. They can equally misinterpret the country's national sporting culture, its practices, traditions, and history. It is not infrequent for natives coaching their own national teams to be dismissed because of their lack of sensitivity and understanding of their sporting cultures and/or the national playing style of their specific sport. On these occasions, native coaches are resisted by athletes, supporters, and, often, by officials and journalists. By the same token, it is plausible that both foreign and native coaches accurately interpret and embody the particularities of a given national sporting culture. A foreign coach can certainly develop a sense of admiration of and attachment to the adopted country's sporting culture and make significant contributions to it. This is especially the case when the foreign coach has coached and lived in her adopted country prior to accepting the job of coaching one of its national teams. Both previous residence in the adopted country's sporting culture and admiration for and attachment to it could be seen as preferable, albeit not required, criteria for hiring foreign coaches to lead national teams.[8]

The second critique points out that hiring foreign coaches violates the unwritten principle of international sport which mandates that national teams be led by compatriots. One answer to this critique is to stress the dubious moral status of unwritten principles. The fact that such principles exist does not give them normative clout. As Robert L. Simon (2000) argues, social conventions lack the resources necessary to assess fundamental moral issues in sport. While they describe what actually happens in sport, social conventions *per se* are unable to specify what ought to be done. Also, in this particular case, it is obvious that the principle is being *de facto* contested by the plentiful examples of expatriate coaching around the world. This situation requires that the legitimacy of the principle be argued for through rational arguments. Otherwise, the principle may become a mere stipulation. There is, once again, the risk of a circular position here by which native coaches are to be preferred only because they are natives, and because they are natives they are to be preferred to lead national teams. I am hopeful that this section and the following show the inadequacy of such a principle.

There are situations in which failure to give a national coaching position to a foreigner may work against the national sporting culture's interests and be morally questionable. For example, if there are no qualified native coaches or the native coaches qualified to lead a national team refuse to do so, it may not be just desirable but necessary to hire a qualified foreign coach. History is telling in this regard. To this date, the Bolivian national football team has only qualified once for the finals of the 1994 men's World Cup. Led by Spanish coach Xabier Azkargorta, 'Bolivia sparkled in the qualifying rounds' (Galeano 1997: 193). The country was enamored with both its national team and its coach. Undoubtedly, Azkargorta, was able to get the best out of an outstanding cadre of players. His example is one among many in the football world. For instance, Ecuador first qualified for the 2002 Men's World Cup while led by Colombian coach Hernán Darío Gómez. Its second appearance in the finals of the men's World Cup four years later was led by Luis Fernando Suárez, another Colombian. Without indicting Bolivian or Ecuadorian football coaches, one wonders, considering the joy of Bolivians in 1994, and Ecuadorians in 2002 and 2006, what proponents of the principle being discussed would say in relation to the hiring of Azkargorta, Gómez, and Suárez. Bolivian and Ecuadorian football officials advanced the interests of their football cultures by hiring foreign coaches.

Moderate patriotism and expatriate coaching in sport

So far, I have responded to the extreme patriots' objections to expatriate coaching in sport. By doing so, I have shown that there is no compelling reason to condemn and oppose such a practice. In this section, I provide a number of arguments demonstrating that expatriate coaching has, potentially, many beneficial effects for both the coach's home nation and the adopted one. As such, they further render expatriate coaching permissible. The arguments in this section are based on the moderate patriots' combination of *amor patriae* with moral regard for foreigners, which allows for actions that promote the foreigners' interests insofar as these actions do not harm, in significant ways, the interests of their native country.

In all probability, globalized national sport officials hire foreign coaches because they are deemed qualified for the job and in the hope that they will be able to represent and improve their adopted national teams' performance. Typically, expatriate coaches tend to come from countries that have been more accomplished and successful on the international stage than their receiving countries. The point is that the work of expatriate coaches can elevate the adopted national teams' performance not only in terms of outcomes but also, more significantly, in their quality of play. Expatriate coaches' expertise and experience can help develop the homegrown talent by increasing its skill level and strategic playing resources. The impact of expatriate coaches can also reach the native coaches, who, with improved coaching abilities, may take over their national teams in the future. In short, expatriate coaching can assist the adopted country's national sporting culture by improving the preparation of native players and coaches as well as the national team's overall quality of training and readiness, and thus its performance in international competition. The commitment to represent and improve the adopted country's sporting culture *in toto* could be seen as another preferable criterion for hiring foreign coaches to lead national teams.

If successful, expatriate coaching can result in more interesting and attractive international sport competition. This is even more the case if competitive sport is understood as a 'mutually acceptable quest for excellence through challenge' (Simon 2004: 27) that is at its best when commensurate opponents are capable of extensively challenging each other.[9] Under this view, the central purpose of international sport competition is to create and compare the relative excellence of teams representing their national sporting cultures through mutual challenge. More accomplished teams bring about the possibility of more accomplished contests. In this sense, by elevating the performance of an adopted national team, expatriate coaching achieves another worthy goal: it narrows international sport inequalities.

The beneficial influence of expatriate coaches on their adopted national team can also be advantageous to the coach's native country's national team. This is so because the improvements of the coach's adopted national team require that her native country continues finding ways to keep improving its own performance. As suggested above, the worthier the opponent, the more significant one's performance. What is the significance of the sense of pride brought about by prevailing over an

ill-prepared opponent? In other words, by increasing the overall level of competition, expatriate coaching tests, and perhaps unveils, the limits of the coach's native
national team's potentialities and opens up spaces for their development. Thus, the
latter can be encouraged to try novel training techniques as well as individual and
team playing patterns not considered before because its rivals did not demand such
imaginative actions. Thus, external pressures induced by expatriate coaching can
indirectly help the coach's native country's sporting culture to prosper.

It is important to note that expatriate coaches may, on occasion, be in a better
position than native coaches to detect, expose, and modify actions and attitudes that
weaken as well as those that strengthen a national team's overall performance and,
therefore, more fruitfully accomplish their jobs. According to José Ortega y Gasset
(1964, 1965), a foreigner can provide a revealing and refreshing portrait of an alien
country. This is so because a foreigner is not so entangled in the life of said country
and has the chance to observe and analyze it from a prudent distance. That is why
Ortega y Gasset notes that Plato used to speak of the 'divine foreigner'.[10] Indeed, in
many of his dialogues, Plato assigns the foreigner the role of interrogator. The
foreigner is, thus, the facilitator of the conversation and simultaneously the one who
questions the conceptions held in the alien country. Expatriate coaches can more
easily take a prudent distance to analyze the strengths and weaknesses of a national
sporting culture, and make their plans accordingly. Being able to take such a distance
can prove of great assistance, for example with choosing the players better suited
for the national team's roster, implementing corrective measures in the team's
functioning, and stressing training practices and playing strategies that could prove
to be profitable. This does not mean that the expatriate coach has to cultivate a cold
and disconnected approach to coaching. Rather, she can adopt an approach that
promotes a reasonable balance between questioning and affirming, corrections and
continuities – an approach that brings a fresh and constructive perspective to the
position of national team's coach. Perhaps the challenge of expatriate coaches in this
regard is to get immersed in the adopted country's sporting culture without losing
the qualities of a foreigner so dear to Ortega y Gasset. This suggests that critical
awareness of the strengths and weaknesses of the adopted national sporting culture
as well as independence of thought could be yet other preferable criteria for hiring
foreign coaches to lead national teams.

Expatriate coaching can also result in increased dialogical possibilities between a
foreign coaches' native and adopted countries. As William J. Morgan proposes for
international sport at large, expatriate coaching seems to be able 'to pry open a space
of interlocution in which national stereotypes can be hashed and contested' (2000:
65). Whether those stereotypes are actually hashed and contested or not, expatriate
coaching carries a morally significant implication: mutual recognition. The fact of
hiring a foreign coach constitutes in itself an example of mutual recognition and,
possibly more than that, at least in the domain of sport the two countries value each
other and share some values. If that were not the case, why would the adopting
country hire a foreign coach and why would the foreign coach accept the adopting
country's job offer? It is worth noting that this kind of interaction has happened

even between countries with a troubled bilateral history. For example, even though Argentina and Chile were on the verge of military hostility in 1978 due to border disputes, Argentine Marcelo Bielsa is, at the time of this writing, the coach of the Chilean men's football national team. Notably, Bielsa has coached the Argentine side in the past and led the team to a gold medal at the 2004 Olympics. He has done so well in his latest coaching assignment that Harold Mayne-Nicholls, the president of the Chilean Football Federation, has declared that Bielsa 'is the cornerstone of the future of Chilean football' (Carvallo 2008). This, and other cases, such as Imura's, symbolizes international sport's moral promise of mutual recognition at its best and why, to paraphrase Morgan, sport morally matters.

The fact that a country's sport officials hire a foreign coach to lead one of its national teams means that they are, at best, willing to engage in intercultural interaction and comparison and, at worst, willing to face the consequences of such intercultural interaction and comparison. Certainly, the meanings assigned to results, favorable or not, achieved by the expatriate coach, the practices, traditions, and history of the national sporting culture as well as native and foreign stereotypes, would certainly be contested and reinterpreted in such overt intercultural processes. Since the openness inherent in hiring a foreign coach, the interlocution it gives rise to, does not assure any particular direction to the conversation, it assists in putting in place a genuine conversation that interrogates pre-existing assumptions and images. This is even the case if the hiring of the foreign coaches has no other purpose than obtaining athletic victories in order to claim national superiority or display dominance. The potential for storylines embedded in international sport is enriched by hiring foreign coaches. Doing so calls people into conversation, provides them with equal conversational standing, and promotes opportunities for all involved to express themselves. If foreign coaches genuinely believe so, all the better.

What all this means is that expatriate coaching has the potential to promote one of the factors that Nussbaum believes are essential to good patriotism: a vigorous critical culture (2008: 83, 86–87). Hiring foreign coaches forces sportspeople to face the 'other', which in no small measure means to face ourselves. In doing so, people can educate themselves not only about foreign cultures but also about their own. The more people are exposed to, study, know, and understand other countries, the more they know and understand themselves. This knowledge and understanding can help in dealing with domestic and international problems, and simply help people to treat each other more justly. The sensible comprehension of 'otherness' and 'ownness', promoted by a vigorous critical culture, is central to moderate patriotism. It is necessary to highlight that expatriate coaching brings about dialogical possibilities and, thus, the promotion of critical engagements between and within the countries involved, but does not guarantee dialogical successes and critical assessments. Nevertheless, such possibilities are valuable as much as is the role of ambassadors. This is even the case if their diplomatic attempts to promote inter-national dialogue and understanding occasionally fail. This, perhaps, is the reason expatriate coaching is usually defended as a kind of ambassadorship. Not coinci-dentally, a Chinese official declared during the 2008 Olympics that 'Both foreign coaches here and Chinese coaches hired by other countries are sports ambassadors and non-governmental ambassadors' (Anon. 2008a). In this respect, some could even argue that patriotism requires that an offer to coach a foreign national team be accepted because it constitutes an opportunity to represent and promote one's country in the hiring country.

There is at least one more way in which expatriate coaching can be beneficial. David Miller (1993) contends that in large and anonymous modern states it is difficult for people to develop feelings of belonging and attachment to the over-arching national community. As a consequence, people tend to resist social, economic, and cultural practices from which they are not likely to benefit directly. Thus, maintaining solidarity among the people of modern states is 'one of the most pressing needs of the modern world' (ibid.: 9). Miller sees in nationalism a way to strengthen such solidarity and the body politic. Nussbaum agrees that

> [the] national sentiment is also a way of making the mind bigger, calling it away from its immersion in greed and egoism toward a set of values connected to a decent common life and the need for sacrifices connected to that common life.
>
> *(2008: 80)*

Hiring expatriate coaches may help maintain and increase solidarity both within the lending and the adopted countries' populations. It can do so, for example, by generating increased attention and interest in the national team's fate on the playing field even if the concern is solely to see it win. It can also do so through the critical examination referred to above. And it can even do so by incrementing the identification with and sense of pride in one's national team's style of play and its successes or by providing new meanings to existing sporting rivalries between countries. The key is that expatriate coaching can engage the national community in novel and varied ways and, thus, promote attachment to the nation 'seen as the embodiment of both memory of past struggles and commitments to a common future' (ibid.: 80). Noticeably, if this happens, it does not need to involve the excesses of patriotism: moral disregard of other countries and their people, animosity toward them, violation of their interests, or arousal of feelings of superiority. On the contrary, expatriate coaching may maintain and expand national solidarity while broadening the scope of people's sympathies and moral concern.

Conclusion

Expatriate coaching in sport has come under criticism from both the receiving and the lending countries. For its critics, who base their objections on the tenets of extreme patriotism, expatriate coaching manifests an unpatriotic attitude. I have responded to these objections and shown that expatriate coaching is not treasonous, disloyal, or harmful to the coaches' native countries. It does not necessarily carry destructive, pernicious, or unfavorable actions toward the coach's country and its people. Similarly, I have also responded to the claims that expatriate coaches are not legitimate representatives of their adopted nation's sporting cultures and that they violate the unwritten principle of international sport mandating that national teams be led by compatriots. While they can certainly come to respect, admire, and represent such a culture, the moral status and the *de facto* applicability of such principles are questionable. In this sense, I have rendered expatriate coaching a morally unobjectionable and, therefore, permissible practice.

Conversely, I have argued, with a distinct utilitarian flavor, that expatriate coaching has, potentially, many beneficial effects for both the receiving and the lending countries. Expatriate coaches can enhance the quality of international sport competition by improving the adopted national team's performance and pressing the coach's native national team to look introspectively in an effort to keep finding ways to improve its own performance. The positive effects of expatriate coaching can undoubtedly extend beyond the playing field into other areas of the country's national sporting culture such as coaching, managing, and spectating. Moreover, by increasing the dialogical possibilities between foreign coaches' native and adopted countries, it can foster genuine intercultural exchanges. Notably, expatriate coaching implies mutual recognition, a salient feature of moderate patriotism. The increased dialogical possibilities that hiring foreign coaches bring about can also contribute to vigorous critical cultures, another vital element of moderate patriotism. Finally, expatriate coaching can increase solidarity in national communities by engaging them in novel and varied ways. Expatriate coaching can promote all this without appealing to the pernicious effects of extreme patriotism. Probably, it can serve as an antidote for such effects.

In light of these advantages, expatriate coaching appears to be not just a morally unobjectionable and permissible practice but even an admirable, although not an obligatory, one. International sport, as Morgan claims, is a paradigmatic articulation and expression of how nations exist for people (2000). When enacted, expatriate coaching can surely help us discuss and comprehend the limits of patriotism and the more appropriate ways in which it can be given expression in international sport and elsewhere. In so doing, expatriate coaching preserves the potential of international sport for combining the best of patriotism and universalism.

Notes

1 While I acknowledge the fact that other moral issues may be relevant to the case, in this chapter I will focus on the issue of patriotism.
2 Tolstoy's ideas on patriotism appear in his essays 'On Patriotism' and 'Patriotism, or Peace?,' both of which are reprinted in Tolstoy (1967: 51–123, 137–147 respectively).
3 See Anderson (1981) for an account of the war.
4 See Dyreson (1998) and Torres and Dyreson (2005) for examinations of patriotism's influence on the Olympic Games.
5 De Coubertin was the main force behind the founding of the modern Olympic Games.
6 See Nathanson's (1993) Chapter 6 for a thorough discussion of this issue.
7 See Nathanson's (1993) Chapters 5 and 7 for a thorough discussion of this issue.

8 Although throughout this chapter I point out several preferable criteria for hiring foreign coaches to lead national teams, I acknowledge that there is more to be said in this regard. Unfortunately, space limitations prevent me from providing a full discussion of the implications of my normative analysis for hiring foreign coaches.
9 See Delattre (1995) for an analysis and justification of facing worthy opponents.
10 Videla de Rivero (1991) has analyzed the function given to foreigners by Ortega y Gasset.

References

Anon. (2008a) 'An age of internationalized sporting', online. Available HTTP: http://en.beijing2008.cn/news/official/noc/oca/n214553530.shtml (accessed 3 April 2008).

Anon. (2008b) 'Seconds out as Henry and Deans step into the ring', *Independent*, 26 July. Online. Available HTTP: http://www.independent.co.uk/sport/rugby/rugby-union/seconds-out-as-henry-and-deans-step-into-the-ring-877879.html (accessed 3 April 2008).

Anderson, T.P. (1981) *The War of the Dispossessed: Honduras and El Salvador, 1969*, Lincoln, NE: University of Nebraska Press.

Black, H.C. (1979) *Black's Law Dictionary*, 5th edn, St Paul, MN: West Publishing.

Carvallo, M. (2008) 'Harold Mayne-Nicholls: "Bielsa es la piedra angular del futuro del fútbol chileno"', *El Mercurio*, 26 October, online. Available HTTP: http://blogs.elmercurio.com/deportes/2008/10/26/harold-maynenicholls-bielsa-es.asp (accessed 3 April 2008).

Cicero (1966a) *The Verrine Orations*, trans. L.H.G. Greenwood, vol. 1, Cambridge, MA and London: Harvard University Press and William Heinemann.

Cicero (1966b) *The Speeches*, trans. H. Grose Hodge, Cambridge, MA and London: Harvard University Press and William Heinemann.

Delattre, E.J. (1995) 'Some reflections on success and failure in competitive athletics', in W.J. Morgan and K.V. Meier (eds) *Philosophic Inquiry in Sport*, 2nd edn, Champaign, IL: Human Kinetics.

Dixon, N. (2000a) 'A justification of moderate patriotism in sport', in T. Tännsjö and C.M. Tamburrini (eds) *Values in Sport: Elitism, Nationalism, Gender Equality and the Scientific Manufacture of Winners*, London: Spon Press.

Dixon, N. (2000b) 'The inevitability of disappointment: reply to Feezell', *Journal of the Philosophy of Sport*, 27: 93–99.

Dyreson, M. (1998) *Making the American Team: Sport, Culture, and the Olympic Experience*, Urbana, IL: University of Illinois Press.

Galeano, E. (1997) 'The duty of losing', in E. Galeano, *Football in Sun and Shadow*, trans. M. Field, New York: Verso.

Heller, J. (2008) 'An expat coach's Olympic game plan', *Christian Science Monitor*, 1 August, online. Available HTTP: http://features.csmonitor.com/backst ory/2008/08/01/qbastian/ (accessed 3 April 2008).

MacIntyre, A. (1995) 'Is patriotism a virtue?', in R. Beiner (ed.) *Theorizing Citizenship*, Albany, NY: State University of New York Press.

Miller, D. (1993) 'In defence of nationality', *Journal of Applied Philosophy*, 10(1): 3–16.

Morgan, W.J. (2000) 'Sports as the moral discourse of nations', in T. Tännsjö and C.M. Tamburrini (eds) *Values in Sport: Elitism, Nationalism, Gender Equality and the Scientific Manufacture of Winners*, London: Spon Press.

Murderball, 2005 [Film] Directed by Henry Alex Rubin and Dana Adam Shapiro. USA: Paramount Pictures.

Nathanson, S. (1989) 'In defense of "moderate patriotism" ', *Ethics*, 99(3): 535–552.

Nathanson, S. (1993) *Patriotism, Morality, and Peace*, Lanham, MD: Rowman and Littlefield.

Nussbaum, M.C. (2008) 'Toward a globally sensitive patriotism', *Daedalus*, 137(3): 78–93.

Ortega y Gasset, J. (1964) 'En la institución cultural española de Buenos Aires', in J. Ortega y Gasset, *Obras completas*, vol. 6, 6th edn, Madrid: Revista de Occidente.

Ortega y Gasset, J. (1965) 'Meditación del pueblo joven', in J. Ortega y Gasset, *Obras completas*, vol. 8, 2nd edn, Madrid: Revista de Occidente.

Orwell, G. (1950) 'The sporting spirit', in G. Orwell *Shooting an Elephant and Other Essays*, San Diego: Harcourt Brace Jovanovich.

Primoratz, I. (2008) 'Patriotism and morality: mapping the terrain', *Journal of Moral Philosophy*, 5: 204–226.

Russell, B. (1928) *Sceptical Essays*, New York: W.W. Norton.

Scarry, E. (1996) 'The difficulty of imagining other people', in J. Cohen (ed.) *For Love of Country: Debating the Limits of Patriotism*, Boston: Beacon Press.

Simon, R.L. (2000) 'Internalism and internal values in sport', *Journal of the Philosophy of Sport*, 27: 1–16.

Simon, R.L. (2004) *Fair Play: The Ethics of Sport*, 2nd edn, Boulder, CO: Westview Press.

Tolstoy, L. (1967) *Writings on Civil Disobedience and Non-Violence*, New York: Bergman.

Torres, C.R. and Dyreson, M. (2005) 'The Cold War Games', in K. Young and K.B. Wamsley (eds) *Global Olympics: Historical and Sociological Studies of the Modern Games*, Oxford: Elsevier.

Videla de Rivero, G. (1991) 'Ortega y Gasset en las letras argentinas: Mallea, Marechal, Canal Feijóo', *Anales de Literatura Hispanoamericana*, 20: 165–178.

Wild, S.E. (2006) *Webster's New World Law Dictionary*, Hoboken, NJ: John Wiley.

INDEX